Creative Dramatics
for the
Classroom Teacher

PRENTICE-HALL SERIES IN
THEATRE AND DRAMA

Oscar G. Brockett, *Consulting Editor*

Robert Benedetti
THE ACTOR AT WORK

Oscar G. Brockett and Robert R. Findlay
CENTURY OF INNOVATION:
A HISTORY OF EUROPEAN AND AMERICAN THEATRE AND DRAMA SINCE 1870

Francis Hodge
PLAY DIRECTING: ANALYSIS, COMMUNICATION, AND STYLE

Charlotte Kay Motter
THEATRE IN HIGH SCHOOL: PLANNING, TEACHING, DIRECTING

Sam Smiley
PLAYWRITING: THE STRUCTURE OF ACTION

Garff Wilson
THREE HUNDRED YEARS OF AMERICAN DRAMA AND THEATRE:
FROM YE BARE & YE CUBB TO HAIR

Ruth Beall Heinig and Lyda Stillwell
CREATIVE DRAMATICS FOR THE CLASSROOM TEACHER

Creative Dramatics for the Classroom Teacher

RUTH BEALL HEINIG

LYDA STILLWELL

Department of Communication Arts and Sciences
Western Michigan University

PRENTICE-HALL, INC., *Englewood Cliffs, New Jersey*

Library of Congress Cataloging in Publication Data

Heinig, Ruth
      Creative dramatics for the classroom teacher.

      (Prentice-Hall series in theatre and drama)
      Bibliography: p.
      1. Drama in education.   I. Stillwell, Lyda
joint author. II. Title.
PN3171.H33   372.6/6   73-21875
ISBN   0-13-189407-2

10 9 8 7 6 5 4 3 2

Printed in the United States of America

Prentice-Hall International, Inc., *London*
Prentice-Hall of Australia, Pty. Ltd., *Sydney*
Prentice-Hall of Canada, Ltd., *Toronto*
Prentice-Hall of India Private Limited, *New Delhi*
Prentice-Hall of Japan, Inc., *Tokyo*

TO LOOK AT ANY THING

To look at any thing,
If you would know that thing,
You must look at it long:
To look at this green and say
'I have seen spring in these
Woods,' will not do — you must
Be the thing you see:
You must be the dark snakes of
Stems and ferny plumes of leaves,
You must enter in
To the small silences between
The leaves,
You must take your time
And touch the very peace
They issue from.

John Moffitt

Contents

2

Simple Activities to Begin On   *21*

3

Stories and Poems for Narrative Pantomime   *40*

4

Techniques for Further Creative Work   *64*

5

Techniques for Strengthening Involvement   *83*

6

Designing Narrative Pantomime Activities   *104*

12
Story Dramatization and Project Work   *230*

13
The Leader and the Group   *249*

Preface

This book has evolved over several years' time and along with the development of our training program in creative dramatics at Western Michigan University. In 1965 we set up a system of demonstration classes in which local elementary schools were invited to participate. Entire classes, along with their teachers, are bused to the campus so that the college students can observe our work with children. At the same time, to conclude the course, we instituted a teaching practicum for the college students. Student teaching pairs are placed in local elementary classrooms during regular school hours and are supervised by us as well as by the regular classroom teacher and frequently the principal. Such a program has enabled us to work constantly with elementary school children, with practicing teachers, and with teachers-in-training and to see their concerns, interests, and needs. Many of the pictures used in this text were taken during these classes.

This text is directed to the teacher-in-training as well as to the classroom teacher inexperienced in creative dramatics. Its aim is to guide the teacher through a step-by-step explanation of various creative dramatics activities. This does not necessarily mean that the teacher must try each type of activity before proceeding to the next. If the teacher feels that he and his students are ready to begin with some of the more challenging material in later chapters, we would encourage him to do so. Ultimately the teacher is encouraged to develop his own personal approach and activities geared to meet the needs and interests of his group.

We have purposely emphasized the techniques of teaching creative dramatics rather than the theories and values of creative dramatics. For the latter the reader is referred to the bibliography materials.

The first chapter is an overview of what creative dramatics is and how it can be used in the classroom. At the end of Chapter 1 is a selected bibliography of other creative dramatics books and related material the reader may find of interest. Chapter 2 presents simple activities for the inexperienced teacher to begin with and includes some preliminary comments on organization techniques and suggestions for adapting activities to accommodate group needs and curricular topics.

Chapter 3 deals with the narrative pantomime, using stories and poems from a variety of sources. This is a fundamental activity and serves as the basis for more elaborate and creative work, which is treated in subsequent chapters. At the end of Chapter 3 there is a bibliography of materials suitable for narrative pantomime work.

Chapter 4 contains techniques for further creative work, with both the narrative pantomime and other activities. Other topics in this chapter include the use of space, orderly playing, and the concept of sharing ideas with classmates.

Chapter 5 is designed to aid the teacher in encouraging in-depth involvement in all creative dramatics activities. Special consideration is given to the selection of material, the presentation of the material, and discussion in preparation for playing, guiding, and evaluating the playing.

Chapter 6 returns to the narrative pantomime activity and teaches the leader how to select, edit, and originate his own activities following this format. At the end of this chapter is a list of longer narrative materials, which can be edited by the teacher.

Chapter 7 is designed to help the teacher elicit further creative work from the children in simple activities. Chapter 8 discusses ways to develop creative pantomime stories based on a variety of topics. Chapter 9 focuses on pantomime for audience feedback.

Up to this point, the teacher is encouraged to allow spontaneous verbalizing if desired. Chapter 10 focuses on guiding simple verbal activities, including sound effects and simple conversations. Chapter 11 deals with the creation of more complex dialogue scenes based on a variety of sources. Included is a list of stories and poetry suitable for dialogue scenes.

Chapter 12 focuses on story dramatization and project work. Included is a list of stories suitable for dramatization.

Chapter 13, the final chapter, is devoted to some thoughts about leadership not covered in earlier chapters. As such, it is perhaps one of the most important chapters. It is placed last only because the teacher may need to become involved in some creative dramatics activities before getting full value out of this chapter. At the end of it is a selected list of books the leader may find useful.

Each chapter except the first includes exercises for the college student. The final bibliography lists story and poetry anthologies containing materials referred to throughout the text and also lists books suitable for dramatizing. All selections and books are numbered, and those numbers are given in parentheses in the text.

Throughout the text we have relied heavily on literature for ideas to dramatize. This is not to suggest that teachers and children will not have ideas of their own. Good literature, however, can be an excellent stimulus for original ideas and often incorporates many concepts related to various areas of the curriculum. For these reasons, literature is particularly helpful to the beginning teacher.

We would like to express our thanks to the many people who have helped to make this book possible. First there are the many students we have worked with in our classrooms — both the college students and the elementary children who have participated in demonstration groups. We would also like to thank the many teachers who have brought their classes to us for demonstrations or allowed the college students to student-teach in their classrooms. Appreciation is expressed to the school principals and to our university colleagues who have helped to make possible our program of training.

We also wish to thank our own teachers, who introduced creative dramatics to us: Agnes Haaga, Mouzon Law, Barbara McIntyre, and Geraldine Siks. We have been influenced greatly by their teaching.

We also wish to acknowledge the many creative dramatics texts that have preceded this one. Our methods have evolved from them, as is evident on each page of this book. At the same time we have tried to expand and elaborate on certain areas that we have found of particular use to the beginning teacher.

Thanks is also expressed to Oscar Brockett and to J. C. Hicks who read an earlier draft of this manuscript and made many valuable suggestions. Additional help, for which we are most grateful, was given by Shirley Stone, Karen Winget, and the editorial staff of Prentice-Hall.

Most of all, however, we would like to express our deepest appreciation to our husbands, Ed and Vern, who have given their encouragement and support throughout this entire venture.

R. B. H.
L. S.

Creative Dramatics
for the
Classroom Teacher

1

Introduction

We are looking in on three classrooms during creative dramatics sessions:

"The Three Little Pigs" is being dramatized in a first-grade classroom. The teacher has divided the class into groups of four. Each group has its specified area to work in. The teacher narrates the story, pausing for the children to act out the appropriate action.

In the background a recording of Henry Mancini's "Baby Elephant Walk" is being played softly. Its lilting beat obviously influences the movements of the children as they play the story. Many of them are walking with a bouncy step as they play in a half-pig, half-human interpretation of the characters.

When the first and second little pigs are eaten, they sit on the sidelines and become the sound effects for the rest of the story. They help the Wolf huff and puff; they rumble for the butter churn rolling down the hill; and they make the noise of the crackling fire under the pot of boiling water.

After the story is played once, there is spontaneous applause from everyone for everyone. The children ask to repeat the story, and some decide they want to switch parts in their group. After reorganizing themselves, the second playing begins.

We move to a third-grade classroom where we learn that the teacher has been dealing with the subject of slavery and freedom. The children have been interested in the story of Harriet Tubman and her work with the Underground Railroad, so the teacher has decided to guide the children in exploring what it would be like to be a slave seeking freedom. Some of the activities the children have already experienced are writing secret messages of escape plans using code systems; learning the song "Follow the Drinking Gourd" and the significance of the gourd as symbolizing the Big Dipper or northward direction; discussions of situations encountered by slaves and the feelings they generate — separation from family, traveling by night under cover, and being assisted by sympathetic people. Today, the children will experience the trip to freedom.

The classroom has been rearranged, and chairs have been pushed back against the walls. The children are sitting on the floor in the center of the room. The teacher specifies that one side of the room is a roadway, the adjacent side is designated as a marshland, the third is a woods, and the fourth side is a clearing and free territory. The window shades are pulled just enough to darken the room and to simulate night. A freedom song is being played softly on the record player. The children are just finishing group discussions about who they are planning to be in their drama and what they think will be their biggest difficulty on the trip. Some of the children are in groups of three and four; some are planning to work in pairs; and a few have preferred to make their freedom flight alone.

The teacher asks the children to decide the order in which they will progress around the room, and they organize themselves accordingly. They begin the experience by pretending to be asleep, waiting until it is dark enough to start the journey. One child, who has suggested that a hooting owl should be the signal for the action to begin, hoots softly on a cue from the teacher. The children, still in the center of the room, silently make their preparations to depart. The first few children start along the "roadway."

The teacher speaks softly as the action begins. She describes the surroundings and suggests the feelings that they might be having as they begin their adventure. She reminds them of the possible dangers that could happen and how they must be cautious. Suddenly she pops a blown-up paper bag, and there is no doubt that it is a gun shot. Everyone huddles closer to the floor, and they proceed even more cautiously than before, continuing on their trip. Some appear to have been wounded and are assisted by others.

Now most of them have reached the "marshland" area, and again the teacher quietly describes what this environment is like and suggests the problems it offers. As before, some of the children listen to her descriptions, while others' are engrossed enough in their own ideas that they need no assistance.

As most of the children approach the end of the trip, the teacher turns up the music and reminds them that they have almost reached freedom — it is only a short way off — within grasp at any moment. The children's faces bear encouraged looks; the walking wounded who are being aided by friends smile faintly. As they pass by the record player, the teacher turns up the volume and begins to sing, encouraging the children to join in. As they sing they return to their original places on the floor. They continue singing until everyone is seated and the teacher fades out the music.

The entire experience has lasted only about three minutes. The teacher now leads a brief discussion about what happened to whom. The children ask to repeat the experience; some have new plans, and the process begins again.

Our third and final visit is in a sixth-grade classroom where we observe the following:

The children are listening to two records, "Alley-Oop"* and "I'm Bugged At My Ol' Man"† brought in by the student teacher. He tells them that the records were favorites of his when he was their age. They talk about the songs for a few minutes, and he suggests that they might want to make up some skits based on the songs or ideas suggested by them. The children seem anxious to try this. They break up into small groups of their own choosing to prepare their skits. After about five minutes of preparation, the following skits are enacted:

Four boys, standing in a row, are each a head taller than the one next in line. The tallest chants, in a deep voice, "I'm Alley-Oop and I'm the tallest and the strongest." The second repeats the chant in a somewhat deep voice. The third repeats in a higher pitch. The fourth, in the highest pitched voice, chants, "I'm Alley-Oop and I'm the shortest and the weakest." Mock fighting for a few seconds between all the boys is followed by the collapse of the three tallest. The little one remains, quietly smiling.

---

*Words and music by Dallas Frazier. Recorded by The Hollywood Argyles, ERA Records, 45 r.p.m.

†Words and music by Brian Wilson. Recorded by The Beach Boys on the album, *Summer Days*, Capitol Records.

In another group there are three boys. One plays the father, one the son, and a third the policeman. The son talks for a long time on the phone. The irate father rips out the telephone. The son goes out to steal and is caught by the policeman and taken to the police station. The policeman calls the father (apparently the phone has been miraculously reconnected) and the father goes to the station and asks how much the bail is. He is told there is no bail allowed for adolescents, but that he must stay in jail in place of the son. The son leaves and the father closes the scene with a, "That's life!" gesture of hopelessness.

Four girls in another group pantomime to the accompaniment of the "Alley-Oop" record. The lead singer holds a ruler for a microphone. The backup singers have worked out a dance step they perform on the chorus of the song.

A fourth group chooses not to show its skit, even though their classmates encourage them. No reason is given, and no comments are made.

Another group of boys also chooses to work on the record "I'm Bugged At My Ol' Man." They, too, select the reference to the father yanking the phone from the son. The boys engage in a verbal argument that seems to have no end. The teacher asks, "Are you finished?" They agree that they are and return to their seats.

After each of the skits the audience applauds appreciatively. As we leave, the student teacher is about to play a record that he says will be "mushy," but that they might like. As the children listen to the first strains of romantic music, they begin to whisper excitedly to each other about their ideas.

What has been described in the above examples is a method of teaching that utilizes drama. Usually this method is called "creative dramatics," although other terms such as "playmaking," "informal drama," "creative play acting," "role playing," "dramatic play," and "story dramatization" are often used interchangeably.*

WHAT IS CREATIVE DRAMATICS?

Creative dramatics involves informal drama experiences. These may include pantomimes, improvised stories and skits, movement activities and exploration,

---

*For a more complete discussion of definitions, the reader may want to refer to Chapter 2 in Siks and Dunnington, *Children's Theatre and Creative Dramatics* entitled "Clarification of Terms," by Ann Viola. See bibliography at end of this chapter for complete information.

and dramatic songs and games. The experiences are planned by the children under the guidance of a teacher.

The purpose of creative dramatics is for the growth and development of the players rather than for the entertainment of an audience. Plays may be created by the children, but the action and dialogue are improvised rather than memorized from written scripts. The only written scripts that might be considered are those that the children write *after* they have improvised a scene and wish to *record* what they have created.

There may be times when the children have a collective desire to share their experiences with other groups outside the classroom society. If a project has so captured the attention and interest of the children that they have spent a great deal of time with it, the activity may appear to have been rehearsed and polished as a formal production.

HOW IS CREATIVE DRAMATICS USED?

Educators have found many values and benefits in using creative dramatics in the classroom. A few research studies have attempted to examine some of them. Among those values are: developing language arts skills; improving socialization skills; stimulating creative imagination; developing an understanding of human behaviors; and participating in group work and group problem solving.

Many educators feel that one of the most important reasons for using creative dramatics in the classroom is enjoyment. Not only do children enjoy playing the creative dramatics experiences, they usually feel successful in them. Perhaps that enjoyment and success stems from the relationship of creative dramatics to the child's natural style of learning and to his basically innate ability to dramatize. The effect of this fun and success in creative dramatics often carries over to other classroom learning as well.

Creative dramatics has also been found useful in many areas of education outside the regular classroom. It has been valuable in alleviating emotional tensions that contribute to reading problems, speech problems, and socialization difficulties. Recreational and library programs often incorporate creative dramatics into their schedules. Religious programs have used creative dramatics as a more meaningful way to teach religious literature and ethical attitudes. In community theatre programs, creative dramatics is frequently offered to give children experience in informal dramatic art.

WHY USE CREATIVE DRAMATICS IN THE CLASSROOM?

Children naturally dramatize. The teacher who uses the creative dramatics method is probably not teaching the child anything that is basically foreign or difficult; he is capitalizing on what the child already knows how to do. For this reason many educators feel that creative dramatics provides an essential style of learning for children. The child of elementary school age is not able to use abstract thinking as easily as the adult. Through dramatization, children are given one way to use information in a more tangible and meaningful way. When children play out an idea, they become an integral part of it. They become kinesthetically involved in experiences that might otherwise remain only words on a printed page.

Through creative dramatics a child can pretend to be the people or things he finds interesting and important to him. He can experiment with societal roles, experience conflicts, and solve problems. In the process of role playing he learns to identify and empathize with others and to experience a part of their lives, confronting their problems. If children can relive the lives of the people they study about, reenact their contributions to history, or find solutions to the numerous problems people have faced, they begin to establish a tangible relationship with the human condition. They can begin to identify with the people and their times. The subject matter comes alive.

Creative dramatics offers numerous kinds of communication experiences. A child's interpersonal relationships depend on his ability to express himself through movement and speech in order to communicate with others. His communication serves the numerous purposes of informing and questioning, forming self-concepts, investigating, organizing and sharing ideas, and enjoying the knowledge, skills, and companionship of others. Through communication the child learns to understand himself, others, and his culture.

Creative dramatics provides learning experience in social interaction. Although children frequently play independently, creative drama most often emphasizes group interaction. Children plan together, play ideas together, share ideas, organize their playing space, and experience human interaction in their dramatizations. Effective socialization becomes a high priority, and the rewards of cooperative group behaviors are often clearly demonstrated to the children.

HOW DOES A TEACHER INCORPORATE CREATIVE DRAMATICS INTO THE CURRICULUM?

Creative dramatics need not be considered a special subject area by itself. Since it incorporates so many skills, it can easily be used in conjunction with any other subject area, whether it be language arts, science, social studies, or the fine arts.

In social studies, the children may enact the conquests of Pizzaro; in literature, the adventures of *Pinocchio* (118).* In music the children might dramatize the folk song "Frog Went A-Courtin' "; in science they may pretend

*See final bibliography for all numbered entries.

to be experiencing a day in the life of a kangaroo rat; and in an oral language experience, they may pretend to be the cheerleading animals in Eve Merriam's poem "Cheers" (39).

Creative dramatics experiences can involve facts and concepts as well as emphasizing problem solving and evaluative and creative thinking. Children can pretend to be molecules reacting to varying physical conditions. They can experience the various facets of work in a logging camp or pretend to be a twenty-first century man solving a problem typical of that speculative time.

Creative dramatics can motivate children to discover new information and skills. For example, children who know they are going to play an experience about digging in old ruins may be motivated to learn anthropological excavating procedures in order to play the activity with greater accuracy.

Drama experiences can also provide one way to check children's understandings. Before introducing children to a unit on simple machines, the leader may give the children movement experiences in pretending to be machines. As the children play he can note understandings and see what concepts he needs to strengthen and what misconceptions he needs to correct.

Learning experiences can be extended or evaluated through creative drama. For example, field trips can be recreated or elaborated. Children can visit a fire department and learn of the work of firemen, see the equipment they use and the way they live at the station house. Back in the classroom those experiences can be played, utilizing the information gained.

A classroom teacher may also want to use creative dramatics as the central activity in an extended project involving a number of curricular areas. For example, the teacher may select a story from a specific country the children are studying and integrate music, dance, art, social studies, or science activities into a long-range project.

WHAT IS "CREATIVE"
ABOUT CREATIVE DRAMATICS?

The activities the leader designs for creative dramatics fall on a line that might be called a "continuum of creativity." At one end of the continuum the children may need many suggestions from the teacher to stimulate their creativity. They may also need very strong structure and guidance in order to achieve their ideas. At the other end of the continuum the children may be overflowing with ideas and need little help from the teacher. They may be able to make many of their own organizational decisions as well.

The teacher is flexible in deciding how much independence a group can handle and how much help it needs. He will find that neither he nor the children are creative to the same degree each time they try. He challenges them but is also willing to change to an easier activity if a difficult one just will not work.

Creativity is fostered by the leader. The effective teacher is one who believes in each child's personal worth and creative potential. His attitude produces a climate of psychological security in the classroom so that the children are not afraid to think and to express their ideas. Often the teacher who uses an activity like creative dramatics is one who already believes in children's creative abilities and is sensitive to the kind of leadership that encourages them.

WHAT IS THE LEADER'S ROLE?

Because creative dramatics is a planned learning experience, the leader has the responsibility of designing and organizing the activities. Often inexperienced teachers are not sure they want to direct or plan creative activities because they feel freedom will be violated. Some teachers are also reluctant to incorporate disciplined attitudes into creative activities for fear of stifling imagination. But groups need organization; people need limits; and creativity needs disciplined structure.

At the same time, the leader will also have the goal of leading the children toward self-direction. As he becomes more familiar with the group and their capabilities, he will let them carry out more of their own ideas and plans and let them make both personal and group decisions on their own. But until the children have had some experience with creative dramatics, the leader has the initial responsibility of planning and guiding carefully and efficiently. Later the leader's main role may be as a resource person who guides the children to make discoveries of their own.

The leader must always design and organize the material for playing according to the group's ability to handle the requirements of the activity. He must also consider the group's personality, age, needs, and interests. To tax the children beyond their capabilities may frustrate them; to underestimate their abilities will stifle their thinking and lead to boredom. Either way, the leader would be unfair to the group and to himself.

The leader must also consider his own personality, style of teaching, and feelings of confidence in his leadership abilities. As he designs and leads the activities, he assesses his own progress as well as the progress of the group so that he can guide with the greatest sensitivity and flexibility.

WHAT ARE THE ELEMENTS OF A DRAMATIC ACTIVITY?

In creative dramatics there are four general areas basic to all dramatization: action or movement; environment and sensory awareness; emotional attitudes and behaviors; and verbal interaction.

Action

Action is basic to drama. In most creative dramatics activities, children will be expressing ideas physically. The leader will want children to learn to move freely and creatively with disciplined, sustained, controlled, and thoughtful movement. He will want children to learn to use space efficiently and to share it democratically.

Sensory Awareness

Creative dramatics is concerned with building children's sensory awareness. The teacher will want the children to expand their knowledge and awareness of environments, both real and fantastical, through the senses and the imagination.

Emotional Attitudes and Behaviors

In creative dramatics children have the opportunity to play a variety of roles and characters and to experience the feelings and behaviors of those characters. The leader will want them to understand what motivates behaviors; to interpret feelings and behaviors; to empathize with others; to put themselves into "other people's shoes"; and to discover the common bond of human emotions that transcends time, age, and geographical boundaries.

Verbal Interaction

In addition to nonverbal communication expressed through movement, creative dramatics is also concerned with children's verbal interactions. The leader will want the children to experience a variety of roles and a variety of situations. He will want to give them opportunities to experiment with the verbal interactions those situations could produce. He will want to help them increase their skills in expressing their ideas. He will also want them to listen to and appreciate the expressed thoughts of others.

WHERE DO THE IDEAS AND MATERIALS COME FROM?

Ideas for dramatization can come from a variety of sources: textbooks, newspapers, tradebooks, literature, and personal experiences. They may also come from audio-visual materials such as television shows, films, pictures, and records. The leader may also write some materials and encourage the children to create their own as well.

Activities may focus specifically on the different drama elements just discussed. For example, a movement activity may be based on Jane Van Lawick-

Goodall's study of African Chimpanzees.* The children, pretending to be chimps, could experience the physical action of agile leaps through trees, juggling fruit and other "toys," poking grass stalks in termite nests, or dancing a chimpanzee raindance.

A sensory awareness activity may focus on one of the basic senses, such as sight, and be based on a sensitive book such as *Sound of Sunshine, Sound of Rain* by Florence Parry Heide (p. 129); or it may involve a variety of sensory awarenesses as the children pretend to experience the discovery of ancient paintings in the Lascaux Cave in France.

Emotional attitudes are emphasized when children have drama experiences in which inner feelings are highlighted, such as the bad tempers of Maurice Sendak's creatures in *Where the Wild Things Are* (p. 248), or the terrifying struggles with false accusations in *The Witch of Blackbird Pond*, by Elizabeth George Speare (148).

A verbal interaction activity may be based on situations in which verbal communication plays an important part. The children might pretend to be one of Lloyd Alexander's characters, Fflam, in *The Truthful Harp* (p. 228), who causes his magic harp strings to break every time he speaks a lie; or they may pretend to be television announcers talking to fill the time waiting for a delayed space launch.

DOES THE ENTIRE CLASS PARTICIPATE?

In creative dramatics it is important to involve as many children in the experience as possible while still maintaining order and control. Frequently the children all work individually without interacting with others, which provides privacy and a minimum amount of distraction from others. It is essential for concentration. Also, when children work alone they have the opportunity to become individually absorbed and to savor their ideas and their uniqueness.

Children may also work in pairs and in groups. Here they have the opportunity to engage in important social interaction. They can stimulate each others' thinking, integrate ideas, lend support, and learn to compromise and cooperate. They may solve problems, create together, discuss, and appreciate each others' contributions. While group process involves trials in power struggles and personality conflicts, it also provides the opportunity to enmesh the creative thinking of several individuals. Individual efforts become part of the greater whole.

Even when the children work in pairs and groups, they may be playing in unison. The pairs and groups play in private, concentrating on their own ideas. Because no undue attention is focused on any one individual or on any group,

*Baroness Jane Van Lawick-Goodall, "New Discoveries Among Africa's Chimpanzees," *National Geographic*, Vol. 128, No. 6, December, 1965, 802.

unison playing creates the psychological security necessary for venturing into experimentation and creative work. There is also less chance for hesitancy or show-off behavior.

Playing ideas for each other is dealt with in two ways. First is "sharing," in which the children experience demonstrating their ideas for their classmates and observing and appreciating the ideas of others. In sharing experiences, self-evaluation is emphasized.

A second method of sharing has as its goal helping children learn to send and interpret messages with increased skill. With this method, the audience is asked to help evaluate the success of the players' communication.

HOW IS THE PLAYING ORGANIZED?

The leader considers several points in organizing an activity:

>the number of players
>whether they will play individually, in pairs, or groups
>whether they will play in unison or with some of the children serving as audience
>the amount of space the children will be given to work in
>how much time will be allotted and how much replaying will be done
>how much in-depth concentration he wants to work for

Although all of the above points are relatively easy and commonsensical, they may take some studied consideration at first. In time, the leader will become flexible and spontaneous with his organization. Ideally he will be able to modify an activity's design on the spot, as the situation calls for it. By understanding all the variables of both the dramatic elements in the activity and the organizational structure, the leader will also be better equipped to help the children plan and organize their own work.

HOW MUCH SPACE DOES
CREATIVE DRAMATICS REQUIRE?

Playing space for an activity may be limited or expansive. Activities can be played at the desk or in larger areas of the classroom. It is strongly suggested, however, that all beginning work in creative dramatics be confined to limited space. The leader should not necessarily associate the limiting of space with the limiting of expression. Rather, he is encouraging the best use of the least amount of space.

"Sometimes we're amused."

"Sometimes we're dubious."

"Sometimes we wonder."

"Sometimes we're shy."

"And sometimes we're satisfied."

In individual playing, the desk area is considered sufficient for any activity. If we are emphasizing the powers of imagination in creative dramatics, there is no reason why the children's desks cannot be a laboratory for a scientist or a ski lift to the Alps. Many activities can be enacted at the side of the desk "in place."

For pair and group work, the space can still be limited, although it may extend beyond the desk area. Expanding space should always be done slowly and by degrees, but one need never go beyond the classroom itself.

SHOULD ALL CHILDREN BE STRONGLY ENCOURAGED TO PARTICIPATE?

A child may participate in creative dramatics in several ways. He participates when he is an observer, a discussant, an analyzer, or a player. His participation will vary according to his interest in the subject, his mood, his confidence, and his awareness of his own needs.

Usually children enjoy playing in creative dramatics when they are secure in the classroom climate and are interested in the activity being played. Forcing a child to participate in creative dramatics is usually a defeating practice. Many children prefer to observe first. They want to see if they like the activity and if they think they can do it. They may also be interested in the responses of their classmates and of the leader. Sometimes they also need to have a model set for them that they can imitate until they have confidence in their own thoughts and creative abilities.

DOES THE LEADER PARTICIPATE ACTIVELY IN CREATIVE DRAMATICS?

Leader participation is possible, can vary, and must be decided by the leader himself. Much of the decision depends on the leader's personality and style of teaching. Sometimes the topic, the age of the children, and *their* personality will be determining factors.

We will be discussing many techniques that involve leader participation. The leader may want to try some of them even though they are optional. The various ways the leader can participate are designed for controlling the playing, enhancing the playing, assisting with dialogue, and helping the children feel more at ease.

HOW OFTEN IS CREATIVE DRAMATICS USED?

The time spent on creative dramatics will probably depend on how many ways the leader can see relationships between drama and other curricular goals. The teacher who is alert to drama possibilities will see topics for dramatization in current events and school and home life, as well as in specialized subject areas. Many of these subjects can be incorporated into activities of pantomime, improvisation, creative story-building, or even extended project work involving the culminating activity of semiformalized enactment.

HOW LONG IS A DRAMA PERIOD?

As to the length of each creative dramatics period, it may be anywhere from a few minutes to an hour or longer. This depends on the leader's lesson plan and on the goals he wishes to achieve as well as the interest and involvement level of the children.

Usually young children work from 30 to 40 minutes. Older children can work from 45 minutes to an hour and even longer. When the activities are interesting and the children are involved, the time passes quickly. Student teachers who feel that an hour in the classroom will last forever often find that they and the children have only just begun in an hour session.

HOW MANY ACTIVITIES CAN BE PLAYED
IN A DRAMA PERIOD?

The number of activities depends on several factors. Chiefly it will depend on the interest the children have for the activity as well as the amount of involvement and concentration the leader is able to help the children achieve. Many activities are replayed in order to deepen the experience. A single activity may take a full session to play, particularly if it is discussed in detail, previewed, replayed, or elaborated. In story dramatization, one scene may be recast with different players several times and may require a full period. If an extended project gets underway, it will have to be divided into its various parts and tentatively scheduled over several days or even weeks.

CAN SEVERAL ACTIVITIES BE PLAYED IN ONE PERIOD?

Often in a drama period the leader uses several activities. Usually they are bound together by a common topic or theme. For example, the children may be studying about Japan. The drama period might incorporate a Japanese game. The leader might narrate an imaginary field trip through the streets of modern Tokyo. Customs might be discussed and pantomimed. A traditional Japanese folk tale such as "Urashima Taro and the Princess of the Sea" (4) (16) might be enacted.

When several activities are used in a period, a feeling of closure and completeness is often helpful. The beginning of the drama period may be a warmup period to prepare the children for becoming involved in in-depth, concentrated playing or for creating and inventing ideas. The ending of the period may need to be a calming or quieting activity of a fairly simply nature.

Usually as the drama period progresses, the leader is able to allow the children more space in which to work and to progress from individual and pair work to group experiences. Usually movement and pantomime work precedes work with dialogue, and simpler materials precede those that require more creative thinking.

For both the teacher and the children, creative dramatics may be an adventure and an exploration into a new style of teaching and learning. It may take time to build the confidence needed to explore new activities and new methods of executing them.

Because he is an educator, the teacher knows that people can grow and change. He knows that experimentation and the leeway to fail and try again are essential to learning. He knows that understanding and patience aid learning. He will allow his students this right. And, just as important, he knows that he must allow *himself* the freedom to experiment, fail, and try again. He must be as patient with himself as he is with the children.

If creative dramatics is to serve in the classroom, it should be practical, meaningful, and enjoyable for everyone. We have tried to keep in mind both the children's and the teacher's needs in order to insure maximum success. It is hoped that this approach will assist the teacher in providing exciting learning experiences for both the children and for himself.

A SELECTED BIBLIOGRAPHY ON CREATIVE DRAMATICS

Barnfield, Gabriel, *Creative Drama in the Schools.* New York: Hart Publishing Company, 1968.

Although a large portion of this text is geared toward the production of plays, there are several useful chapters on dance-drama, movement, and improvisation.

Burger, Isabel B., *Creative Play Acting* (2nd ed.). New York: The Ronald Press, 1966.

This text outlines a useful and practical approach for teaching play acting and improvisation. The second half of the book is concerned with play production.

Crosscup, Richard, *Children and Dramatics.* New York: Charles Scribner's Sons, 1966.

An autobiographical account of a teacher's work with a variety of dramatic forms with children, including pantomimes, shadowgraphs, and improvisation.

Durland, Frances Caldwell, *Creative Dramatics for Children.* Yellow Springs, Ohio: The Antioch Press, 1952.

A manual for drama leaders that includes both creative dramatics and a creative approach to formal play production.

Edwards, Charlotte, *Creative Dramatics*. Dansville, New York: The Instructor Publications, 1972.

A brief but helpful guide for beginning creative dramatics work in the classroom.

Fitzgerald, Burdette, *Let's Act the Story*. Palo Alto, California: Fearon Publishers, Inc., 1957.

A booklet describing methods for beginning story dramatization.

_____, *World Tales for Creative Dramatics and Storytelling*. Englewood Cliffs, N. J.: Prentice-Hall, Inc., 1962.

A collection of over one hundred interesting and unusual folk tales from many lands that are suitable for dramatization.

Haaga, Agnes, and Patricia Randles, *Supplementary Materials for Use in Creative Dramatics with Younger Children*. Seattle: University of Washington Press, 1952.

A helpful manual containing summaries of twenty-seven sessions with five- and six-year-olds.

Haggerty, Joan, *Please, Can I Play God?* New York: The Bobbs-Merrill Company, 1966.

The delightful experiences of a beginning teacher's struggle to learn ways to introduce children to drama.

Hutson, Natalie Bovee, *Stage: A Handbook for Teachers of Creative Dramatics*. Stevensville, Michchigan: Educational Services, Inc., 1968.

A practical, helpful handbook for beginning teachers.

Lease, Ruth, and Geraldine Brain Siks, *Creative Dramatics in Home, School and Community*. New York: Harper Brothers, 1952.

A description of the use of creative dramatics in a variety of settings.

McCaslin, Nellie, *Creative Dramatics in the Classroom*. New York: David McKay Company, Inc., 1968.

A text written especially for the classroom teacher and inexperienced leader of creative dramatics.

McIntyre, Barbara M., *Informal Dramatics – A Language Arts Activity for the Special Pupil*. Pittsburgh: Stanwix House, Inc., 1963.

A guidebook for beginning work in creative dramatics written for the special education teacher.

Pemberton-Billing, R. N., and J. D. Clegg, *Teaching Drama*. London: University of London Press Ltd., 1965.

A British text explaining creative drama with elementary school children.

Sanders, Sandra, *Creating Plays with Children*. New York: Citation Press, 1970.

A booklet giving one teacher's approach to creating plays. Includes several short scripts that children wrote *after* the playlets were created.

Schattner, Regina, *Creative Dramatics for Handicapped Children*. New York: The John Day Company, 1967.

A variety of dramatic activities, both formal and informal, are discussed by a special education teacher.

Schwartz, Dorothy Thames, and Dorothy Aldrich (eds.), *Give Them Roots and Wings.* Available through American Theatre Association, 1317 F. St., N.W., Washington, D. C., 20004, 1972.

This manual is the combined work of several creative drama teachers. It contains more than fifty sample lesson units for primary and intermediate grades.

Siks, Geraldine Brain, *Children's Literature for Dramatization.* New York: Harper & Row, Publishers, 1964.

An anthology of stories and poems for the creative dramatics teacher. Each selection is introduced with suggestions for dramatization.

————, *Creative Dramatics: An Art for Children.* New York: Harper & Brothers, 1958.

A widely used text, Siks's book describes characteristics of children and relates the drama activities to them.

————, and Hazel Brain Dunnington (eds.), *Children's Theatre and Creative Dramatics.* Seattle: University of Washington Press, 1961.

An index of the basic principles and practices of child drama, written by nationally known leaders in the field.

Slade, Peter, *Child Drama.* London: University of London Press, Ltd., 1954.

A pioneer worker in the field of child drama in England discusses his philosophies and theories.

Spolin, Viola, *Improvisation for the Theatre.* Evanston, Illinois: Northwestern University Press, 1963.

This book describes numerous theatre games for adults and children, written by a leader in improvisational theatre.

Ward, Winifred, *Playmaking with Children.* New York: Appleton-Century-Crofts, 1957.

A standard text by the founder of creative dramatics in America. Discussion includes dramatics in the classroom, in recreation, religious education, and therapy.

————, *Stories to Dramatize.* Anchorage, Kentucky: Children's Theatre Press, 1952.

A collection of stories and poems suitable for dramatization with children of all ages.

Way, Brian, *Development Through Drama.* New York: Humanities Press, 1967.

A British text that contains many suggestions for improvisational work with children.

SELECTED RESEARCH IN CREATIVE DRAMATICS

Ayllon, Maurie, and Susan Snyder, "Behavioral Objectives in Creative Dramatics," *Journal of Educational Research*, LXII, No. 8 (1969), 355.

This study measured the effects of verbal prompting and the use of a child as a model on the behavioral responses of five first-grade children in a creative dramatics situation.

Courtney, Richard, *Play, Drama and Thought.* London: Cassell and Company Ltd., 1968.

A source book written for students and teachers of drama education. The text examines the relationship of drama to other fields such as anthropology and psychology.

Irwin, Eleanor Chima, "The Effect of a Program of Creative Dramatics Upon Personality As Measured by the California Test of Personality, Sociograms, Teacher Ratings, and Grades." Ph.D. dissertation, University of Pittsburgh, 1963.

When compared with a control group, significant improvement in personal and social adjustment was made by third graders involved in a creative dramatics program.

Karioth, Emil, "Creative Dramatics as an Aid to Developing Creative Thinking Abilities." Ph.D. dissertation, University of Minnesota, 1967.

Creative dramatics aided in developing creative thinking abilities in culturally disadvantaged fourth graders although problem solving attitudes remained unchanged.

McIntyre, B. M. and B. J. McWilliams, "Creative Dramatics in Speech Correction," *Journal of Speech and Hearing Disorders,* XXIV, No. 3 (1959), 275.

A discussion of the use of creative dramatics in a speech clinic setting, emphasizing its value in psychotherapy, diagnostic observation, and auditory training.

McIntyre, Barbara, "The Effect of a Program of Creative Activities Upon the Consonant Articulation Skills of Adolescent and Pre-Adolescent Children with Speech Disorders." Ph.D. dissertation, University of Pittsburgh, 1957.

Creative dramatics was included as one of the creative activities and helped alleviate a common speech problem.

Prokes, Sister Dorothy F.S.P.A., "Exploring the Relationship Between Participation in Creative Dramatics and Development of the Imagination Capacities of Gifted Junior High School Students." Ph.D. dissertation, New York University, 1971.

Creative dramatics was shown to be effective in developing the imagination capacities of participants.

Shaw, Ann M., "A Taxonomical Study of the Nature and Behavioral Objectives of Creative Dramatics," *Educational Theatre Journal,* XXII, No. 4 (1970), 361.

A summary of Shaw's doctoral dissertation.

Shaw, Ann Marie, "The Development of a Taxonomy of Educational Objectives in Creative Dramatics in the United States Based on Selected Writings in the Field." Ed.D. dissertation, Columbia University, 1968.

A delineation of the educational objectives, including cognitive and affective behaviors, of creative dramatics.

Smilansky, Sara, *The Effects of Sociodramatic Play on Disadvantaged Pre-School Children.* New York: John Wiley & Sons, Inc., 1968.

A report of a study on the use of dramatic play with disadvantaged youngsters in Israel.

Tucker, JoAnne Klineman, "The Use of Creative Dramatics as an Aid in Developing Reading Readiness with Kindergarten Children." Ph.D. dissertation, University of Wisconsin, 1971.

Participants in a creative dramatics program developed readiness skills comparable to those developed in participants in a reading readiness program.

Wright, Mary Elin Sommers, "The Effects of Creative Drama on Person Perception." Ph.D. dissertation, University of Minnesota, 1972.

Sixth grade boys (not girls) improved in role-taking skills after participating in creative drama.

Ziegler, Elsie Mae, "A Study of the Effects of Creative Dramatics on the Progress in Use of the Library, Reading Interests, Reading Achievement, Self-Concept, Creativity, and Empathy of Fourth and Fifth Grade Children." Ed.D. dissertation, Temple University, 1970.

Creative dramatics did not enhance the fourth and fifth grade children's skills in the areas tested.

2

Simple Activities
to Begin On

When both the teacher and the children are new to creative dramatics, it may be helpful to try simple activities first. Simple activities include games, action songs, and simple narratives.

Simple activities can also be used for warmup activities in longer drama periods. They can help children in working with more demanding or difficult material later in the period. They may also involve some skill building or "rehearsing" for the major or most difficult material in the period. Simple materials are also helpful in ending a period, particularly if they also have a calming or quieting effect on the group.

The emphasis of simple activities is on having fun and on creating the appropriate climate for psychological security. They can relax the group, generate good feelings, and promote a sense of group cohesiveness. Often they can unite the group in a common effort, which becomes strong enough that individuals forget themselves and participate freely.

Another value of simple materials is that they almost organize themselves. Usually the rules of the game and the organizational procedures built into them are helpful. When the children learn the rules of a game or learn how an activity is to be played, they help keep each other "in line." The student teacher who has not had much experience working with groups of children will usually find it easier to teach the simpler activities.

Although simple activities are helpful in building confidence for the inexperienced teacher, they should not become a crutch. The leader should also understand that the activities, while they should be simple enough for the children to be successful with them, should also be challenging enough so that they do not become boring. Many of the simple activities can also be adapted to include curricular concepts, a task that will take some imagination and work on the leader's part.

Most experienced teachers know how to organize classroom activities and games. For the student teacher, however, this may be a new experience. Giving directions, rearranging the classroom, and keeping order and control are tasks that require some thinking ahead and planning.

Warming up with a simple activity.

The inexperienced teacher will benefit from practice, but practice without good lesson planning will waste everyone's time. When activities are disorganized, energy is spent, tempers can flare, and a general attitude of "What's the use?" can prevail. Just one experience with unorganized and chaotic "running around" is enough to discourage any future attempts with creative dramatics. The new teacher must recognize and accept his responsibility for guiding and controlling even the simplest activity. He cannot expect it to happen magically or automatically. This chapter is designed to help the inexperienced teacher learn some initial skills in planning simple activities.

DIRECTED ACTIVITIES

The kind of activity that keeps the most control, is the easiest to organize, and is the simplest for the children to play is one in which a leader tells or shows the children what to do. The teacher should be the first one to lead the group, although in subsequent playings he may wish to give the leader role to secure children. It is always important in leader-directed activities that the leader's movements and directions are clear and exact so that the children do not have trouble understanding what they are to do. Following is a discussion of several kinds of leader-directed activities.

Finger Plays

Finger plays, for those who are not familiar with them, are little rhymes, songs, or chants that the children act out as they recite them. They are very popular with young children.

The actions are done with the fingers and hands. There are many, however, which include other body motions as well. Some classic examples of finger plays are "The Itsy Bitsy Spider" and "I'm a Little Teapot."

Finger plays are readily available in numerous sources. Many are traditional and are passed along by word of mouth. Many may be made up by the teacher himself from favorite nursery rhymes. For example:

Hickory Dickory Dock	(Arms hand down, hand clasped, swaying like a pendulum
The mouse ran up the clock	(Fingers run quickly upwards)
The clock struck one	(Hold up index finger)
The mouse ran down	(Fingers run quickly downwards)
Hickory Dickory Dock.	(Repeat first motion)

Single-Action Poetry

Some poetry suggests a single, rhythmic movement such as running, hopping, or galloping. While the leader reads the poetry, the children may simply perform the one action. They may be seated at the desk or standing at the side of it. Actions such as running are done *in place.* This means the children remain in one spot and do not move forward..

Some examples of single-action poetry are: "Hoppity" by A. A. Milne (4); "Running Song" by Marci Ridlon (50); "Jump – Jump – Jump" by Kate Greenaway (4); "Trot Along, Pony" by Marion Edey and Dorothy Grider (4); "Merry-Go-Round" by Dorothy Baruch (4); "Rocking Chair" by John Travers Moore (11); and "Paul Revere's Ride" by Henry Wadsworth Longfellow (4).

Action Songs

Action songs are also fun to sing and play. These are songs that have action words in them and can be acted out. Many are traditional such as the following: "Did You Ever See a Lassie?" "Here We Go 'Round the Mulberry Bush" (or "This is the Way We Wash Our Clothes"), "If You're Happy and You Know It," "She'll Be Comin' 'Round the Mountain," and "This Old Man, He Played One."

There are also some songs that can easily be made into action songs by the teacher and the children. For example, the traditional African folk song, "Kum Bay Yah" has a very strong, steady, and slow rhythm. The words are constantly repeated in the different verses with little variation.

> Kum Bay Yah, My Lord, Kum Bay Yah
> Kum Bay Yah, My Lord, Kum Bay Yah
> Kum Bay Yah, My Lord, Kum Bay Yah
> Oh, Lord, Kum Bay Yah.

The second verse is "Someone's singing, Lord, Kum Bay Yah." The third verse is "Someone's cryin' " and the fourth is "Someone's prayin'." Simple gestures of singing, crying, and praying can be added to the song in addition to the clapping and swaying that is usually inevitable when a group sings such a song. *Very simple* dance movements are also easily added when the group is strongly moved by the song. These may be simply moving from side to side on the lines of the verse and extending arms upward on the lines "Oh, Lord, Kum Bay Yah." Children can be grouped, and each group can perform different movements. When more space is used, circles and other formations are possible.

Another example might be a song such as "Michael, Row the Boat Ashore." One teacher discussed with the children all the activities that sailors must do on a ship. Verses were added that included the children's names and various tasks that everyone acted out: "Sally, help to swab the deck," "Andy, pull up the anchor slow," etc.

Additional songs that lend themselves to acting out are traditional ones such as "Frog Went A'Courtin'," "I Know an Old Lady Who Swallowed a Fly," "Old MacDonald Had a Farm," "Sing a Song of Sixpence," "Twelve Days of Christmas," and "Waltzing Matilda."

Action Games

Action games are also useful. Traditional ones might be "Follow the Leader" and "Simon Says." In each of these games the leader specifies the actions he wants the group to do. In "Simon Says", however, the child is not to perform the action if the leader does *not* say "Simon Says." If he does, he is out of the game, by the traditional rules.

"A good fast game is a good warm-up."

Such a game that eliminates players, however, should be revised. Ironically, the child who is eliminated is the child who probably could benefit the most from remaining in the game, practicing the skill he has difficulty mastering. Furthermore, eliminated players can cause discipline problems and understandably so. The children may become bored and frustrated with inactivity and with watching classmates excel where they have failed. As a result, they may create diversions to amuse themselves, which are labeled discipline problems. Games need not eliminate players at all; or, a player may be eliminated for one turn.

Games like "Follow the Leader" and "Simon Says" can be played with variation. One teacher invented a game using sizes and shapes. For example, the directions were such commands as:

Simon says, "make yourself shaped like a box."
Simon says, "walk in place taking steps like a giant."
Simon says, "make yourself shaped like a piece of pie."
Simon says, "make yourself small as a mouse."

Action Stories

There are some traditional stories that have actions in them for the children to perform. As the leader tells the story and does the actions, the children follow along. Most teachers are already familiar with such traditional stories as "Lion Hunt" or "Bear Hunt" or "Brave Little Indian."

The leader can also make up his own action stories. He may select traditional stories and assign actions to the characters in the story or to any frequently used words. All the children may act out each word, or specific words could be assigned to rows or groups. Sometimes children like to help the teacher think of the actions to use.

For example, the leader might narrate a brief version of "The Three Billy Goats Gruff" with the following actions:

Words	*Actions*
bridge	Stand, stretch out arms, sway back and forth and say "creak"
Little Billy Goat Gruff	Stand, take tiny steps in place and make two tiny horns with fingers
Middle-Sized Billy Goat Gruff	Same as above but with larger actions
Great Big Billy Goat Gruff	Same as above but bigger and use two fists for horns
Troll	Stand, hunch over, squint eyes, stroke beard and growl once

Older children can enjoy similar kinds of activities with more "sophisticated" subject matter. Some topics might include stories with melodramatic themes (complete with villains and swooning lasses), spy stories, or cowboy and rustler adventures. Following is one original example.

Villain: strokes mustache, twirls "cape" and says "Aha!"
Heroine: clasps hands and says, "Oh dear, oh dear"
Hero: flex muscles and pound chest
Mother: wipes eyes with corner of apron and shakes head sadly
Sheriff: twirls two six-guns, shoots them in the air and says, "Bang"

Story: This is the tale of a young girl named *Nell,* her *Mother* and a *Villain* named Evily Pete. And, a show-off *Sheriff* named Sam and a *Hero* named Hal. Our story takes place in the town of Junction City. Nell and her widowed Mother have fallen on hard times and have no money left to pay the rent. The landlord (none other than our *Villain* Evily Pete) goes to demand payment. *Pete* knocks at the door, but *Nell* and her *Mother* are too frightened to answer. *Pete* goes off to get the *Sheriff* to arrest them.

Meanwhile, the *Sheriff* and his friend, *Hero* Hal, are at the saloon having their afternoon drink of sarsaparilla. . . .

GAMES

Games are also useful for beginning creative dramatics work. In fact, games have been used predominantly in the work of Viola Spolin in her book *Improvisation for the Theatre* (p. 18). The games she has devised are specifically intended for instructional purposes with actors in training. There is also a section devoted to work with children. The leader will find many of Spolin's games helpful. In addition, many traditional games are also usable.

The games selected for drama work should be exciting. They should involve action or the development of some skill needed for further dramatization. Many games can also serve double duty if the leader incorporates additional curricular concepts into them.

There are some cautions about games, however. Many traditional games encourage competition, and when competition is overemphasized, the learning of the skill of the game can be lost. Children are more interested in gaining points, getting to the finish line first, or jeering those who lose or who cannot qualify for playing. In some games the winner gets to become the next leader or gets to choose the next player. Many children will never be able to be the winner or will never be chosen by their classmates. Such games should be avoided or redesigned.

The leader may also have to use his imagination in adapting a number of activities to the playing space available in his particular classroom. Frequently teachers are told that they should use gymnasiums or activity rooms if they are going to do creative dramatics. In fact, if large rooms are not available, a teacher often assumes that he cannot do creative drama at all. The suggestion of using games often leads the teacher to assume that he will need a large room to work in.

However, it has been our experience that one of the prime reasons for many of the leader's difficulties with creative dramatics is his inattention to the use of space. It is our belief that the classroom provides sufficient space for the beginning teacher, and even the use of that fairly well-defined space requires a number of considerations.

It seems to us that expanding space by degrees is important. For this reason we begin by using the desk area before moving to larger areas of space, This procedure seems more practical, safer, and definitely easier on everyone's nerves.

There are games designed for playing at the desk, for example:

Balance Movement Game. While standing by the sides of their desks, the children can perform a variety of movements the leader calls out. For example, he could command them to stand on tiptoes, crouch and touch both knees, take one step forward, one step back. All of the actions are to be done while the children balance a book on their heads.

The leader can also create his own activities to be played at the desk:

T: As I beat the drum (or tap on the desk) you move in your desk in as many ways as you can think of. The only rule is that you must move *only* when the drum beats. I may try to catch you off guard, so be sure to listen carefully.

First . . . lots of little short taps . . . Halt! . . . now one long loud beat. . . .

Expanding Space

A number of games may require the use of more space. As we indicated earlier, expanding space requires preparation and foresight. In the traditional classroom, where the desks are in rows, the usual procedure in expanding space is to move the furniture against the walls. This sounds simple, and the experienced teacher can make it look ridiculously easy; but for the new teacher it may be an awesome experience.

Frequently a novice will tell an entire class, "Quietly push your desks against the wall," and then expect that this can be done in absolute silence. The sound of thirty desks scraping and thirty pairs of feet scuffling, added to spontaneous whispering and quiet chattering, may be enough to convince the new teacher that the seasoned teacher possesses supernatural powers.

The new teacher, whose voice often lacks assurance, unfortunately makes a direction sound more like a question. This, in itself, can cause perfectly normal children to take advantage and "cut loose." They can create pandemonium with zestful abandon and never hear it at all. But the rest of the school probably will!

What the new teacher often does not realize is that the seasoned teacher usually sets up an efficient procedure for moving desks and the children have rehearsed it many times. It *seems* spontaneously organized, but often much work has gone into it. Until the new teacher sets up a similar procedure, there is no substitute for caution. It is much wiser to take a little more time and proceed step by step.

T: Row one, pick up your desks and place them here. (When they have finished and are seated, continue.) Row two, over here, etc.

Sometimes teachers try to make a game out of moving desks. They may suggest that the children pretend that the desks are "explosives," which have to be moved carefully so that they don't blow up. However, such a direction may be too tempting for some children. "Exploding" may be more interesting than the planned activity! It is usually best to be honest and straightforward about getting the furniture rearranged.

Controls in Space

Once the space is expanded, the leader should consider control features for each activity. For example, games played in a circle keep the children in a specified area. This formation is a built-in control that aids organization and orderly playing.

Numerous circle games lend themselves to playing in the classroom. An action song game such as "Hokey Pokey" (or "Looby Lou"), for example, keeps the children in a circular formation even though there are a variety of actions the children are asked to perform.

Another circle game that is excellent because it combines both actions and development of observation skills is "Who Started the Motion?" For this game players form a circle. One child leaves the room. A leader in the circle is chosen to perform actions that the other players must imitate. The "It" child returns to the room and must guess who is the initiator of the actions.

The circle formation can also be used as a basis for developing other kinds of games. One teacher developed the following:

> *Circle Game.* Two concentric circles are formed. They rotate in opposite directions. Players are to remain equally spaced as they march around the circle to lively music. When the leader calls out "Change" the players must reverse directions. After this much of the game is learned, the next stipulation can be added.
>
> The added challenge is for the leader to move around the circles and tap players on the shoulder. When he does, the tapped person must move to the opposite circle and change directions while still marching. Other players must adjust the spacing so that the space is still equidistant between players. The leader may continue to call out "Change" at any time.

Another way to control is to design a game in which the children must stop and "freeze" at various moments on signal. For example, a game called "Freeze" might be designed. The children might be allowed to move about the room in any way they wish (without bumping into each other) but on signal they must freeze into a position or an expression. The leader might ask them to look funny, to be historical statues, or to be animals.

The signal for freezing should be definite and clear, and in order to teach the signal and test it out it would be wise to use only a few children for the first brief playing. Additional children may be added gradually.

A variation of freezing might be for the leader to beat a drum and allow the children to move only when the drum is beating. In this way the leader can stop the children by stopping the drumbeat.

Another way to control is to have the children root their feet in one spot. A game called "Caught in the Act" incorporates this control. The children move in any way they wish while their feet remain stationary. A signal is given to stop. On a second signal they must move about the room as fast as they can in their frozen position. On the next signal they are again rooted to the spot and are free to move the rest of their body.

Slow motion is another good way to control movement. It is also an excellent exercise in disciplined, thoughtful movement. Children are encouraged to move as slowly as they can as in slow motion camera work or as if they were moving through heavy molasses. Playing slow music can help set a slow pace. Continual reinforcement from the teacher may also be necessary:

> T: That's it. Keep it slow. Freeze. Now this time go even slower — three times as slow as you just did.

Many activities can be played in slow motion. A simple game of tag is Viola Spolin's suggestion in her book. The leader will have to help the children guard against the tendency to speed up as they try to tag one another.

Incorporating Curricular Concepts

The leader may also adapt games to incorporate curricular concepts and topics. Following are some examples:

> *Grouping Game.* The leader taps a steady beat or plays music as the children march, hop, skip (or other movement) around the room. The leader calls out a number, and the children group themselves accordingly. Any "remainders" also group. They may stop momentarily after each grouping or the leader may prefer to have them continue to move around the room in their groupings.
>
> Variations:
>
> a. Groups can be formed on the basis of solving simple math problems. For example, rather than calling out "6," the leader might say, "5 plus 1."
> b. Groups could be formed according to geometric shapes: triangles, squares, octagons, etc.
> c. *Nickel Game.* Everyone represents a nickel. The leader calls out "Dimes," "Quarters," or "Half-dollars." Other denominations of currency could also be used.
> d. The leader might call out "days of the week" for the number 7; "months in the year" for 12; or "seasons of the year" for 4, etc.
>
> *Fruit Basket Upset.* Children are in a circle in chairs. They name off around the circle as "apple," "peach," "banana," and "pear." One child without a chair calls out the name of a fruit and all those bearing that name must exchange seats while the "It" tries to get a chair. He may also

call out "Fruit Basket Upset" and then everyone must change chairs. The child left without a chair becomes the new "It."

Variations:

a. The leader can assign children specific numbers that are the solutions to math problems. Then he calls out the problem, which the children must quickly solve before they know who is to change seats.

b. An "Early Explorer" game could have the children assigned as "French," "English," "Spanish," etc. The leader calls out the name of a specific explorer and the children must recall what country he represented and change seats accordingly.

c. A geographical game can be played by matching countries with continents.

d. Children could represent consonant blends, and the leader could call out words containing them. (e.g., "*church,*" "*sh*eep," etc.)

e. An "Animal Classification" game could have the children divided into "vertebrates" and "invertebrates." Each child has the name of a specific animal, such as "sponge," "snake," "scorpion," "whale." In addition to calling out "vertebrates" or "invertebrates" the leader could further classify by calling out "mammals," "amphibians," or "anthropoids."

Sensory Games

Some games can teach a variety of skills helpful for further creative dramatics work as well as for other benefits. For example, games that emphasize developing skills in sensory awareness are useful in many areas of the curriculum.

SEEING

Scavenger Hunt. The children are given a list of articles to collect within a given time limit. The articles may be: a green pencil, a paperclip, a rubberband, a book with a picture of a Toltec temple, a paragraph with the word "magnet" in it, or a picture of a scientist conducting an experiment. The children may work on their own, in pairs, or in groups.

Concentration. (a) Arrange a variety of items on a table and allow the children to study them for a minute. Then have them write the names of the items on a piece of paper from memory. (b) A variation could be to rearrange some of the items and remove one or two while the children close their eyes. See if they can guess which item has been removed. (c) A third variation is to arrange items in a sequence, rearrange them while the children's eyes are closed, then see if the children can replace them in the original order. (d) This observation game can also be played by adding or changing an item in the classroom every day for a week and see if the children can detect the changes.

HEARING

Guess the Sound. The leader (and the children) can tape record a number of familiar sounds. Or, the sounds could be made behind a screen. Examples of sounds might be: tearing a piece of paper, snapping fingers, the sound of a vacuum cleaner, a running faucet, and so forth. As the children listen to the sounds, they are to guess the source. When they think they know what it is, instead of telling they may act it out. The fun of the game is in the variety of identifications that can be made of one sound.

Who's My Partner? The leader distributes to each child a slip of paper with directions for a specific sound such as: "mew like a cat," "whistle a bob-white call," and so forth. Each sound has two (or more) children performing it. On a signal everyone begins making his sound softly, repeating it until his partner is found. When the partner is located, the sounds stop, and the pairs wait where they are until all partners are discovered. Papers may be redistributed for repeated playing.

TOUCHING

Guess the Object. Have the children try to identify numerous items by their shape and texture. The objects might be in paper bags; the children might be blindfolded; or they may sit in a circle and the objects passed behind the children's backs. Objects might be a fingernail file, a toy truck, a key chain, and so forth.

Leading the Blind. Have children work in pairs, one with eyes closed and the other the leader. They explore the classroom, discovering that what is usually taken for granted is different when "viewed" in this way. Usually it is best not to allow any talking during this activity in order to aid concentration.

TASTING

Discuss the differences in tasting and smelling with such items as onion, chocolate, peppermint, potato, etc. We taste only sweet, sour, salt, and bitter. We smell rather than taste many foods we eat. If one holds his nose and tastes he has difficulty guessing a number of foods and flavors.

SMELLING

Put a variety of items with distinctive odors in small containers. Have the children guess the items by sniffing *gently*. Items might be vinegar, ammonia, turpentine, coke, banana oil, vanilla, cedar wood, onion, etc. Items can be diluted with water to subdue the smells for safety as well as to make the game more challenging.

Communication Games

Some games also help children to increase their communication skills, both in speaking and in listening. The games are designed to help the children realize the importance of sending and receiving messages as accurately as possible.

What's This? One person describes an object such as a safety pin, a paper clip, a lightbulb, or an article of clothing without naming what the item is. The listeners must draw each part of the object as they listen to the description. They cannot ask questions. When the listener thinks he knows what the drawing is, he may guess. This game could be played in pairs, in small groups, or with the entire class.

Giving Directions. This is similar to the above game. Two children stand back to back with a desk or table in front of them. On each desk two or three identical objects are placed. For example, each child may have a pencil, an eraser, and a book. A third child arranges the objects on one child's desk. That child must then tell his partner how to place his objects so that the arrangements are identical. Again, the listener cannot ask questions. Note: To help children see how questioning for clarity is of value, one partner may be allowed to question when the game is repeated. In a third playing, both partners may be allowed to question.

Character Voices. Different types of people speak with different voices. Even an inanimate object might have a voice that is affected by the material it is made of. For example, tin produces a metallic sound while cotton has a muffled quality.

Place a number of simple sentences on cards and distribute them. On another set of cards, different characters could be listed. Children try to say the sentence as the character might sound. Simple sentences might be: "Good morning." "Hello." "How are you?" Characters might be Papa Bear, Paul Bunyan, a Grandfather clock, a tin soldier, a weeping willow, or a wooden spoon.

Ye Olde Junke Shop. Children pretend to be items in an old junk shop. They create sounds for each item to make as it moves. For example, one child may choose to be a squeaking old rocking chair; another a scratchy gramaphone; another an out-of-tune musical box. Replayings might focus on sounds and movements appropriate for a "cheerful" junk shop, a "gloomy" one, etc.

SIMPLE PANTOMIME

Simple pantomimes are brief ideas that can be acted out without dialogue.* All the children can play them at the same time. They are not to be guessed but are designed mainly to give the children a chance to explore and experience pantomime action on their own.

Pantomimes must involve action. In addition, they may also include sensory awareness and emotional attitudes. Particular learning benefits are that they require the children to concentrate on remembering past experiences, to

---

*Extensive discussion of techniques for designing pantomimes can be found in Chapter 6. Pantomimes for audience guessing and evaluation will be discussed in Chapter 9.

recall information they have read or heard about, and to form mental pictures. These skills are necessary for most learning tasks and can be sharpened through exercises that simple pantomime activities provide.

When creating pantomime activities for children, the teacher should try to make them as intriguing as possible. While the everyday, ordinary ideas are interesting when played in pantomime, an unusual idea such as "Be a crayon drawing a picture of yourself" can be particularly captivating.

Variety of action in pantomimes is also important to keep in mind. For example, the leader may focus on creating action to involve the entire body.

> T: Wonderperson! There isn't a thing you can't do! You can leap tall buildings . . . run faster than a speeding bullet . . . break chains with a snap . . . hang by your teeth . . . twirl a rope on the end of your little finger . . . now with both hands . . . and rotate a hula hoop around your neck at the same time!

Movements can involve levels and directions. Up and down, back and forth, left and right, bending over, turning around, going in reverse, and so forth. The following example uses directions in movement while the children pretend to be a power shovel in operation:

> T: . . . you drive over to your job. Now swing the cab around to the left and lower the dipper (outstretched arms) to that mound of dirt. Slowly now . . . scoop up the dirt. Now raise the dipper and swing back to the right . . . that's it . . . Now, very slowly and carefully swing the dipper over the dump truck . . . be very careful not to spill. Now open the dipper and drop the dirt in. . . .

The leader can also concentrate on changes of tempo. Actions can be done in double time or even triple time, speeded up like an old-fashioned movie. Or, they may be done in "slow motion time" as if one were in space, or performing in a television replay. In the following example, the timing is varied as well as reversing the action.

> T: Pretend you are a bow-legged cowboy walking in his frontier town's dusty main road . . . Now do that same walk a little faster . . . a little faster . . . Now stop! In slow motion take your pistol out of the holster . . . Now reverse that action . . . Take out the gun even slower . . . Now reverse that action just as slowly . . . Practice taking the gun out in double time . . . triple time. . . .

In addition to focusing on a variety of action, pantomimes can also involve a variety of characters.

"See how slowly you can sink."

A. COMMUNITY HELPERS

T: Let's imagine we are people who work and help others in our community. First let's pretend to be doctors giving children shots to help their bodies fight disease . . . Now let's pretend to be the milk man, driving his milk truck and stopping to deliver some milk . . . The foresters who trim the city trees are important. Let's pretend to be these people who are carefully sawing limbs from tall trees. . . .

B. STORYBOOK CHARACTERS

T: Let's try on some different characters we all know from storybooks. Let's first pretend to be the Wolf, sneaking through the woods, looking for Little Red Riding Hood . . . Now let's be the Giant in "Jack and the Beanstalk" coming home for dinner and sitting down to eat a mountain of food . . . Now we're Pecos Bill lassoing a cyclone to ride. . . .

Senses

Pantomimes can also focus on sensory awareness. The following are some examples:

T: Pretend that you are:

(Tasting)   Taking a dose of bitter medicine.
              Biting into a piece of your favorite cake.
              Eating a dill pickle.

(Touching) Threading a needle.
Shuffling cards.
Playing a musical instrument.

(Hearing) A bird listening for a worm.
Asleep and the alarm rings and wakens you.
Hearing a small voice inside your pocket.

(Seeing) Observing the actions of a small insect on your desk.
Peeking through a knothole in a board fence.
Flipping through a magazine looking at food ads.

(Smelling) Opening a carton of milk and finding it sour.
Peeling onions.
Smelling smoke coming from inside your desk.

Emotions

Pantomimes may also include emotional feelings. For example:

T: Pretend that:

You are watching a scary television show.

You are a cautious rabbit. You never take chances. You are eating a carrot for the very first time.

You are a mean witch mixing a powerful brew in your cauldron.

You are a very shy person at a party drinking a cup of punch.

Conflict

Pantomimes can also be made more interesting with the addition of conflict or a problem. Notice this in the following comparative listing:

Pantomime Activity	*Pantomime with Conflict*
Eat an ice cream cone.	Eat an ice cream cone; the temperature is $100°$.
Pretend to read a book.	Pretend to read a book; a pesky fly keeps bothering you.
Pretend to be listening to a very boring speech.	Pretend to be listening to a very boring speech; your boss is giving the speech and he will be upset if you don't act interested.

Conflict is the basis of the following activity focusing on a science lesson:

T: Let's pretend we're people who contribute to the various environmental problems of today. Imagine you're a person eating a candy bar with one hand while the other hand casually throws the wrapper on the ground . . . Pretend you're a vegetable gardener with a small plot of ground. DDT has been outlawed but you've been using it for years and this spring day finds you outdoors spraying . . . You're a person busily measuring a cup of harsh detergent into a clothes washer.

Now let's pretend we're suffering from the various problems man creates. Imagine you are a duck floundering helplessly in water contaminated by an oil tanker spill that occurred months ago . . . Pretend you're out jogging. The smog is very thick today. Your eyes begin to smart; your head begins to hurt and you have difficulty breathing . . . Imagine that you are a recently hatched baby bird. You're aware that your mother is circling nervously overhead. There is a growing sound of bulldozers and men. The strip miners are coming closer and closer. Your tree begins to tremble and suddenly your world rips apart. . . .

As the student teacher gains practice in developing pantomime activities, he will find it relatively easy to create many of his own ideas and to modify an activity to make it fit his particular needs. In the following example, a student teacher used an idea he called a "Time Circle Machine." He wanted to give his class a lot of controlled action. He also wanted to cover some historical events at the same time. He selected several events and arranged them in the activity in chronological order. The children all participated in the activity, standing at the sides of their desks.

"Statues can't move a muscle."

T: We're going to take a quick historical tour through time in a Time Circle Machine. For each period of time we change to, we'll have to go through certain actions in order to make the machine work for us.

To go all the way back in time, turn in a circle once. Now you are back in prehistoric time . . . you are a cave man looking about, hunting for food . . . Look all around . . . up and down . . . search. . . .

Now stop. Turn around in the smallest circle you can. Now crouch down. Now stand up. Now we are in another time period. You are on the *Mayflower,* traveling to a New World. The boat is rocking back and forth . . . back and forth . . . You've been on the ship for many days . . . Oh, boy, we'd better go to another time period before we get seasick. . . .

Now stop. Stand perfectly still. Close your eyes. Turn around once to the right, now once to the left. Wiggle your nose. Snap your fingers once — only once. Now open your eyes. You are Paul Revere riding your horse. You are galloping, faster and faster, because the message must be carried through that the British are coming. Hurry, make your horse go faster. Halt! Whoa! The Time Machine moves on. You will now be someone else.

The activity continued through being the Wright Brothers flying their plane at Kitty Hawk and Neil Armstrong landing on the moon. Almost any event, however, could have been included in such a format.

QUIETING ACTIVITIES

A creative dramatics period should come to a quieting end. There will probably have been a lot of action, concentration, and hard work. It is usually helpful, if not essential, to calm the children down rather than to let them go on to their next work at a high pitch.

One technique that is often helpful is to narrate a very quieting selection. There are several poems suitable for this purpose. The characters in the poems are relaxed or tired; thus, the actions are subdued. Some examples are "Fatigue" by Peggy Bacon (36); "Lullaby" by Robert Hillyer (39); "Slowly" by James Reeves (59); and "Sunning" by James S. Tippett (4) (39).

Usually it is helpful to have the children close their eyes as they enact the poem. The leader should try to capture the quieting mood in his voice or perhaps use a quiet record for accompaniment. The poems are effective even if the children simply listen quietly as the teacher reads them in as calming a voice as possible.

The leader may also create his own simple quieting activities. He may narrate a few sentences about a candle burning and slowly melting away. Or he may ask the children to pretend to be floating on a sea of tranquility. It is also effective just to have the children close their eyes with their heads on the desks while the leader plays a quieting musical selection.

The importance of the quieting experience is to relax the group and to calm down any hyperactivity. Perhaps more than that, however, it helps the children to absorb the concepts, experiences, and feelings covered during the drama period.

EXERCISES FOR THE COLLEGE STUDENT

1. Collect or design five of each of the following:
   a. finger plays
   b. single-action poetry
   c. action songs
   d. action games
   e. action stories
   f. quieting activity
2. Find a game or design one of your own that has action in it but can be played at the desk.
3. Select a game to lead your classmates in. Give the directions for playing the activity. Organize the group for playing the game. Bring the playing to a close. Afterward discuss with your classmates what your strengths and weaknesses were. Brainstorm for ways to improve the activity.
4. Select or design three games that illustrate the use of controls.
5. Select a traditional game and redesign it to incorporate additional curricular concepts as was done with "Grouping Game" and "Fruit Basket Upset."
6. Select or design five sensory games, one for each of the senses.
7. Select or design a communication game, emphasizing either speaking or listening skills.
8. Write a pantomime, of at least 50 words, which emphasizes a variety of actions.
9. Write ten sensory pantomimes, two for each of the five major senses.
10. Write five pantomimes emphasizing emotions.
11. Make a list of ten brief pantomimes; then in a second list add conflict to each.

3

Stories and Poems
for Narrative
Pantomime

The pantomime materials we will focus on in this chapter are those that the leader can narrate for the children to interpret in their own way. There are a number of stories and poems describing interesting and dramatic action that the children can easily play as the teacher reads them.

> T: As I read the "Winnebago Origin Myth," you pretend to be the Earthmaker. You pretend to see what he sees, think what he thinks and do what he does. For example, when he picks up a piece of clay, you pick up an imaginary piece of clay. . . .

At the end of this chapter we have listed a number of selections suitable for playing in narrated fashion. Some of the better-known pieces include the folk tale, "Teeny Tiny," Beatrix Potter's *Peter Rabbit,* James Weldon Johnson's poem, "The Creation," and Dr. Seuss's *How the Grinch Stole Christmas!* Many selections can be found in basal readers. Some of the selections are realistic adventure stories of people and animals and could correlate with science and social studies lessons. Our listing is only a representative sampling of the many that exist in textbooks and trade books.

All materials referred to in this chapter are listed at the end of this chapter.

VALUES OF NARRATED MATERIALS

Narrated pantomime provides an expedient, efficient, and enjoyable way to dramatize a number of materials. It is a useful activity regardless of the amount of experience the children and the leader have had in creative dramatics. Narrated materials are also a foundation for further creative work. Later, dialogue can be added to these materials or they may be elaborated in a variety of ways. These techniques will be discussed at later points.

Values to Children

Narrated activities are relatively easy to do. Many children feel pressured if they are required to think and make decisions on their own before they are psychologically ready. In narrated activities everyone can be successful since they need only follow the actions the material prescribes. Thus, narrated materials help build confidence and develop positive self-concepts in the children.

Values to the Leader

Narrated materials are orderly and consistent and provide a built-in organization. This is an important aid for the beginning teacher. As the leader narrates the action, he gives the cues for playing. The children must listen carefully to the material in order to know *what* to do and *when* to do it. For this reason, narrated materials are also excellent for developing listening skills.

Narrated materials also provide a basis for developing the leader's skills in guiding other creative dramatics activities. After the leader is proficient in guiding simple narrative materials, he will probably feel more comfortable editing passages from longer materials and writing his own materials. This will be discussed further in Chapter 6.

One of the most important skills for the leader of creative dramatics is sidecoaching. Sidecoaching is the encouraging commentary the leader gives as the children play their ideas. We will speak of sidecoaching many times, but for now the leader is simply alerted to the fact that the technique of sidecoaching is similar to the techniques discussed with narrated materials.

Individuals, Pairs, and Groups

Narrated materials may be played individually, in pairs, or in groups. Individual playing means that everyone plays his ideas alone, without interacting with others. As we mentioned before, this aids concentration and provides privacy. Each child is the solo performer in his own private drama. He may play the main part in a story without having to share the role with someone else. For many children it is important to have this immediate gratification. Once they have had a chance to be the main character they are usually more interested in the other roles the material suggests.

Also, when children play individually they need only a small amount of space. This can be the desk area, which minimizes the need to reorganize the classroom. Unlike individual playing, pair and group playing involve both social and physical interaction. These two factors will necessitate additional considerations in organizing the playing. Although the social interaction provided by group work is a valuable factor in creative dramatics, it also poses special considerations that the leader must keep in mind.

When each child plays alone, there is more of a one-to-one interaction between the teacher and each child. With pair and group playing the children will be dividing their attention between relating to the teacher and interacting with a partner or with other group members.

In pair and group work there is usually physical interaction as well. As the children work, plan, and play together, they will be in close physical proximity to each other. The materials they are dramatizing will also have suggestions for social interaction and sometimes for physical contact.

If the inexperienced teacher is not already aware of it, he should be alerted to the fact that children frequently introduce aggression and physical contact if there is the slightest suggestion of it in the material. A seemingly innocuous line such as, "When John headed for the door, Sam stopped him," might seem to be a good line for practicing a flying tackle! The children often see such action in dramatic shows. For them it is logical and impressive. Since this attitude is normal and quite typical, the teacher need not worry that the children are trying to get away with something. The problem is that someone could get hurt; therefore, it will be necessary to find acceptable and safe ways of enacting physical contact.

Because of the possibility of physical contact, it is usually best to begin with individual playing and work up to pair and group playing and interaction gradually. When both the teacher and the children feel comfortable with or have become accustomed to individual playing, pair and group playing can follow more easily.

Unison Playing

It is important, particularly in the beginning stages of creative dramatics, for the children to play in unison. As we described earlier, unison playing means that several or all of the children in the class are playing at the same time, whether in pairs, groups, or by themselves. Each individual, pair, or group works privately, independently concentrating on their own ideas.

Unison playing also allows children a chance to experience their thoughts for pure and simple enjoyment without worrying about audience evaluation. It

"Individual playing means I work by myself."

"Individual playing means I can enjoy my own ideas."

allows them an opportunity to sort out their own thinking and to rehearse and polish their ideas in case they later decide they would enjoy sharing their ideas with their classmates.

*Children like to include
physical contact.*

Another benefit of unison playing is that it reduces the time spent waiting to take turns. For active groups who cannot bear to sit and wait, convinced that their turn will *never* come, unison playing is most satisfying.

Limited Space

As a general rule, the leader should not give more space than is absolutely necessary for first playings. Expanded areas of space should be saved for replaying only.

Individual playing should take place at the desk area. The children's desks can become the auto for Lois Lenski's story about Mr. Small. The desk can also be the table, the sink, and the easy chair, as well as the truck for *The Man Who Didn't Wash His Dishes.* At the side of the desk all sorts of actions can be done in place.

The desk area is a convenient and concrete tactile boundary. The desks separate the children from each other physically, and this factor keeps them from distracting each other.

There are also psychological reasons for using limited space. The desk area is familiar territory and a home base to the child. It may give him the sense of security needed to risk participation. Furthermore, if a child has an idea he is not too sure of, it seems easier to try it out in a small amount of space first.

In the first playing, the teacher has an opportunity to gauge the confidence of the children and their depth of involvement in the material. Then he has a better awareness of their ability to handle increased space.

Beginning pair and group work should also be done in limited space. For some classrooms there may be sufficient space without the need to rearrange furniture. The space between aisles or at the sides, back, front, and corners of the room may provide plenty of space. Some extremely crowded classrooms may have to be rearranged. This rearranging must be done with extreme care and planning, as we discussed in the last chapter and will discuss further in the next chapter.

CREATIVE INTERPRETATION

Although narrative materials contain numerous ideas of *what* to do, the children are not told *how* to do them. Thus they may interpret their ideas through pantomime in whatever way they choose. When they do, we call it "creative interpretation." One of the most important aspects of creativity is the uniqueness of each individual; creative interpretation can encourage this concept.

The narrative materials selected should be simple, straightforward, and basically action-oriented. Even though the materials may also include sensory descriptions and detailed emotional reactions, action should always be the underlying ingredient.

Many of the lines of the material can be played easily and simply. The characters may skip (action), eat a sour apple (sensory), or tremble with fear (emotion). Yet, even with a simple idea, there is no one way to perform it. Creative interpretation is possible even with a fairly explicit line such as "frogs hop." Some children may choose to enact their frog in an upright position, hopping on hind legs. Others may want to be on all fours, perhaps even crooking their arms to represent the frog's bowed front legs.

Some lines may be more challenging. For example, in Carl Sandburg's "Lines Written for Gene Kelly to Dance To," the children are asked if they can dance a question mark. This could be interpreted in a variety of ways: the feet might draw a question mark on the floor; the hands might inscribe one in the air; or the whole body might form one, dissolving and reforming in a rhythmic dance.

Sometimes the material calls for action that has to be interpreted symbolically rather than literally. The children have the opportunity to exercise their creativity and imagination and think of ways to interpret "disappearing," "being swallowed," "dissolving," "swinging from a rope," and so forth. Certain physical actions can be potential problems unless they are interpreted in symbolic ways. For example, "falling in a fright," "spitting," and "collapsing" must be worked out in acceptable ways.

Any physical contact called for in the material will have to be faked. The seasoned teacher knows that this kind of action can get out of hand, and he cannot allow the children to endanger themselves or hurt others. For example,

The cats stalk the mouse.

"The Crack in the Wall" by George Mendoza is fun to play with one child being the hermit and one being the expanding crack. But the hermit pounds and kicks the wall. The kicking and pounding can be done *close* to the "wall" without actually touching it. This means that the players will have to be careful about judging their distance from each other. And the hermit will have to have enough control to contain his actions. If such action poses problems it will have to be eliminated. Or, the teacher may want to refer to the section "Creating Fights and Battles" in Chapter 7.

Dialogue

Although the material focuses mainly on action, some selections have bits of dialogue. If the lines are very short and compelling, the children may want to repeat them after the leader reads them. For example, most children will probably want to say, "Gwot, I ate it!" which is the final line of George Mendoza's "The Hairy Toe." Or, in Russell Hoban's *The Little Brute Family,* the lines "How Nice," or "May we keep it?" may be fun to repeat.

If the leader feels that repeating the lines will be distracting, he may omit the dialogue or ask the children to pantomime the lines.

T: If your character says, "No," you might just shake your head or something similar to indicate "no."

PREPARATION

There is no set way for the leader to prepare the children for narrative pantomime. The nature of the material and personal preferences will play an important part in the final decision. The following are suggestions for procedures the teacher may want to consider when he guides the children through narrated materials.

Presenting the Material

First, the leader may want to read the material aloud to see whether the children like it well enough to play it. The teacher's reading will affect the children's initial interest as well as their interpretative playing of it. It may be necessary to give one's all to making the material sound exciting, interesting, or funny — whatever the material calls for.

A prior reading is particularly beneficial when there are certain concepts in the material the teacher wants the children to understand. For example, there is a small science lesson in Jean George's *All Upon a Stone:*

> **T:** As I read the story, you listen to the description of the mole cricket and the things he does. A lot of what he does will be different from the way you do things. That's because his sense organs are different from yours. He hears with his knees, and breathes through his belly, and smells through his antennae. You'll have to keep all that in mind when I read it the second time for you to play it.

Or, if the material is lengthy and it would be too time-consuming to read it through, the leader may prefer to give a brief synopsis of it. Still a third variation might be to read a passage up to a particular point and then begin the narrated action of only one portion of the material.

Discussions and Preview Playing

Before the material is played, the leader will want some assurance that the children will be successful. This means that:

> a. they have some idea of what they will do for the challenging and/or symbolic lines;
> b. they understand how to use limited space;
> c. they can handle the physical action safely.

Discussions and preview playing generate ideas and help the teacher assess the children's readiness. In discussions both the teacher and the children have the opportunity to explore ideas. In preview playing they *see* ideas in action and have a chance to work out any problems that might arise.

The following examples illustrate how the teacher can guide children to discuss and preview play:

A.

T: In the poem "Boa Constrictor" you will be pretending to be swallowed up, starting with your toe until you are completely swallowed. How could we pretend that is happening to us? You may all have different ideas.

C: I could stand behind my desk, see, and then go down behind it a little bit at a time.

C: You could sink down on the floor.

C: You could just crumple until you were a ball of nothing.

B.

T: In Ray Bradbury's story "There Will Come Soft Rains," how might you play the part of the machines that are like little mice cleaning the house while you remain at your desk area?

C: I have suction cleaners on my feet that neatly and quickly eliminate all dirt. When I scoot to the front of my desk, I clean the living room; at this side, I clean the bedroom; this is the kitchen; and this side is the study; and up here, you find the bathroom. I clean that last.

C: I'll be a giant machine here in the middle of my desk. I'm all folded up but when I begin to work, I slowly unfold. My long arms extend throughout the house. One arm is equipped with a vacuum cleaner hose and the other has furniture polish and cleaning spray.

C.

T: There is one line in *Hildilid's Night* that tells us she hated the night so much she "spat" at it. Those in Row 1 who think they can pretend but not really spit, let's see how you'd do that. On the count of three – 1, 2, 3!

D.

T: In the story *Oté*, the devil gives you a command and you fall in a faint. How can you pretend to fall so that you don't get hurt?

C: The coach has taught us guys to fall part by part so you land on your muscles.

T: That sounds very safe. Would some of you like to demonstrate how you would do that?

E.

T: Also in the story *Oté*, the devil hops on Oté's back and makes him take him home. How can that be done?

C: We better have Jimmy play the devil; he's the littlest.

T: But there may be several people who would like to play that part. How could that part be played without anyone having to carry anyone else?

C: The devil could just walk real close behind Oté and maybe put his arms around his neck like he does in the picture.

T: Les, could you and Mack show us how that could be done? Jenny, how about you and Ted? Sam and Otis? Fine.

F.

T: In "The Crack in the Wall" the man pounds the wall and kicks it. This will have to be faked — just like it's done in the movies and on TV. Who thinks they can *pretend* to hit and kick without touching? (Picks 3 volunteers.) How about trying it right next to this back wall; then we'll have someone be the wall the second time. Remember, "No Contact."

Usually children prefer to keep all the exciting action in the story and rehearse it carefully. Knowing they will have to forfeit the privilege of playing exciting drama if they cannot follow the rules motivates them to comply.

The leader soon knows his group well enough to estimate what they can handle. For some groups, all the leader needs to say is:

T: This line sounds as if it could cause a problem. If we're not careful, someone could get hurt and I can't allow that. Can we use caution? Do we need to rehearse it?

If the discussions and preview playing reveal that the children are not ready to handle particular lines or action, they may be omitted or reworded. Or, the leader may demonstrate exactly how he wants the line played without giving the children any leeway. He may, for example, substitute "made a face at the night" for spitting. He may demonstrate that the children are simply to crouch on the floor to indicate "fainting." Instead of pounding and kicking the wall, the hermit could "stamp his feet" or "clench his fists."

It may be necessary to demonstrate only one idea from the selection as in the examples above. Sometimes it is helpful to play the entire selection in a preview playing.

The demonstrators for preview playing should be volunteers since they will probably be the most confident children. It is also a good idea to have more than one demonstrator. In this way there is no pressure on any one child. For paired playing, three pairs might be a good number for a preview. For small group playing, one or two groups may be sufficient.

Since preview playing has a tendency to be a model for the entire class to follow, it is important that it be successful. Usually several children will volunteer to be demonstrators so it is valid and desirable for the leader to use some selection procedures. The leader may explain that those who are selected must be able to remain involved and not be distracted by the fact that others are observing them. Confident and even "hammy" children might feel at ease in front of their classmates if the material is humorous. If the material is serious, however, the "comedian" may not be a wise choice. He may be secure with clowning, but serious material may turn to a farce in his hands. Then, the entire class may decide that they want to play the material in the same way! Sometimes it is the shyest person in the class who, if he volunteers, can make the serious scenes convey the poignancy they call for.

It is important to give the children a chance to make the decision of whether or not they can accept this responsibility. However, the leader should clearly describe his expectations. And, once the demonstration begins and it proves too difficult for some children, they should be given the chance to take themselves out of the activity.

> **T**: I'm going to stop reading the selection because I can see that we're having difficulty with it. Perhaps it is harder to do than you thought it would be. We're losing the mood of the material. Let's start again and see if a second try will be easier. Anyone who prefers to wait until later should sit this one out. Okay?

Audience for Preview

Even at this early beginning it is good to establish the audience rules. Any time that children are observing their peers, they are doing so to learn something and to share ideas. In preview playings, they are seeing material enacted in one way. They should remain quiet and not be allowed to boo and hiss even in a playful way because such action will interrupt the demonstrators' concentration on their work.

Perhaps it is important to point out at this time that "work" is a good word for the leader to use. The play and fun part of creative dramatics is obvious enough to them. Usually children are surprised, yet pleased, to think that something they enjoy can also legitimately be called "work." And it *does* take concentration and involvement to produce the most satisfying results.

PLAYING

Children should be invited rather than forced to participate. Some children will be relieved to hear the teacher say, "*If* you would like to play. . . ." Feeling that they *have* to play can cause anxieties. Extending an invitation encourages children to make their own decisions. When they do join in, it is more likely to be because the activity looks like fun and they want to be a part of it.

Reluctant children may wish to sit out during the first playing and enter in on replayings. Watching their peers lets them see ideas they can imitate. The

"Look at the world upside down . . ." (Photo courtesy of
the Kalamazoo Gazette.)

leader's continual acceptance of children's ideas and interpretations will
eventually give the reluctant children the courage to try on their own. Forcing
reluctant children to participate only increases their reluctance.

On the other hand, there are many children who need and want to be
involved in as much of the playing of the story as possible rather than watching
their classmates. Although they can appreciate each other's contributions and
can work cooperatively together, the fun of drama is so compelling they usually
want immediate involvement. As we pointed out previously, individual playing
can answer this need.

Individual

Individual playing can be utilized both with material with one character
and sometimes with material with several characters. Some materials have only
one character. Sometimes the character lives by himself as does *The Selfish Old
Woman.* Or, the character may be alone on an adventure as is the Navy ensign in
"Man Alone." Or, attention may be drawn to one person as in the poem, "Base
Stealer," which focuses on a crucial moment of a baseball game.

With some material, although there are several characters, there is a main
character who appears throughout the story. *Peter Rabbit* is such an example.
All the children can play this part by themselves and simply imagine all the other
characters.

Some material has several characters who act independently of each other. For example, *The Pond* describes the movements of several characters, one at a time: the water, a dragon fly, shadows, and so forth. In these materials the child can play all of the parts, changing from one to the other.

Even though the children may be playing at their desk by themselves in individual playing, it is important for the leader to plan the playing and to explain it to the children. Here is an example of specific directions for one plan:

> **T**: Now that we've discussed the story, we'll pretend that each of you is the Grinch who is out to steal Christmas. We are just using the desk area the first time. First you'll be in your cave, making the Santa Claus suit and getting dressed in it. Your desk will be the sled you ride in to Whoville. When you ride to Whoville, I'll play "Sleigh Ride" on the record player. Are their any questions?

Pair and Group

Because of the consideration of social and physical interaction with pair and group playing, the leader may need to take some precautions. At first the leader should select stories with one main character throughout. Then, the first playing can be done individually, working up to interaction slowly. For example, in a first playing of "The Sorcerer's Apprentice," all the children might be Fritzl. A second playing might be in pairs, adding the broom since it creates the conflict and causes all the excitement in the story. Then, for trio playing, the Sorcerer may be added. In any replayings the children can switch parts.

Another way to reduce the problem of physical interacting is to let different children play the different parts, but in isolated space without interacting. For example, in a story with two characters one half the class can play one character while the other half plays the second character. But, instead of interacting as pairs, they play at their desks imagining their partner. They can see the other part being enacted, but they remain separated from each other.

This same method may also be used for material with several characters. For example, the children might play "Goldilocks and the Three Bears" with Row 1 (or one group) being Goldilocks; Rows 2, 3, and 4 being each of the Three Bears. The desks could be the table, the chairs, and the beds in the story.

It is not necessary to cast all parts in the material. In scenes where horses or other animals carry riders, children will often ask to play the animal. However, it is usually best to avoid this. The animals can easily be imagined. The reason is not so much that children cannot follow the rules of caution, but the sight is an unreal one and the children know it. They get amused and then have trouble concentrating on the story. Even if the story is a humorous one the antics resulting from one child riding on the back of another overshadows everything else.

Playing More Than One Part

Rather than casting one child for each part in the story, it is often helpful to let children play more than one part. For example, in the stories in which a character is taking a trip or going on an adventure and meets a series of different people along the way, the story can be played in pairs. One child can play the adventurer, and the partner can play all of the people that are met along the way.

Even in a story like "Goldilocks" one child can play the part of all three bears, simply by switching back and forth. Or, in a story like "Gertrude McFuzz" the same child who plays Lolla-Lee-Lou could also play Uncle Dake.

Double Casting

It may be desirable to cast more than one person in certain parts. For example, there can be two wives and two husbands in *Brownies – Hush!* and any number of elves. Since each child usually considers himself the character, no matter who else is playing it, he never seems to be bothered by double casting. The leader probably won't even need to change the wording to "husbands" and wives."

Additional Narration

The leader may want to narrate a few words of additional action to give children increased involvement or attention in their part. For example:

T: While Fritzl stayed at home to do the housework, Liesi did the work in the field, *cutting and stacking the hay.*

Or, if the leader wants to give the children something specific to do, but doesn't want them to be physically active, he might add to the narration:

T: The bears walked so long in the woods, waiting for their porridge to cool that they became tired and *sat down under* a tree to sleep. Meanwhile, Goldilocks.. . . .

Waiting One's Turn

The leader may want to specify where the children should remain when they are not in the scene. If the material is long or if the children are to be out of the picture for a long time, it may be helpful to define a nearby offstage area where they can sit and wait. In this way they can become a small audience for each other.

When the children and the teacher become accustomed to group playing, can use space without problems, and like to watch one another play a story, the teacher may want to select a story with a great many characters in it and cast the entire class into one grouping. *Ittke Pittke* is one story that has a number of interesting characters. Although they do not always have a lot of involvement in the story, all of them are important. In addition to Ittke Pittke there is the Prince, the wife, four sons, the Prince's messenger, the doctor, the funeral director, and all the customers and mourners. Some parts may be double cast. The different groups of people may remain in a specified area in the classroom. Ittke Pittke and the messenger are the only ones who need to move about.

Another story that can be planned in this way is *Brownies – Hush!* This can be cast with three wives, three husbands, and the rest of the class the Brownies. The wives can remain in one area, the husbands in another; or they may work as three pairs in their own specified house. The Brownies can remain at their desks. When they are seated they are in hiding in their houses. When they stand at the side of the desk, they are in the old couple's house, performing their good deeds.

Selecting and Casting

Usually it is best at first not to cast children into groups larger than five. The interaction process usually becomes too complicated with additional members.

For pair and group playing the children can be grouped by the teacher or they may group themselves. Usually children work best if they can choose their co-workers themselves. Some classes can pair and group themselves with few arguments.

The leader may assign the parts to the children or they may decide this matter for themselves. Particularly if they know there will be replayings of the material and they have the opportunity to switch parts, the decision about who will play which part can be made more easily. It merely becomes a matter of who will play which part *first*. Some children in repeated playings prefer to keep their original role. If the group agrees on this, there is no reason to force the children to switch parts.

When children do have problems with group decisions, the leader will need to step in. During these moments it is best to make the decisions quickly and get on with the playing. If the teacher acts as if he expects the groups to get along with each other, they frequently live up to that expectation. Sometimes the excitement of acting out the material is strong enough to help them forget about arguing over co-workers and casting. Further discussions of group interaction will be taken up in the final chapter.

Reading the Material

The leader should be familiar with the material so that he can read it by glancing down *occasionally* rather than having his eyes glued to the page. This gives him more opportunity to watch the children and to time his pauses to last only as long as the majority of the group needs to complete their playing of the idea.

One student teacher learned the value of good reading most graphically. She began by selecting a poem too difficult for her kindergarteners to understand. She asked the children to stand and play the poem as she read it and to close their eyes so they could "think better." Then she read the poem, haltingly and without once glancing up. The children stood patiently, listening, but had no idea of what to do. At the end of the poem and after a moment's silence, during which the student tried to figure out what had happened, one little voice piped, "Is that it?" Although the student had made an error in selecting the material, it would have helped to know that the children were doing nothing. A couple of glances up from the page would have made this clear.

The leader should also take his own voice into consideration when deciding how many children will be playing the material. For the teacher with a strong voice, it may be possible to read loudly and clearly enough even when the entire class is playing. Many teachers, particularly the inexperienced, may not have strong enough voices to be heard when more than ten are playing. Some experimenting and practicing may be necessary to determine one's vocal capabilities.

Some material may need a number of pauses while other material needs little, if any. Generally, it is best to make the pauses too short rather than too long. Pauses can always be lengthened on repeated playings when the children have more ideas and feel more comfortable with the material. Since the narration contains the cues to the action, the children must be cautioned to participate quietly enough to hear the leader. The leader's timing and intensity in reading can help control the noise level. If the children become a little boisterous, he can pause for a moment. When the children become more quiet in order to hear the next cue, the leader can speak in a softer voice, and the children's playing will become quieter. When he reads fast or slow, the children will pick up those cues as well.

Music

The use of recorded music during the playing, while not required, has advantages. It can lend atmosphere and sustain involvement as well as encourage ideas. The selected music should be appropriate to the spirit of the material.

The music might be played throughout the activity or may be regulated to come in only at the beginning and end or during certain pauses. The leader will have to realize, however, that if the music is played throughout, his voice will have to be projected over it.

There is probably no one answer to what is appropriate music, but since pantomime is being emphasized, the leader should generally be most concerned with the timing and beat of the music. The movements the children create will be more flowing or casual with music that does not have a definite beat. If the music sounds more rigid in time as in a march, it would encourage more precise kinds of movements.

Repeating the Material

Often children will want to play the material more than once. The first playing can be a sort of run through, and the leader should not expect detailed pantomime and depth of meaning. In repeated playings the children may deepen the experience on their own.

In additional playings the children can be encouraged both to repeat the ideas they like and to try new ideas as well. The leader might say,

> **T:** This time when we play, you may decide to change the way you played the idea the first time and try something new. If you really liked something you did the first time, you might want to repeat it.

In repeated playings the leader and children may experiment with more space, sharing experiences, and working for in-depth involvement. We will discuss specific procedures for these goals in the next two chapters.

Evaluation

Throughout the discussions, preview playing, and the eventual playing, the leader should convey to the children his general enthusiasm and enjoyment. While there is a spirit of hard work, there is also a spirit of fun.

Comments can be made that acknowledge children's ideas, but no one idea need be praised over another. Statements should be made in a general way.

> I see.
> That's another way it could be done.
> I saw many different and good ideas.

The leader can express his appreciation whenever children handle space or difficult lines creatively or when they follow the audience rules:

> I like the way you listen to each other.
> You did very well putting all of the actions into one tiny area.

Perhaps the most important evaluation, however, is the children's own. Self-evaluation can be encouraged by asking:

> What's the one thing you did that you liked the best?
> What do you think was your best idea?

What was the hardest part for you?

What can we do about the hard parts? In what ways can we help one another with them?

When a spirit of working together to create an enjoyable experience can be established in any learning situation, the highest achievements are gained.

EXERCISES FOR THE COLLEGE STUDENT

1. Select a story and a poem suitable for a narrated activity. Prepare it to read aloud to your classmates. Practice and experiment with pauses, timing, vocal pitch, and quality to make the selection as interesting as possible. Find some background music suitable to the mood of the selection and play it as you read.
2. Select a narrative poem or story suitable for individual playing. Lead your classmates through a playing of the material you have selected. Consider whether or not a discussion will be necessary; whether preview playing is required. Give all the necessary instructions for organizing the playing. Consider the possibility of special effects of lighting, sound effects, etc. Evaluate the playing.
3. Select a narrative poem or story to be played in pairs following the format in 2.
4. Select a narrative poem or story suitable for group playing. Proceed as above.
5. Find as many other suitable materials for narration as you can. Keep a file of these materials. Select from reading books, social studies, health, science, and other trade books used in the classroom.

MATERIALS FOR NARRATIVE PANTOMIME

The following stories and poems are suggested for narrative pantomime. They are arranged in alphabetical order according to title. Numbers in parentheses refer to sources listed in the final bibliography.

The following symbols are used to indicate the age level the material might be best suited for:

Y   young children in kindergarten, first, and second grades
M   middle-grade children in third and fourth grades
O   older children in fifth and sixth grades

Y   *Alligators All Around,* Maurice Sendak. Harper & Row, 1962.
Something to do for each letter of the alphabet.

M   *All Upon A Stone,* Jean Craighead George. Crowell, 1971.
Picturebook. A mole cricket searches for and finds his fellow crickets.
After a brief meeting he returns to his solitary life once again.

Y-M   *Andy and the Lion,* James Daugherty. Viking, 1966.
Young boy reads about lions and imagines himself in an adventure similar
to that of the fabled Androcles.

M   *The Barn,* John Schoenherr. Little, Brown, 1968.
Picturebook. In an old barn, a skunk searches for food; yet to the Mother
Owl, the skunk is food for her babies.

O   "Base Stealer," Robert Francis.   (39)
Baseball player's actions described as he hesitates — then decides to run.
Poem.

Y   *Beady Bear,* Don Freeman. Viking, 1954.
Beady Bear, a stuffed toy bear, thinks he should live in a cave so he gives
it a try. Picturebook.

M-O   "The Bear in the Pear Tree." Alice Geer Kelsey.   (35)
The Hodja meets a bear and hides from him in a pear tree.

M   *The Big Yellow Balloon,* Edward Fenton. Doubleday, 1967.
Picturebook. With his yellow balloon Roger manages to lure an unlikely
parade of a cat, dog, dog catcher, lady, thief, and policeman. Organize
this one carefully.

Y-M   *Brownies-Hush!* Gladys L. Adshead. Henry Z. Walck, 1938.
A version of "The Elves and the Shoemaker" story. There are some
fourteen elves, but it can be played with fewer.

Y   "Boa Constrictor," Shel Silverstein.   (34)
Very brief poem. The complaint of one being eaten by a boa.

Y   "Busy," A. A. Milne.   (33)
A little boy plays at pretending to be different people. In between he
turns roundabout.

M   "The Cares of a Caretaker," Wallace Irwin.   (34)
A nice old lady has her work cut out for her trying to take care of life on
the seashore. Poem.

Y-M   "Cat," Mary Britton Miller.   (4)
In this poem a cat's movements are described.

O   "The Cougarfish," George Mendoza.   (15)
A fisherman is determined to catch the wild and savage cougarfish.

M-O   "The Crack in the Wall," George Mendoza.   (15)
A hermit loses his house to a crack in the wall that won't stop spreading.

O   "The Creation," James Weldon Johnson.   (21)
One description of the procedure God used to create the world and man.

Y-M   "Dippy's Day by Moonlight," Cynthia Stone Richmond. Ginn Reader
How It Is Nowadays.
A kangaroo rat spends his day at night.

M   *The Dragon of Santa Lalia,* Carol Carrick. Bobbs-Merrill, 1971.
Grandmother takes care of a fiery dragon with the help of some popcorn.

Y   "The Elf and the Dormouse," Oliver Herford.   (46)
An elf borrows a toadstool from a dormouse and invents the first
umbrella in this story poem.

Y   "The Elf Singing," William Allingham.   (46)
A story poem about a wizard who almost catches an elf.

M–O   "Foul Shot," Edwin A. Hoey.   (39)
Sensitive poem that describes all the minute details of a basketball
player's actions before making the foul shot. In solo playing the children
can be both the player and then the ball.

Y   *Frances Face-Maker,* William Cole and Tomi Ungerer. World, 1964.
Frances doesn't like to go to bed at night. Daddy plays a game with her,
trying out all kinds of faces.

M   "Gertrude McFuzz," Dr. Seuss.   (62)
Gertrude finds that growing a big beautiful tail may not be what she
really wants after all.

Y   "Goblin Story," Else Holmelund Minarik.   (29)
Something scares a little goblin; then he discovers it was only his own
shoes running after him!

Y   "Goldilocks and the Three Bears," Robert Southey.   (3) (46)
Classic story of little girl who visits a bear's house.

M–O   *Gone Is Gone,* Wanda Gag. McCann, 1935.
The old tale of the man who swaps chores with his wife to discover her
work isn't as simple as he had thought. Another version is "The Husband
Who Was to Mind the House" (4).

Y–M   *The Great Big Enormous Turnip,* Alexei Tolstoy. Watts, 1968.
Picturebook. Grandfather, grandmother, granddaughter, dog, cat, and
mouse finally succeed in pulling up a turnip. The story is simple. One
child could be the turnip as well. Can also encourage character
development.

Y–M   *Gregory,* Robert Bright. Doubleday, 1969.
Proud Gregory is fast, can jump high and holler loud; but he has a
problem listening. He wants to show off his talents and Grandma only
wants him to gather eggs. Solo or group.

M–O   "The Hairy Toe," George Mendoza.   (24)
Deliciously weird tale similar to the tale of Teeny Tiny. Picturebook.

Y–M   "The Handre," Dorothy S. Thomas. Ginn Reader *How It is Nowadays.*
Ugly goblin is tricked by two little cats.

Y–M   *Harold and the Purple Crayon,* Crockett Johnson. Harper & Row, 1955.
A little boy has many adventures with the help of a purple crayon to
draw them with. Solo playing.

Y   *Harry the Dirty Dog,* Gene Zion. Harper & Row, 1956.
Harry won't take a bath until his family doesn't recognize him.

Y-M   *Hildilid's Night,* Cheli Duran Ryan. Macmillan, 1971.
Woman tries everything she can think of to get rid of the night.
Picturebook.

Y-M   *How the Grinch Stole Christmas!* Dr. Seuss. Random House, 1957.
The classic story of a spiteful character who learns the true meaning of
Christmas. Picturebook. Can be done in solo or in pairs with Max, the
dog.

Y-M   "How the Rhinoceros Got His Skin," Rudyard Kipling.   (28)
A Parsee gets even with a rhinoceros who keeps stealing cakes from him.

Y-M   "How the Robin's Breast Became Red," Flora J. Cooke.   (46)
The tale of the brave robin who saved the precious fire.

M-O   "Hungry Hans," Keller-Untermeyer.   (46)
Use the second half of the story. The lock turns and Hans is left to tend
the roasting pig. His hunger overcomes him and bit by bit the suckling
pig disappears into his expanding stomach, until he realizes what he has
done and sinks to the floor in despair. Both tragic and comic.

Y-M   *If You Were An Eel, How Would You Feel?* Mina and Howard
Simon. Follett, 1963.
Picturebook. Various animals described according to their characteristic
actions.

Y   *Indian Two Feet and His Horse,* Margaret Friskey. Scholastic, 1964.
A little Indian wishes for a horse and gets one.

O   *Ittki Pittki,* Miriam Chaikin. Parents', 1971.
Ittki Pittki, a merchant, fears he has been poisoned.

Y   "Jump or Jiggle," Evelyn Beyer.   (4)
Brief poem naming animals and their style of walking.

Y-M   *Just Suppose,* May Garelick. Scholastic, 1969.
Suppose you were a number of different animals, doing what they do.

M-O   "Lines Written for Gene Kelly To Dance To," Carl Sandburg.   (13)
Poem asks famous dancer to dance different ideas. First section is the
most fun to do.

Y   *The Little Auto,* Lois Lenski. Henry Z. Walck, 1934.
Mr. Small has a little auto which he cares for and drives all around.
Picturebook.

Y-M   *The Little Brute Family,* Russell Hoban. Macmillan, 1966.
Picturebook. Papa, Mama, Brother, Sister, and Baby Brute consistently
have grumpy and unpleasant days until a little lost feeling enters their
lives. Group playing.

Y   *The Little Cowboy,* Margaret Wise Brown. William R. Scott, 1948.
A big cowboy does a number of things and a little cowboy repeats them
in smaller style.

Y   *The Little Fire Engine,* Lois Lenski. Henry Z. Walck, 1946.
Mr. Small is a fireman in this story.

O   "Man Alone," Author not indicated. SRA Reader, *The Big Abzul-
Raider Game,* 1967.

A Navy ensign, testing a new type of survival fishing kit, accidentally goes overboard and spends several hours in the Pacific Ocean before being rescued.

M   *The Man Who Didn't Wash His Dishes,* Phyllis Krasilovsky. Doubleday, 1950.
Picturebook. A lazy man's neglect in washing dishes poses problems in housekeeping.

M   *Mousekin's Christmas Eve.* Edna Miller. Prentice-Hall, 1965.
Picturebook. Mousekin leaves an empty house and finds a new one on Christmas Eve.

Y-M   *Mousekin's Family,* Edna Miller. Prentice-Hall, 1965.
Picturebook. Mousekin tries to teach survival methods to a mouse he thinks is a member of his family. Fun for pairs.

M   "The Old Wife and the Ghost," James Reeves.   (5)
A poem about a ghost who plays tricks on a deaf woman.

Y-M   "On Our Way," Eve Merriam.   (6)
In this poem children experiment with the walks of various animals.

M-O   *Oté*, Pura Belpré. Pantheon, 1969.
Picturebook. A Puerto Rican folktale about a man and his family who are plagued by an unwanted, nearsighted little devil.

M-O   *Painting the Moon,* Carl Withers. Dutton, 1970.
Picturebook. The Devil wants to get rid of the moon, which shines so brightly that he can't do his dirty work. He and two helpers have a solution. Begin where they begin to paint.

O   "The Passer," George Abbe.   (41)
Brief description of a football pass. Try this one in slow motion.

Y   "(The Tale of) Peter Rabbit," Beatrix Potter.   (3) (46)
The timeless story of a misbehaving bunny who finds adventure in Mr. McGregor's garden. Solo and in pairs with Mr. McGregor.

M   *The Pine Tree,* George Maxim Ross. Dutton, 1966.
A pine seed fights the elements for its life. Played in solo; or in pairs one child can be the pine tree and the partner can portray the various elements in nature.

M-O   *The Pond,* Carol and Donald Carrick. Macmillan, 1970.
Sensitive, poetic description of movements of water, insects, and all life near and in a pond.

O   "Rodeo," Edward Lueders.
Description of a cowboy readying to mount and ride a Brahma bull.

M-O   "Saved by a Turkey," Ellis Credle.   (49)
On his way home in the boat with his prized turkey, Jess loses the oars. He can't swim, but he can think, and with the turkey's help they get to shore. Begin with the trip home.

M   *The Selfish Old Woman,* Toshiko Kanzawa. Bobbs-Merrill, 1971.
An old woman bakes a pie and has a strange adventure when her bonnet falls down over her face and she has to guess what happens next!

O   "The Skunk in the Pond," George Mendoza.   (15)
A henpecked man finally takes care of the problem of a skunk in the
pond by cooking it for his nagging family to eat! Solo or in groups.

Y   *The Snowy Day,* Ezra Jack Keats. Viking, 1962.
Picturebook. Peter plays in the snow.

M-O   "The Sorcerer's Apprentice," Richard Rostron.   (46) (3)
The young apprentice to a magician remembers only part of a magic spell
and finds himself in much trouble. Begin action when the Sorcerer leaves.

Y-M   "The Spaghetti Dream," Beatrice Schenk de Regniers.   (10)
A fantastic dream about eating spaghetti and ice cream.

Y-M   *The Story About Ping,* Marjorie Flack. Viking, 1961.
The adventure of a little duck on the Yangtze River.

Y   *The Tale of Two Bad Mice,* Beatrix Potter. Warne, 1932.
Two mice find a doll house and create havoc when they find the play
food is not real.

Y   "Teeny Tiny," English folktale.   (46)
A little lady has a problem after taking the scarecrow's clothes.

Y-M   "Theodore Turtle," Ellen MacGregor. McGraw-Hill, 1955.
Forgetful Theodore first loses one of his rubbers and then misplaces
almost everything else he lays his hands on.

O   "There Will Come Soft Rains," Ray Bradbury.   (30)
Sensitively written science fiction story about an ultra modern house
that falls apart, piece by piece, after humanity is destroyed with the final
bomb. Difficult but worth the effort.

Y   *There's a Nightmare in My Closet,* Mercer Mayer. Dial, 1968.
Picturebook. A little boy solves a problem with a scary nightmare-
monster, who really isn't as scary as he seems.

O   "Three Fridays," Alice Geer Kelsey.   (3) (35)
On three Fridays the Hodja, who has problems thinking of a sermon,
manages to get by with saying very little to his congregation. Begin with
the third paragraph.

M-O   *The Three Poor Tailors,* Victor G. Ambrus. Harcourt, Brace & World,
1965.
Three tailors go off to see the city and find fun, adventure, and trouble.
Groups of four: three tailors and the fourth can play the soldier, the
innkeeper, and guards.

M   "Ticky-Picky-Boom-Boom," Philip M. Sherlock.   (2)
Begin where Tiger is chased by the yams from Anansi's fields. He tries to
hide behind the Dog and the Duck. Brother Goat saves him. Some
chanting of repetitious dialogue. Be sure to play this one running in place
at first.

M-O   "Trinity Place," Phyllis McGinley.   (36)
Description of actions of pigeons in a city park, comparing them with
men.

M-O   "Two Feasts for Anansi," Harold Courlander.   (25)
The spider's plan to attend two feasts backfires. His sons pull and tug at the rope tied to his waist until his middle becomes very small.

M   *The Village Tree,* Taro Yashima. Viking, 1953.
Picturebook. A poetic description of children at play by the river and the great tree in Japan. Middle portion is the easiest to play.

M-O   "A Visit from St. Nicholas," Clement V. Moore.   (4)
Traditional story-poem about what happened the night before Christmas.

M-O   "Wait Till Martin Comes," Maria Leach.   (53)
A man has a scary adventure in a haunted house.

M   *The Way of an Ant,* Kazere Mizumura. Crowell, 1970.
A young ant keeps climbing because there always seems to be something higher, until he grows older and wiser and understands the order of things.

M   *We Were Tired of Living in a House,* Liesel Moak Skorpen. Coward-McCann, 1969.
Some children decide to investigate other places to live and find that their house might not be so bad after all.

Y-M   *What Do You Do, Dear?* Sesyle Joslin. Young Scott, 1961.
Unusual situations still require social manners.

Y-M   "What Was I Scared Of?" Dr. Seuss.   (40)
One of Seuss' characters is frightened of a pair of pants with nobody in them, until they find that each is frightened of the other. Pairs.

Y   *Whistle for Willie,* Ezra Jack Keats. Viking, 1964.
Peter wishes he could learn to whistle for his dog.

M-O   "Winnebago Origin Myth."   (45)
The myth of the creation of the world and man from the Winnebago Indians.

M-O   "The Witches' Ride," Lupe de Osma.   (4)
A youth's adventure with perhaps four witches who also play the robbers later.

4

Techniques for Further Creative Work

In the previous chapter we focused mainly on creative interpretation of narrated materials, unison or private playing, and limited space. In this chapter we will discuss how the leader guides the children so that they contribute their own ideas to the material; encourages them to share their ideas with each other; utilizes larger areas of space within the classroom; and organizes the playing in an orderly fashion.

FURTHER CREATIVE WORK

Earlier we used the term "creative interpretation." We said that the material gave the children ideas of *what* to do but not *how* to do it. Once the children have played the material as it is written, they may like to replay it, adding some of their own ideas. Particularly with materials for pairs and groups, the leader might even like to encourage the children to play it on their own without his narration. In this way the narrative material can become a basis for a new activity.

For beginning work in creative thinking, the narrated materials are particularly useful since the children have the original ideas to fall back on. Also,

All materials referred to in this chapter are found in the preceding bibliography.

the leader has the original material to use for any narration or sidecoaching the children may need.

It is important that the leader not expect outstanding ideas or very lengthy ones. This is initial work in opening up for elaboration. A climate of acceptance of all ideas is important. Once this climate is established in beginning work, children's confidence in their ideas will grow, and the foundation will be laid for more creative work later.

On the other hand, it is important to remember all the rules necessary for playing that will keep order and control. Limited space can control action. Keeping the size of groups small at first and gradually expanding with more people minimizes problems with social and physical interaction. The leader should not try to do everything at once, or chaos and confusion will take over where creativity was the goal.

Additional Action

After the children have played a narrated story, the leader can question them about any additional ideas they may have for playing it. Generally the leader stimulates them to think of additional action. Notice the following examples:

A.

T: Gregory was very fast and could jump very high. Besides being able to catch the honeybear and move the mule, what might be some other jobs he might have to do before he gets griddle cakes to eat?

C: He might pick a lot of strawberries for the jam and have to go 'way up on the hill to find them.

C: He could plow some fields with the mule.

C: Because he could jump up high, maybe he could paint the barn up at the top where his Granny couldn't reach.

B.

T: In Dr. Seuss' story, "What Was I Scared Of?" the person is always afraid that when he goes out to do errands or go fishing or whatever he sets out to do, he will meet the pants with no one inside them. This time when we play the story, perhaps you can think of some other things the person might be doing when he meets the pants. What might you do?

C: You could go grocery shopping and see him pushing a cart toward you.

C: You could go to the movies and be finding a seat and get all settled and then look up and there he is next to you!

C: You might be picking berries and he comes riding by on his bicycle.

Using the procedure above, the leader and children can develop ideas for creative work based on narrative material from a variety of sources. Notice the following example from a narrative passage in a social studies text:

> **T:** Our text doesn't describe what the Eastern Woodland Indian women and some of the Indian men do while the hunters search for game. The text does describe grinding corn, weaving a blanket, making a wigwam; but after these tasks, while the hunters are stalking the deer, what else could they do? The picture may help you form some additional ideas.
>
> **C:** I think that baby in the picture is going to cry, and one of the women will feed it.
>
> **C:** It looks like one of the women is going toward the canoe. Maybe she could go fishing or check to see that the canoe is in good repair.
>
> **C:** Since it's autumn, some of the Indians might search for fall berries that make good dye.

For some materials the children can be encouraged to create their own ideas of what happens just before a story takes place, or what happens at the moment just after the ending. For example, in a story like "The Three Bears," the leader could ask for ideas of what Goldilocks is doing while the Bears are eating their porridge and finding that it is too hot. The children might suggest that she is picking flowers in the woods; that she is on her way to visit someone; or that she goes for a walk, gets lost, and stumbles on the Three Bears' house by accident.

The ending of the story says only that Goldilocks jumped out the window and ran home. Sometimes it is fun to add just one more thing for each character to do.

> **T:** At the very ending of the story, Goldilocks runs home. We don't know what the Bears did after Goldilocks ran away. Let's think of one thing for Goldilocks to do when she gets home and one thing each of the Bears might do at the end of the story.
>
> **C:** Goldilocks hides under her bed when she gets home.
>
> **C:** She could call the cops and tell them some Bears are missing from the zoo.
>
> **C:** Mama Bear takes an aspirin.
>
> **C:** Baby Bear cries because he wants her to stay and play.
>
> **C:** Papa Bear calls the cops and reports a break-in.
>
> **C:** All the Bears faint.

Additional Characters

In replaying narrated materials there is an opportunity to invent additional characters. For example, there can be guards, servants, crowds, passersby, pets, friends, or onlookers in almost any story. And the leader should not overlook the possibility of creating interesting inanimate objects. For example Richard

Rostron's "The Sorcerer's Apprentice" would seem to have only three playable characters: the Sorcerer, Fritzl, and the Broom. But children delight in being various articles such as magic books, bottles, baskets, or flasks found in the Sorcerer's cellar which bob around, sink, or float in the rising water.

Children should not be cast as inanimate objects, however, unless the object has importance or can move in some way. For example, there is nothing exciting about standing with arms outstretched to represent a gate unless the gate has some significance (all who pass through are changed) or can move (it is unlatched and a storm causes it to be blown back and forth.)

In adding characters, the leader generally asks about what these people or things will be doing when the other action is taking place. For example:

> **T:** Several of you have mentioned that you would like to be the Sorcerer's magic book. Let's think about that for a moment. Where is the book and when does the water reach it? What happens when the water does get high enough to float the book? What happens to the book, does it float or sink? Who has thought through what will happen to you as a magic book in a flood?
>
> **C:** I'll be open, lying on the table.
>
> **T:** How high from the floor will that be? (Child indicates height.)
>
> **C:** Then, because I'm magic I can see the water getting higher and higher. So I will close slowly so my insides won't get wet. Then I float until the end of the story.
>
> **C:** I'm on a shelf like a library book. The water never gets up as high as I am. But I fall off the shelf because there's so much commotion. And because I'm magic, I grow legs and arms and swim out the door.
>
> **C:** And up the steps. You're in the cellar you know.

In the story *The Little Auto,* some groups might like to enact the auto itself. Along with Mr. Small there would be a group of five children, which might be as many as could be handled easily. In each group, four children on their hands and knees can be the tires of the car. To give them a little more to do, they can also be the engine humming and the horn beeping. The action can be controlled if the auto bounces along "in place" rather than moving about. A sixth person could act all the parts of the other characters mentioned: the policeman, the gas station attendant, and even (although he is not mentioned) the person who sells the newspaper to Mr. Small.

Planning and Playing

Particularly for pair and group playing, the children may need a brief planning time together to decide their ideas. The time given for such planning should not be so lengthy as to suggest that the children must create a great deal of new material. A minute could be sufficient for the first attempts.

The leader may continue to narrate the material as before, merely pausing for a little longer time in the places where he has encouraged any additional action. Now it will be even more important for the teacher to be very familiar with the material so that he can carefully observe what is being added to the material and so that his pauses can allow time for the additional ideas to be played.

If the leader decides that the children might be able to play the material without his narration, he will need to give a signal to begin and end the playing. The signals might be the first and last lines of the story.

T: Once upon a time there was a little old lady who. . . .

. . . and she never went looking for trouble again.

Or, the leader might like to use music to signal the beginning and the ending of the playing. If music was used during the first narration, the same music might be used again.

T: This time, instead of narrating the story, I'll just play the music we used before. When the music starts, you may begin playing. When the music stops, you must end your playing.

Now that the children are incorporating their own ideas into the playing and are not waiting for the leader's narration, the playing time may be varied. If the leader wants them all to end together, he may say, "Bring your story to an end," or he may say, "The music is coming to an end; you'll have to complete your story." Then he ends the music smoothly and perhaps states the story's last line.

It is quite possible that the children will repeat the same ideas they dramatized in the first playing of the material. Often they feel their original ideas warrant repeating. On the other hand, sometimes the children change the story line — either in a planned way or spontaneously. One of the tailors in the story, *The Three Poor Tailors,* for example, might decide to escape punishment. Or, they may all decide to get caught, escape, and get caught again. They may even escape punishment altogether!

In these replayings, particularly in pairs and groups, children frequently initiate verbalizing.* If the children can talk among themselves quietly, verbal interaction should be allowed. If talking makes the playing too noisy, a rule of "pantomime only!" may have to be enforced.

Sidecoaching

Whenever the leader encourages the children to contribute their own ideas to the playing, he should be prepared to sidecoach. In sidecoaching, the leader

*Further work in verbalizing is undertaken in Chapters 10 and 11.

"talks the children through" the activity, suggesting action or sensory or emotional reactions they might include. It is a remedial technique used when the children need suggestions from the teacher.

Sometimes sidecoaching is needed by all the children, and sometimes only a few need help. Usually the children who do need help are the ones who listen for it. It does not seem to distract those children who have their own ideas.

Usually the teacher does not know for sure, until the children have begun playing and he is observing them, whether they will need sidecoaching. It is not unusual for children to discuss an idea with great enthusiasm and appear to be very ready to enact it, and then during the playing suddenly become unsure of themselves and appear to be at a loss. On the other hand, there are times when although only a few ideas are mentioned in a discussion, the children begin to have numerous ideas as they play.

As we noted in the previous chapter, if the leader uses narrative material, he can rely upon it for his sidecoaching. He may also include some of the ideas the children mentioned in their discussion or some of the ideas he observes:

> **T:** It seems as if the fishermen have all arrived at the spot where they will try to catch the cougarfish. Some are already baiting their hooks. I wonder how long they'll have to wait to catch something . . . Some seem to be having trouble hauling their catch in . . . Some don't seem to like what they have caught. . . .

When the teacher sidecoaches, sometimes just the sound of his voice in the background reassures the children that he has not left them entirely on their own. It is similar to playing background music; and, in fact, the two go well together.

SHARING

Often when children play an idea in creative dramatics and particularly enjoy it, they want to share it with others. The teacher will want to give children the experience of both sharing their ideas and of appreciating each others' ideas. He will want them to have the opportunity to note the diverse interpretations of ideas as well as the similarities. He will want them to have the experience of giving and receiving in an interpersonal relationship.

The philosophy of creative dramatics focuses more on personal development and communication skills than it does on theatrical skills. For this reason an audience situation must be handled with care, or it can arrest rather than aid personal development.

It must always be stressed to the children that they are not performing or entertaining or evaluating each other. Almost everyone, even the youngest of children, has had the unhappy experience of having to entertain and being judged for it. For example, a young child spontaneously sings a song with gay abandon. Then when Daddy comes home at night or visitors are present, the child is asked to repeat his song. Now he clams up or sings with fear. The environment has now changed, and the psychological security has disappeared. The insensitive parent is disappointed and says so.

Fearful of repeating an earlier unhappy experience, many children feel anxious when others are watching them, even their own classmates. Many will behave toward each other as they have been treated in the past themselves. If the players are less than great, they may be made fun of through booing, hissing, and sarcastic remarks. What may be happening to the audience is that they are identifying with the player and are afraid that they too might be less than great when they are called upon. Before others make fun of them, they will make fun of others.

Even if children are not uncomfortable in an audience situation, they may have only one idea of what an audience should be. Frequently children are in an audience at a sports event or a movie or watching television. In these situations they may behave in ways that go unnoticed by the performers. They talk out loud, cheer, boo, and scream without much disturbance or detriment to the performers. And these behaviors are generally acceptable for such events.

Being an audience for a sharing experience may not be that common for children. The teacher usually needs to lead toward a different kind of attitude and behavior. He will have to be concerned with the player's confidence and with the audience's sensitivity. Some patience may be necessary for changing children's established attitudes.

Usually it is best to use first playings for unison, private work and replayings for sharing. After several initial experiences in unison playing, the children will probably feel more comfortable and confident. They will also have gained a greater degree of concentration and absorption in their ideas.

It is important that children be allowed to make their own decision about sharing. Although a child may not be uncomfortable working in front of his peers, he may sometimes feel his *ideas* are too personal and private to share.

Frequently those children who do want to share ask the teacher to allow it. If the teacher is not certain about everyone's readiness to share, he may ask,

T: Are there some people or groups who would like to share their ideas with the rest?

Whenever sharing is done, it is always important that no undue attention is focused on any one person. For individual playing, it is possible for one half of the class to share their ideas with the other half. For pair playing, there can be three or four pairs at a time. Even for small group playing there can be two groups, rather than one group at a time.

At first it is important to keep the sharing time brief. This is particularly helpful when children may have only vaguely formulated ideas. The players usually feel less threatened by the short period of time. Observers can become understandably bored by lengthy sharing periods – from inactivity if nothing else.

It is also important that the leader convey the philosophical attitude about audiences for creative dramatics by his use of the word "share" rather than "show" or "perform." There need not be a judgement placed on the ideas presented, and no evaluation is required. The teacher may need to say no more than,

> T: You may see a lot of different ideas and you may see some ideas that are similar to your own.

As in preview playings, the audience should be guided to help the players concentrate by not distracting them in any way.

> T: While the players are working to share their ideas with us, let's help them concentrate by being as quiet as we can.

SPACE

There is a common misconception about the relationship of space to the successfulness of creative dramatics. For one thing, there seems to be a tendency to feel that children will have more ideas if they have more space. Some teachers rationalize that the children need space to express their ideas. This results in the false conclusion that the more space the children have the more ideas they will have and the better they will express them. But, if the stimulus for ideas is inadequate or the guidance of ideas is lacking, no amount of space is going to work the magic.

In fact, space can actually become overpowering, inhibiting, and unmanageable. If children have no idea of how they will use the space given to them, they can become uneasy about it. They may stand immobilized, giggle, crowd against each other, or behave as if freed for the first time in their lives. All of these behaviors can be indicative of embarrassment and a sense of insecurity about not knowing what to do. During times like these, space can be oppressive.

Some children have very little trouble using space. Their motor control is excellent, they sensitively adjust their movements to accomodate a variety of spaces – the gym, activity room, and classroom. They can move freely and with astonishing control. They can run in random patterns and never collide or even touch each other. They can work closely together, maintaining control and sensitively respecting the needs of their peers.

It would be ideal if all children could operate in this fashion. Realistically, however, many children will not. Such factors as age, motor control, and social and emotional maturity will play a significant role in determining their ability to use space. The teacher has the responsibility for guiding children who have greater needs.

Expanding Playing Areas

In the previous chapter it was suggested that individual children should remain at their desks and that partners and groups should work in small defined areas such as corners of the room. To expand the space further, the leader will move the children from these tactile boundaries. For individual playing the children can move to those open areas at the front and sides of the room. There the children probably can occupy a space large enough to turn with outstretched arms without touching anyone else. For pair and group playing, the leader will probably have to rearrange the classroom furniture to allow more open spaces. This has already been discussed in Chapter 2.

When the space is expanded and former tactile boundaries are no longer used, new boundaries will have to be set so that the playing areas do not overlap. The specific areas must be clear to everyone. The teacher may designate these areas, or he may give the children this responsibility.

When it is possible for the entire class to play at the same time, it may be wise to let individual children or small groups select their areas one at a time. This procedure gives both the children and the teacher the opportunity to see the remaining available spaces.

> **T**: For this story, everyone will have a space to work in by himself. You can select that space, but be sure your space doesn't get in the way of anyone else's. People in Row 1, find yourself a place here in the front . . . Row 2, it looks as if there are still some available spaces in that same area. . . .

This procedure also keeps the excitable noise to a minimum. When children are selecting their areas, there is usually some amount of interaction. While this is a natural response, some groups are noisier and more excitable than others.

It is wise to keep in mind that some children easily distract each other, and those children should probably be separated.

> **T**: Before you find a space, it might help your concentration if you avoid standing next to someone you are apt to talk to or giggle with.

For some children it may be necessary for the teacher to assign specific areas.

> **T**: Sandy, this can be your place; Ralph, here's yours; Betty, you stand here. I think this arrangement might make it easier for you to concentrate.

Some rooms may not be large enough to accommodate all of the children playing simultaneously. If so, the leader may create some activity for the seated children to do. Often they can make appropriate sound effects for the playing children.

When children are settled in their playing area, the teacher should explicitly explain that they are to remain in that space *throughout* the playing. Otherwise, they may think they can begin there and then move on to other areas later.

The leader can aid their efforts to remain in those areas by selecting or designing materials in which the characters are logically anchored. For example, scarecrows can be tacked to a pole; clothes can be pinned to a line, etc. Children are able to move, but their movements are restricted to a specific area.

It is also helpful to give them time to explore their separate areas. The teacher may clearly define them and help the children see their imaginative possibilities.

A.

T: Before we begin to play the story of "Peter Rabbit," take a few minutes to imagine that your area is Mr. McGregor's garden. Staying in your area, find the lettuce . . . radishes . . . don't forget the parsley. Now where will you put the gooseberry net? . . . How about that important watering can? . . . And the gate? . . . Where in your area will you put your own home? . . . and comforting bed? . . . .

B.

T: Now that you're all in your specific area, you and your partner explore that area. If you can, determine where you'll pitch your camp and the spot where you will pretend that you two, the first men ever, reach the top of Mount Everest.

Slow Motion

The leader may want to give the children the experience of moving in slow motion. Slow motion is useful for several purposes. It can control difficult action by slowing it to a more manageable pace. It is helpful in demonstrating the relationship of the moving body in space, accommodating other moving bodies. And, when it is mastered, it can be fascinating to watch and to be involved in.

Moving in slow motion is not always easy and requires the guidance of the teacher. Children have to be reminded to keep the movement slow; in the excitement of moving, the tendency is always to speed up. Children can be encouraged to be aware of each movement and each body position. It is also helpful to compare slow motion to the replays of televised sports events or to time-lapse photography.

Any activity can be played in slow motion. The following is a narrated short poem:

> **T:** I'm going to read the poem, "The Passer," and as I do, one of you will pretend to be the football player who secretly hands the ball to his partner. But all of this will be done in slow motion. You'll both run in slow motion; the passer will hand the ball to the end, and the receiver will take the ball in slow motion. Try to be aware of every movement you make. . . . (It might add to the fun of this particular poem if the leader were to pretend to be the sports announcer. After one playing, he might officially request a "repeat of that action for the folks at home.")

Encouraging Children
to Organize Space for Themselves

It is possible for children to become and remain involved in what they are doing without the aid of the separate working areas. The leader can encourage and guide children to allow their physical needs and their ideas to determine the use of space. They may move wherever they feel they need to and where their ideas take them, provided they can remain involved and can be aware of the others in the group.

When children are allowed to organize space for themselves, the boundaries are considered flexible and constantly changing to accommodate the needs of the individual, the partners, or the groups. Some children might choose to move throughout the room. Others might prefer to remain in a specific area during the entire activity.

Such an experience in democratic responsibility is extremely valuable. Self-discipline and respect for others become primary issues. Each child is encouraged to express himself fully while at the same time being aware that his classmates are also self-seeking and yet respecting his needs also.

Such an experience may need to be approached systematically. Discussions can help. The teacher and the children may discuss what people do in order to share space. For example:

> **T:** When people move about in crowds, how do they manage to share their space with each other?
>
> **C:** They watch each other.
>
> **C:** Sometimes they have to speed up or slow down; sometimes you have to stop so you won't bump into someone.
>
> **C:** Sometimes you pass around them and sometimes you let them pass you.

The teacher may have the children practice moving without colliding or without touching. For initial practice sessions, it may be easier if the movement is simple, such as walking. It may also be helpful if the teacher plays "walking" music, or music with an easy, specific rhythm the children can follow.

> **T:** Let's see if it is possible for all of us to walk in this area and share the space. We'll start with just a few people and then add more and more. Row 1, you start first. Walk to the music and in a few minutes I'll give the signal for Row 2 to join you and then Row 3 and Row 4 until we're all in it together. Are there any questions? OK, Row 1, here we go.

After the simple activity of walking, it is also good practice (and fun!) to increase and vary the speed. It may be necessary to begin with only a few children at a time and then add more.

> **T:** This time I'm going to vary the speed of the music. When it speeds up, you speed your walking; when it slows, you slow. We'll start with just a few people and then add more. . . .

ORDERLY, ORGANIZED PLAYING

It is very important that the leader communicate his procedures for playing as clearly as possible. Children need to know what he wants and expects. From their point of view there is nothing so frustrating as having to second-guess what the teacher has in mind. From the teacher's point of view, clearly stated directions can avoid many problems.

Giving Directions

Often inexperienced teachers want to appeal to the children's imagination by sugarcoating directions in fantasy. For example, they may want the children to remain in a designated area; yet they warn:

> **T:** You're like a sticky gum, so don't touch anyone or you may stick together.

For most children this kind of statement is like a "Wet Paint" sign. It becomes an interesting possibility and announces itself as a challenge to be tested. "Really?" they may say to themselves. Then they are ironically beguiled into doing exactly what the teacher was trying to avoid. Not only do they touch each other, they may clump in a huge mass before the teacher ever figures out what happened! Being straightforward about directions is usually safer:

> **T:** During this activity you are to remain in your own space. Give yourself enough room so that you will not touch anyone.

We enjoy watching our classmates' ideas take shape.

We listen for instructions.

We go supermarket shopping as quickly as we can without bumping into each other.

Often the leader will also have to be explicit about no talking. This is hard for some teachers to do, and they will try to sugarcoat these directions. For example, the material may be a poem about snowflakes, so the teacher says,

T: Remember now, snowflakes don't talk.

But if a child can imagine he is a snowflake, he can also imagine that his snowflake is capable of speech. It makes perfect creative sense! And, in fact, the teacher might just ask for this kind of imagination on another occasion. Being straightforward, the teacher should say simply and directly,

T: For this activity I want you to move as silently as possible. There should be no talking at all. When everyone is quiet, we shall begin.

Getting Attention

To help the teacher in giving directions, he may need some attention-getting device. This device may be a sharp sound, such as the ring of a small bell or the beat of the drum; it may be a visual signal, such as the flicking of lights or the raising of a hand.

A cue other than the teacher's voice is often most effective in gaining attention. When the teacher tries to shout above the group's noise, he only adds to the din and confusion. The children often have no idea that the teacher is talking to them. Furthermore, when teachers try to raise the volume of their voice, they raise the pitch of their voice as well, which contributes to cacophony.

In time, however, with patience and guidance, the group can become sensitive enough that the leader need only say:

T: Groups, go to your areas and when you're settled, I'll give you some further directions.

Directions can be fun and still challenging and effective. For example, children usually like the word "freeze" to indicate stopping. They seem to enjoy halting in a rigid position. It becomes more of a game rule than a command. However, "freeze" can easily become overworked. If the teacher finds himself using it more than two or three times in one period, he should reexamine the situation.

Nonverbal Directions

The teacher should also be looking for ways in which to remain in control and yet not be scolding or constantly reminding children of how he wants them

Devices for getting attention.

to behave. Much of this control can be done nonverbally.

Student teachers have noted that the experienced teacher can do much with a glance, a definite shake of the head, or other simple tactics that convey as strong a message as a verbally stated one. Many of these tactics will take time to learn and to perfect. But student teachers will do well to think of some possibilities for themselves. One student teacher who was having a hard time getting the children's attention because of her soft voice drew a large colorful sign saying in bold letters, "Cool It!" Whenever she wanted the group to be quiet and listen for futher directions, she simply held up the sign and waited for a few seconds until everyone saw it. Then she proceeded with the activity.

The new teacher should also get into the habit of taking direct action when it is needed. Frequently student teachers prefer to look in the other direction rather than face a problem. There are many situations that can be overlooked, but when an activity is getting raggedy around the edges because of the behavior of some children, the whole session may begin to deteriorate quickly unless action is taken immediately.

For example, some children have a tendency to chatter to one another or to engage in horseplay. Often they will stop when the teacher moves over in their direction. The close proximity of the authority figure speaks for itself. A hand on the shoulder might also be helpful.

Repeating Directions

The teacher probably should not assume that directions can be given once and are then internalized by the children immediately. For example, experience has taught most teachers that even though careful precautions are taken, it may be difficult for the children to stay in their area once the playing begins. The children *understand* that they are to remain separate, and their intentions are well meaning, but it is very natural to gravitate (sometimes friends are tempting), and soon social and sometimes physical interaction completely overshadows the activity. Of course involvement is usually lost.

When this happens it is best to stop the activity. Inexperienced teachers are often hesitant to do this; they try to muddle through and get it over with rather than trying to solve the problem. But insistence upon remaining in separated areas is not an arbitrary decision; it is an aid for involvement. It may take practice to stay in a separate area, particularly for young children who are very active and whose bodies are often constantly in motion. Directions and the reasons for them may need to be repeated a number of times before children can follow through.

> **T:** We'll have to stop for a moment. Some people have moved from the area they began in. Please return to your starting area. It is very important that you stay in that area so that you have your own place to work and concentrate in. When you get near your friends, you have trouble concentrating. I know it may be difficult to do this the first few times we try it, and we need a little more practice in it. Let's try it again. Everybody ready? . . .

After several experiences in this step, and when children see that keeping their concentration makes the playing more interesting, it will be easier to accomplish.

Understanding Problems

When children play creative dramatics, they can often get excited and hyperactive. Sometimes it is difficult for them to listen to and follow directions. Sometimes the leader contributes to children's hyperactivity. Sometimes he takes too long to get to the playing, causing the children to be restless and fidgety. Sometimes he proceeds too quickly with an idea before the children are ready to handle it. Recognizing and admitting one's own mistakes is important in letting the children know that the difficulty may not be their fault.

A.

T: I think I've kept you sitting a long time while we've discussed this, so let's all do one small part of this together in order to get the kinks out before we play the whole thing.

B.

T: Sometimes I get so excited about what we're doing that I try to rush you too fast. I think that may be what happened just now. We were just really getting ahead of ourselves. I'll see if I can "cool it" this next time and you help me.

When things do go wrong, the best thing to do is to stop before they get worse and try to sort out what has happened and how to remedy it. There are ways to keep the excitement down without scolding the children for something that is a quite natural response. This can be done good naturedly.

T: Whoops, I can see we've got a problem. Let's work on it.

But the problem usually cannot be worked on until everyone is quiet, and the children have stopped moving. The teacher should be sure to get these things accomplished before going on with extensive discussion. If the movement is stopped first, the children's talking usually stops automatically. If not, a finger to the lips for a moment or two should be all that is necessary. Then the teacher is ready to find out what went wrong.

A statement of the situation and the consequences can put things into perspective.

T: Look, I know you're excited. But you know the rules. We can't begin until everyone settles down. I'll know that you're ready when everything is quiet.

Then the teacher waits until things do quiet down.

Even the children are aware that this wait can be helpful. One of the authors vividly remembers a helpful suggestion from a five-year-old during a chaotic moment with kindergarten children. As the children were pretending to be baby animals, they suddenly turned into ferocious tigers and lions, fighting one another. The leader recalls standing in a kind of daze until "out of the mouths of babes," a child suggested:

Teacher, I think we need to sit down in a circle.

Sometimes things go wrong in spite of all one's precautions. A leader's directions may sound logical and clear to him; he could assume that they are clear to everyone else. However, this is not always true. Once one of the authors, in trying to organize a group, became exasperated with one child who was talking with a friend. Accusingly she asked, "Can you do this?" and pointed a finger at him. He, puzzled but cooperative, nodded his head and pointed his finger also! At a time like this a sense of humor is very helpful.

In summary, we remind the teacher that by beginning with the most restricted area and expanding space by degrees, and by using organization, planning, and the clearest directions, children can learn to function with less teacher control and greater self-control.

The following is a description of a narrated poem that was elaborated in two one-hour periods with a class of fifth-graders. These sessions were the first time the children and the teacher had worked together; and it was the first time the majority of the children had experienced creative dramatics. The teacher began with narrated material, and by the end of the second hour, the children had progressed to creative activities involving group planning and verbalization.

The leader began by reading the poem "Foul Shot," and a brief discussion followed. Through her questions the leader emphasized the player's conflict: he has the opportunity to break the tie score and win the basketball game. After the discussion the leader narrated as the children pretended to be the player. This experience was repeated three times. During the three playings, the children were limited to their desk area.

During these repeated playings the leader worked for involvement by: (a) use of voice, particularly timing, when she read the poem; (b) positive feedback on what she had observed while they participated; (c) asking the children to evaluate the good things they themselves had done and how they felt when they had been involved.

For the next activity, the leader asked the children to invent the other players. Where were these players while the foul shot was being thrown? What was their attitude about the shot? The leader divided the class into groups. Each group was to decide who would be the player making the shot, who would be on his team, who would be on the opposing team. The children suggested having a referee who would hand the imaginary ball to the player and blow a "whistle." Desks were rearranged to give more space for the basketball teams. After the groups were organized, the leader again narrated the poem while the children participated.

The third experience based on the poem opened the second period. The leader and children invented the spectators. What kinds of people would attend that basketball game? While the game is going on, what do they do besides sit and watch? The children had some time to do any group planning and organizing they needed.

After this planning time, the leader gave each group a number. There were five groups. When the leader called a group's number that group was to pretend they were spectators. They could talk, use the classroom space, and do activities they felt appropriate for their character. All the other groups were to watch. The leader randomly called numbers and varied the time each group participated.

The final experience based on "Foul Shot" was initiated by the children. The groups wanted to do half-time entertainment. The leader gave them time to decide who they would be and what they were going to do. When all the groups had planned, each group shared their ideas for the rest of the class. There were tumblers, trampoline artists, a Scout drill team, and a marching band.

EXERCISES FOR THE COLLEGE STUDENT

1. Discuss various classroom physical environments. Consider such factors as fixed desks, rows of desks on runners, large rooms with movable furniture, small rooms with tables and chairs, carpeting, thin classroom partitions and walls, sky lights, and shades. Consider ways to accommodate any of these physical features. Include selection of material, planning and organizing space, and giving directions.

2. Plan to replay a selection of narrated material encouraging the children to use larger areas of space. Sketch a floor plan of a classroom, indicating the placement of desks and free space. Assuming that all of the children will be playing the activity, map out the areas the children will use. Write the directions you would give to a group of children in order to organize them in their assigned playing areas.

3. Lead your classmates in playing the above activity.

4. Plan to replay a narrated selection in which you will enourage the children to add their own ideas. Ask three to six specific questions stimulating their ideas. For each question, write three answers you think the children might give. Specify the grade level.

5. Plan to replay a selection of narrated material and rearrange the classroom. Write the directions you would need to give to the children to organize the rearrangement. Also write the preliminary instructions you will need to give before playing the material.

5

Techniques for Strengthening Involvement

Up to this point the teacher has been introduced to simple games and to narrative materials. With the narrated materials, we have also suggested methods of replaying with variations. We have referred to the importance of the children's involvement in playing. For example, we noted the importance of selecting volunteers for preview playings who could be unselfconsciously involved. We also mentioned the importance of expanding space only when involvement would not be affected adversely. In this chapter we will examine some additional techniques the leader can use to aid in-depth involvement in the playing of these and *all* materials for creative dramatics.

The importance of aiding in-depth involvement cannot be overemphasized. Generally speaking, the success of drama experiences, as measured by both the teacher and the children, is dependent on the degree of involvement of the players.

Usually the leader measures a child's involvement by observing certain behaviors. Generally he is sure of involvement when children are so absorbed or engrossed in their playing that they are unaware of anyone observing them. Perhaps they enjoy the material so much that they forget about everyone else, or perhaps they are able to block out distractions successfully.

When children are involved in dramatizing they often demonstrate their awareness of the imagined environment. For example, a child pretending to walk a tightrope may walk very carefully, exactly placing one foot ahead of the other,

"Involvement means believing what you are doing."

balancing his body with outstretched arms. He may stop momentarily, gently swaying, eyes fixed straight ahead, arms moving as if in an attempt to regain a loss of balance, and then slowly move ahead. All these movements demonstrate that he is very much aware of the narrow rope suspended high above the ground.

Another clue might be the spontaneous addition of details that the material has not specified. For example, the child pretending to walk the tightrope might also pretend to hold an imaginary umbrella for balance and bow and throw kisses to an enthusiastic but imaginary audience.

Involved children may concentrate intently and are usually highly pleased

"When you're involved, no one can distract you."

with the experience. Frequently they ask to repeat the material.

Behaviors indicating a lack of involvement might be: hesitant looking at other classmates to see what they are doing, moving aimlessly, or appearing to be puzzled by the activity. They may also involve embarrassed giggling, whispering to each other, crowding together, and other indications of insecurity.

There are times when the entire classroom seems to respond as one person, all with the same depth of involvement or lack of it. Usually, however, each child's involvement differs. Sometimes half the class is involved while the other half is only superficially involved. Sometimes only one or two are involved; sometimes only one or two have difficulty becoming involved. Some children will need a great deal of assistance; others may need little help at all.

The teacher can be very instrumental in making an experience and the playing of it as meaningful as possible. From the time he selects the material itself until the time the material is being replayed for the third or fourth time, the leader has the opportunity to affect the involvement the children will have in it. We shall discuss those steps and some of the considerations the leader can make for aiding involvement in each step along the way.

SELECTING MATERIALS

The first consideration the leader must make is in the selection of appropriate, enjoyable and meaningful material. Children work best when they are intrigued.

When the material is appealing, the children can become involved more easily. No one can respond to or concentrate on an idea that seems to be a waste of his time.

The materials should capture the children's attention and create interest. They should be fun, intriguing, or exciting. They may be subjects that thoroughly entertain, and the children want the enjoyment of playing them again and again. Or, they may be subjects that encourage intense discussions and stimulate sincere concerns.

The leader usually has to learn from his group what kinds of situations and materials it will find most appealing. Many listings of materials will specify which age groups they are most appealing to. However, it should be remembered that these are only guides and not sacred rules. While a leader should be aware of the interests of certain grade levels, he should also learn which material is most interesting and meaningful for his particular group, regardless of their age level.

Groups also vary in personality. Some groups are satisfied only when the material tickles their funny bones and has a joke in it they can enjoy together. Others want to be involved in more serious situations and stories. Some groups enjoy romantic stories; others will reject any hint of a love element. Some groups like anything and everything; others are very finicky about what they will respond to. Tastes and interests can be expanded, but that may take time and some careful planning.

As the children begin work in creative dramatics, it may be helpful to start first with materials that are humorous. The gay and lively situations relax them with laughter and lift the spirits. If the characters are funny, there is less pressure on the child to play the part in a suave, polished, and formal way. Also, if the material is humorous, a little silliness or laughing does not destroy the mood as easily as it does with serious material.

Obviously the material should also appeal to the leader since his own enthusiasm and involvement is usually contagious. The leader should select an activity in which he can have confidence and interest. He may need to be enthusiastic about it in order to sell it to a group who needs proof that the activity is worth its attention.

A leader's choice of material will naturally reflect his personality and values. For this reason, the leader should take stock of himself periodically and examine the nature of his favorite materials to see if they are meeting the needs of the children. He may discover that the children have other interests, values, and concerns. He may have to challenge himself to reach beyond his own sphere of interest, to keep alert to new materials, and to listen with a sensitive ear to both the spoken and implied interests of the children.

PRESENTING THE MATERIAL

Although we have used only literature so far, there are many materials that can motivate drama experiences. All material, whether it is music, props, pictures, or literature, is only as good a stimulus as the leader's presentation makes it.

The greatest aid in presenting material is the leader's interest in it. His own enjoyment motivates him to share it with enthusiasm. As he tells a story, leads a discussion, or even gives directions, the teacher's attitude can begin to create an appropriate atmosphere for the eventual playing.

All material has some general categorization of mood. For example, a story may be exciting, music may be peaceful, a picture may be humorous, or a prop may be curious. When presenting the material the leader can reinforce its mood by reacting appropriately. He may smile and laugh along with a humorous story, or he may tell it tongue-in-cheek. When playing recorded music he can carefully fade it in and out rather than dropping or lifting the needle abruptly. Or, he may react to a curious prop with surprise in his voice when he asks, "Who do you suppose owns this? Have you ever seen anything like it before?"

When the leader selects materials that arouse his personal interests and feelings, his voice and body will more naturally communicate the material's ideas and meanings. Vocal quality, pitch, timing, or loudness and softness of voice are all tools the leader can use in contributing meaning and understanding.

The voice can add to sensory description. For example, the leader's voice can become quiet and convey a soft quality when referring to the feel of a kitten's fur. He can say the word "warm" and make the children feel it; or say "tangy, crisp apple" in such a way that they almost taste it. His voice can creak like the door of the haunted house, moan like the wind, or boom like thunder. The voice can also convey feelings. The word "lonely" can be drawn out; sorrowful passages may need a low voice; or anxiety can be conveyed when he reads about someone trapped in a mine shaft.

The leader should always be thoroughly familiar with the material. This is especially important in presenting literature. Even if the poem or story is well known or the teacher has used it several times before, it should always be quickly reviewed before it is presented again. Familiarity with material eliminates the irritating tendency to omit crucial points, to mispronounce words, or to be halting and hesitant in the presentation. It also allows the teacher the ability to establish rapport with the children and to judge the effect of the material on them.

There are advantages to telling a story or reciting a poem, rather than reading them. Granted that time does not permit us to commit great bodies of literature to memory, face-to-face contact is superior to reading with one's nose buried in the pages. If material is to be read, the leader must be able to glance up at least occasionally.

It also helps concentration if the leader does not begin presenting the material until the children are ready to listen and participate. Some leaders are particularly adept at captivating children's attention with storytelling. They begin a story and allow the first sentence or two to calm down or to entice a wiggly or listless group. Most teachers have to establish the rule that the material will not be shared until the children are ready:

>   **T**: I'll tell the story when everybody is ready to listen.

Then they patiently (not impatiently!) wait a moment or two until the children settle down. They may also ask children to put their heads on their desks or close their eyes to aid listening.

It is helpful if the room and the children are arranged in a way that accommodates both the presentation of the material and the playing. For example, if the children are to play at the desk area, there is no need to have them sit on the floor in a circle to hear a story and then move back to their desks to play it. This can break the mood of the material and the children's concentration on it.

All material should contribute to rather than detract from the experience. If music is used, the instrument played or the recording should be of good quality. The instrument should be in tune; a record player or tape recorder should be of good fidelity. If props are used they should be sturdy, durable (or easily replaceable) clean, safe, and interesting enough to stir the imagination. Pictures should be clear, large enough to be seen, and well mounted. If a picture book is being used, the illustrations should be clear and large enough to be easily seen by the group. Film should have a clear sound track and be free of scratches and dirt.

UNDERSTANDING THE MATERIAL

A child cannot play an experience if he does not understand it. There are several techniques the leader can use to aid understanding.

Stimulating Awareness

Understanding and involvement is reinforced when children are given materials related to the activity that they can touch, taste, smell, listen to, and carefully examine. For example, before playing an experience on scuba diving, the teacher may have available some object associated with scuba diving. He has fins, a mask, oxygen tank, and perhaps some shells and a piece of dried seaweed. He shows them to the children, and they talk about them and handle them. For some children these materials may be new experiences that help them understand the topic a little better.

Or, before guiding children to pretend to be young Helen Keller, who must depend on her sense of touch for understanding and knowledge, the teacher may first choose to have the children close their eyes and examine various objects with their fingers. Before an activity in slow motion, a film such as *Dream of the Wild*

*Horses** can demonstrate the beauty of slowed movement. Or the pictures in a book such as Edward Steichen's *Family of Man†* can demonstrate the universality of human emotions. These materials can create images and awarenesses that words alone cannot always communicate.

Analogies

Sometimes the use of analogies is helpful in dealing with unfamiliar subjects. For example, before pretending to explore the moon's anti-gravity environment, the teacher might help the children recall the floating sensation of wading in deep water.

Children can think of their own analogies also.

T: Our story takes place in a desert. We already know some things about a desert, even though none of us has ever been there. Can you think of something you have seen or experienced that would be like something in the desert?

C: It would be hotter than it was in here the day the heat was turned on too high and we almost suffocated.

C: My Grandpa says when it gets really hot you can fry an egg on the sidewalk.

C: It would be even hotter than it was this summer when we had the hottest day ever recorded.

C: Those chameleons the first grade has look like the gila monsters in our book about the desert.

Discussions

Discussions can be very useful in promoting greater understanding of the material, in clarifying perceptions, and in bringing the experience closer to the children's own.

Sometimes the language of material needs clarification. For example, in the poem "Foul Shot" (p. 59), the basketball player is said to be "squeezed by silence." He also "measures the waiting net." It may help to talk about these phrases; the children may want to explain them in their own words.

C: "Squeezed by silence" means you feel cramped because it is so quiet and everyone's watching you.

C: He "measures the waiting net" by sizing it up and aiming the ball real good.

*"Contemporary Films." McGraw-Hill. Nine minutes, color.
†(New York: Museum of Modern Art, 1955.)

For material with strong sensory awareness, the teacher helps them understand the descriptions and the imagery.

> **T:** When "Hungry Hans" (p. 60), imagines himself to be at all the great feasts in history, what do you suppose comes to his mind?
> **C:** The first Thanksgiving.
> **C:** A big Roman banquet.
> **C:** I don't think any feast ever had as much as we had at our family reunion this summer. There was stuff there I had never seen before and probably won't see again.

For material that centers on emotions, the leader may want to help the children understand the material's description of feelings. For example:

> **T:** In the Beatle's song "Eleanor Rigby" the lyrics describe a lonely person who keeps her face in a jar until she's ready to wear it. What do you think that means?
> **C:** She doesn't want people to see she's sad.
> **C:** It's like she's not real; she wears a mask.
> **C:** Maybe she's got a lot of faces hanging by the door.

He may want the children to understand how the characters express their emotions:

> **T:** The story doesn't tell us, but I wonder how "Gertrude McFuzz" (p. 59), has her temper tantrum? What does she do, do you suppose?
> **C:** When my brother has one he pounds his fists on the floor and screams.
> **C:** I think she goes to her room and slams the door.
> **C:** She gets real angry. My dad, when he gets angry, says he could "spit nails."

Often it is helpful to focus on the motivation of the character's feelings and expressions:

> **T:** Now that we've read all but the last chapter of the book, *The Black Pearl* (p. 127), we know quite a lot about Ramon. Now that he has regained the pearl and is returning home, what do you think he's going to do with it? What are his feelings about that pearl?
> **C:** He knows it's not jinxed. He's going to give it back.
> **C:** He's going to put it back in the Madonna's hand.
> **C:** He might hide it until he can go to Guaymus someday by himself.

Discussions may be necessary if the experience is a culturally different one for the children.

T: James Huston vividly describes a very serious moment when Tiktalik-tak (p. 129), gives up hope for living and builds himself a coffin. Why do you think the Eskimo youth did that? According to the story, what are his last thoughts as he carefully arranges his weapons by his side? Why do you think he would want his relatives to understand the reason for his death?

C: He had to build a coffin; he was going to die. There was no choice.

C: If they didn't find his weapons, they might not ever know what happened to him.

C: Also, I think he wanted to tell them that he didn't commit suicide. He just starved to death.

Serious Material

Playing serious material is often the most rewarding of drama experiences children can have. There is no question that it is worth the time it takes to understand the material and to work at becoming involved in it. Sometimes it is a surprise to find that the most unlikely children are the ones who lead in the requests for challenging material once they have had the experience of becoming involved in it. Working with serious material does, however, take additional and special considerations.

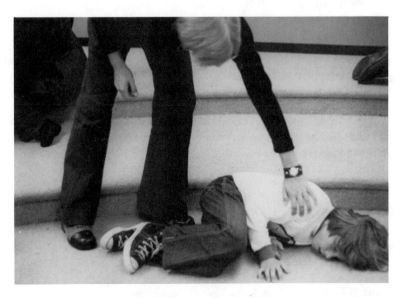

Checking for concentration.

First, the leader must create an appropriate climate for beginning the work. Sometimes teachers assume that children will know the material is serious and that they will automatically respond with a serious mood. Often this is not true. It may be helpful if the teacher simply alerts them immediately to the fact that the material is serious:

> T: Today we're going to be talking about the relocation of Indian tribes. We might be able to understand these tragic moments a little better if we enact the march along the Trail of Tears. This will be serious material and it may take some effort on our part. . . .

A child can become more involved in serious materials when he can discover the similarities between his own feelings and the feelings decribed in the materials. Discussions are an important process for identifying with the emotions in serious materials.

> T: I've adapted a passage from Maia Wojciechowska's *Shadow of a Bull* (129), about Manolo's fears. As you know, there is one descriptive scene when all the boys merrily jump from a wagon of hay. All but Manolo; he's too afraid. What thoughts do you think are in Manolo's head when the boys suggest jumping? How do you think he feels? Have you ever been afraid of something the way Manolo is afraid of jumping?

Children can sometimes feel more comfortable about discussing serious topics if the teacher shares his feelings also.

> T: The "Star-Bellied Sneetches" (40) don't play with the Sneetches that don't have stars. They don't invite them to their wiener roasts. I remember how I felt when a girl in my class at school didn't invite me to her party. I think I know how those Sneetches without stars must have felt. . . .

In discussing emotional feelings it is helpful to word the questions, "What do you think?" This allows children to express their feelings and interpretations in their own way. They may also discuss topics dealing with emotions from their own background of experience.

> T: How do you think Johnny Tremain (105) felt when Isannah screamed that his scarred hand was "dreadful"?
>
> T: Before we dramatize some sections from *Call it Courage* (p. 127), let's talk about courage. What is courage to you? What are some things a courageous person might do?

Through discussion, children have the opportunity to discover that others share their ideas and their powerful and often overwhelming feelings. While children may not say it, they often think to themselves: "So that's your idea. I feel the same way! I thought I was the only person in the whole world who felt like that."

"Close your eyes to help you think."

Sometimes it is necessary for the leader to acknowledge that there may be different perceptions and that it will be important to respect each other's ideas. It may be helpful if the teacher openly and sincerely acknowledges the difficulty and concern everyone has when talking about and planning serious material.

> **T:** In a few moments we're going to be talking about some serious feelings. As we talk and play we may hear ideas that surprise us, and we may be tempted to think the answers are silly or wrong. It will be important for everyone to be able to give his opinion without anyone making fun or criticizing. We will need to respect each other and each one's feelings and opinions.

In addition to clarifying the material to be played, preparatory discussions can begin to establish the mood necessary for involvement during the playing. They help to set the stage for the eventual enactment.

PLAYING THE MATERIAL

One of the questions teachers frequently ask is, "How do you keep the kids from acting silly?" Silliness or "goofing off" behaviors are usually the result of uncomfortable feelings. Rarely will anyone be silly for the sake of being silly. But without understanding the causes of these behaviors, the teacher may lose patience. And that adds to rather than solves the problem.

A good story will capture attention.

The behaviors may be caused merely by the fact that the children are doing something different from what they have been accustomed to doing. Even with careful preparation in the planning of the material, it may still be difficult for the children to play it. They may simply need time to experiment and to find out what creative dramatics is all about.

We also believe that children have a keen awareness of how the material should be presented. They often know as well as the teacher the importance of what they are doing. And it is just this awareness that makes things difficult. If their ideas are not turning out the way they want them to or think they should be, they become embarrassed. They may feel inadequate to meet the challenge of the material and try to cover it over as if it really were not that important. Often they fantasize the way the material will look when it is presented, and if reality doesn't measure up, they are more disappointed than anyone else.

It is also important for the leader to be patient with himself in trying for in-depth involvement. He must recognize that his attempts may not always work. In such cases, it is important not to suggest either verbally or nonverbally that the children have failed. We are all familiar with the indignant look of the teacher, which indicates a loud and clear reprimand. Children can easily reflect this attitude and give up or become defensive and indignant themselves.

The leader must try to establish the most appropriate playing conditions possible. There must be a climate of acceptance, yet firm guidance, in following whatever rules are necessary.

Psychological Security

A sensitive teacher is well aware that a comfortable classroom atmosphere is conducive to a good learning environment. Children must feel secure in their physical and social environment if they are to be free, confident, and unselfconscious enough to use drama as a tool of learning, thinking, and personal expression. They may need a great deal of encouragement in playing particularly when they are trying out a new idea, when they are typically shy, or when they lack confidence in their ability to think of and express ideas.

At the same time it is important to have a good *working* atmosphere in which to create the drama experience. It should be unhampered by the noise and chaos of people not knowing what they are to do. The leader should know what he wants and what he expects and then insist on it. This is most crucial in the use of space and with rules for no talking.

Brief Playing

For initial attempts at in-depth involvement it is helpful to keep the experience fairly brief. The leader may choose a short piece of material or select a very brief episode out of a longer piece of material. If children know the experience will be short, they may be more apt to participate in it and may be less anxious about it. They can be assured that they will not have to concentrate on in-depth involvement *forever*. The experience will be over before they have had time to be embarrassed by it. And, if they are somewhat successful, they have bolstered their confidence to try for a longer experience the next time.

Short experiences are also easier on the teacher. He, too, will not have to work so long and hard at sustaining the mood and creating the appropriate atmosphere. His initial success will also bolster his confidence for a longer experience the next time around.

Sometimes the leader will want a brief playing in order to get a total perspective. Playing an idea briefly gives the teacher and the children a chance to see its possibilities and how it could be further developed.

Replaying

Often there will not be in-depth involvement in a first playing. The best of creative thinking and understanding may be impossible to achieve immediately. Even the most experienced teacher with experienced children may not achieve all their depth of playing with one try. The teacher should keep this fact in mind and inform the children of it so that no one becomes overly discouraged when things do not turn out as well and as rapidly as they had hoped. If an idea is worthwhile, it is worth taking some time to experience it. Continued work on an idea often produces the most satisfying results in the long run, and makes everyone's time and efforts worthwhile.

Some teachers, when guiding for greater depth of involvement, play the activity three times. For a first playing, the leader may concentrate on just experiencing the action or the *doing* part of the material. The first playing may be treated as a run-through to give everyone a total perspective and chance to see the possibilities.

When the teacher views the first playing experience as experimentation, it is helpful to share this attitude with the children. For example, it is extremely comforting to the children if the leader says, "We've never done this before. Let's just try this and see what happens." The mere statement, "Let's experiment," relaxes everyone (including the teacher) and reduces unnecessary anxiety.

After experimenting in a first playing, both the teacher and the children have gained a familiarity and sense of security to bolster their courage for repeated playing. With each new playing they have the opportunity to learn more about the material, the people in it and about themselves as well.

Evaluation

When the leader and the children evaluate the playing, there is increased possibility of involvement in subsequent playings. When the children are asked to think about what they have done, and what they liked about it, they are positively reinforcing themselves.

When the leader makes evaluations, they must be specific enough so that the children know how to duplicate what is good. Saying "good" by itself is probably not helpful since the children really don't know what they are doing that is good. And if "good" is said to one child ("Good, Tom") and not to another, the second child may draw the conclusion that his work was bad or at least less than good.

But if the leader is more specific and says, for example, "Good, your puppets are walking very stiffly — just as if you were made out of wood," then he is praising stiff movements. He is describing action that can be observed.

Believability of expression is also a key concept to consider in evaluation for involvement. Something about the dramatizing should have the look of being *real*.

T: I began to get the feeling that I was really watching an instant replay on television, you were moving in slow motion so carefully — as if each step was measured — smooth — floating. . .

Concentration

Concentration will need to be encouraged. Although the teacher will be tempted to caution the children to think or concentrate, the admonitions by themselves will serve little good. Unless the children know what they are to think about or to concentrate on, or indeed what they are supposed to do when they think or concentrate, they cannot possibly oblige.

As we have mentioned previously, designing the playing so that children work separately and privately can lessen distractions and aid concentration. In countless experiences the authors have observed that this technique alone can stablize children and help them focus on their ideas. The leader may consider that the first playing could be experienced in a specific, limited area, and as involvement deepens, the areas may open. In addition the leader can dim the lights in the room so that isolation and privacy are futher aided.

> **T:** I think it would be helpful for us to pretend that we are alone in this experience. I'll turn the lights off so that the room is not as bright and that may help us pretend that we are by ourselves.

Another technique is to ask the children to close their eyes. Sometimes this helps them in forming the mental pictures in their mind, which adds to the experience. By closing their eyes the children are also able to block out distractions.

Particularly when they are playing individually and are in limited space, having their eyes closed will not pose a problem. And it is amazing how readily some children adopt this aid and use it on their own, even after they have become experienced in creative dramatics. Many children will be able to judge for themselves when such a technique will make the playing more involving and hence more satisfying for them.

It is helpful if the leader and the children discuss what aids and what interferes with their concentration. Usually children know what distracts them. Often it is other people just being near them, touching them, or purposely trying to distract. Or they may be bothered by just being aware that others are around them. After playing ideas, the leader can ask the children to evaluate the conditions they were working in and find ways to make it better.

> **T:** How many of you think you were able to concentrate more this time by closing your eyes? Would it be helpful if we played the story again?

The leader will also encourage the children to recall when they felt themselves really involved in and understanding the material. Particularly after the children do give behavioral evidence that they are involved in the material, it is helpful to have them verbalize about it and describe it for themselves.

> **T:** There was one moment when most of you seemed to be very absorbed in what you were doing. I think perhaps concentration might have been the strongest at that moment. At the moment when Jonathan Livingston Seagull (p. 128) was desperately trying to perfect his diving skills, what

were you thinking or feeling? Do you know why that was a particularly strong moment for most of you?

Selecting Volunteers

Just as the leader used care in selecting volunteers for preview playing, he should use the same care in selecting players for serious material. While it is true that the leader will want to have all children participate in the playing, it is always a wise precaution to begin with just a few or with those children who can be most easily involved. Particularly when one is trying out new material, or is not sure of the response the group will have to it, there is no point in taking chances with an entire classroom.

The first playing of the material is experimental; the first players can also be a model for subsequent playings. Also, when the first players can become involved and a mood is set by them, it is much easier to sustain that mood.

Involvement may also be aided if the leader allows each individual to judge when he is ready to participate in the material.

> **T:** Not everyone may feel ready to try this yet. Some may feel they want to try now; others may feel they want to wait a bit. We'll start with those who want to give it a try. As we continue to play the scene, just join in when you feel you can concentrate on it. We'll leave some spaces around for you to step into and work in. Who would like to start out? . . .

If a child cannot follow the rules for playing, particularly when dealing with something as concrete as the use of space and no talking, the leader may have to ask him to remove himself from the playing. This is important in keeping the climate of playing orderly and the mood of the material strong. If a child distracts from that, he is getting little from the experience and may also be hampering others from enjoying the experience.

Removing a child from playing can be done very quickly and privately to the child in order not to cause him embarrassment. The leader need only say,

> **T:** I think the rule to remain in your own space and not distract others must be too difficult for you to follow just now. When you think you can follow it you may return.

It should be pointed out that when a child does not follow the rules, removing him from the playing is only a symptomatic solution to the problem. The leader needs to consider why the child exhibited problematic behavior.

Even though the child has been removed from the playing, he can continue to watch the others. Many children need to see the other children playing in order to understand the activity and see what it is they are to do.

Throughout any handling of problem behaviors, the leader should remain objective. If the activity has been made intriguing and challenging, the fun of playing it will often be the drawing card for the child to comply with rules.

Music, Lights, and Sound Effects

The use of music, lights, and sound effects can also aid involvement. They can add to the mood, create a wealth of pictorial images, and stimulate the imagination. Appropriate music can make a carnival scene gayer; it can make a haunted house scarier; pastoral scenes more peaceful; or create the mood of solitude and loneliness.

"Tiktiliktak lifts the stone cover of his coffin into place."

Lighting can lend very special effects. It is surprising what children can imagine with the simple technique of flashing the classroom lights on and off. Lightning and electrical storms, movie spotlights, neon signs, or the sparkling sights in outer space are only some of the possibilities. When the lights are off and the room dimmed, children can more easily imagine dark tunnels, mysterious underwater worlds, ancient ruins, the Arctic.

Music, along with the imaginative use of classroom lights, can also encourage involvement. For example, if the room is darkened and appropriate music is playing, it is much easier to pretend to be seeds tucked away in the ground awaiting the arrival of the warm spring rains and soft sunshine. Or, with bright lights and energetic music, the children may be able more easily to

"The slaves disembark from the ship."

imagine visiting a bustling city department store, trying on hats and shoes, sampling display cologne, and snacking at the stand-up counter.

Sound effects have similar influence. They can add to the mood, stimulate the imagination, and aid in the involvement. For example, in some social studies textbooks it is noted that the sound of fife and drum accompanied Nathan Hale to his place of execution. If the children were to dramatize this moment, it might be intensified by the ominous sound of drumming on desktops.

The leader and the children can invent their own sound effects. Most children enjoy this challenge and can discover appropriate sounds from all sorts of improbable sources. They may suggest slamming a desk top (one only!) for a burst of cannon fire, rattling beans in a tin can to give rain effect, or squeeking the classroom door for a haunted house.

The following is an extended example of a 30-minute activity with a fifth-grade class during their fourth session of creative dramatics. It demonstrates many of the techniques discussed in the chapter.

Noteworthy is the fact that there was lengthy preparation in order to guide the understanding and to establish a strong, serious mood and a sense of deep involvement. The physical activity itself involved walking only about six feet. The drama event was focused literally on only about three sentences of text. But the understanding of the event as well as the emotional feelings involved required much discussion and work.

The leader guided the children through three discussions and three playings. After thirty minutes of work, all the children had become involved in what was to be a very moving experience.

The children and the teacher grouped themselves on the floor at one end of the room. The teacher introduced the book *Venture for Freedom* (142), explaining that it was a retold, true story based on the experience of a captured African tribe and of an African king's son whose English name was Venture Smith. She read short, specific episodes describing the fatal beating of Venture's father; the day Venture sneaked down to the ship's hold to find his mother; and the moment the Africans disembarked into the blinding Barbados sun and slavery.

Then the teacher and the children discussed the following questions:

What kind of people do you think they must have been to have a King who died rather than betray his tribe?

The story gives us some idea of the grim condition in the ship's hold, but expanding on that with your imagination, what do you think the hold was like?

How must Venture have felt knowing his mother was in that hold?

His mother told him to go back on deck and stay alive. How do you think she felt saying that? How did Venture feel?

What do you think it was like to come out of the ship's hold, after so many weeks in the dark, into the blinding sun? What thoughts and feelings do you think they had?

How must Venture have felt knowing that this would be the last time he would see his mother and his people?

After the discussion the leader played a recording of "Sometimes I feel Like a Motherless Child." She explained that the song grew out of and reflected the sorrow of the slave trading days.

The teacher told the children that they were going to put themselves back into this time and into the lives of these Africans. The lights were turned off. They were to imagine that they were in the ship's hold and that the two chairs she had placed close together in the middle of the room represented the ship's disembarking plank. Slowly, one at a time or in pairs, they were to come out of the hold, walk the plank, and then sit and wait for their brothers.

She told them to think about who they were; their physical condition; their attitudes about seeing the earth again; about the slave seller who would bark his orders to them as they slowly emerged into the day; their feelings about each other; their feelings about slavery.

In order to help establish a mood, the teacher asked the children to close their eyes and softly hum, "Motherless Child," as they thought about their characters. After a few moments the teacher stood and in a rough and callous voice growled, "All right, look lively! Come on out!"

As the first children reached the plank, the teacher threw open the curtains to reveal the very bright sunlight. They slowly walked between the chairs; some seriously involved in the activity, some snickering to their partners. After they had all assembled, the leader turned on the lights.

She talked to them for a few moments, commenting objectively. Quietly, and in the mood of the material she said,

"As we played this the first time, some of you were involved in the moment and some of you found it difficult. It's not easy to play something as serious as this, but I think we can do it if we work at it some more. Let's try it again. Now that you know what it's about, let's have you decide if you think you can remain involved in it this next time. If you think you cannot, you may sit and watch."

Six children sat down. The activity was repeated. The involvement was stronger this time, but the leader noted that it might be even more serious.

"What do you think? Shall we try it once again?"

They all agreed they wanted to try the experience again, and the leader offered them the choice again if they wanted to play or to watch. All the children got up to play. This third playing was the most successful; and the children spontaneously expressed their satisfaction with it.

When children have once experienced in-depth involvement in a drama experience, often they will not be satisfied with superficial playing again. However, they may still need much assistance in arriving at that goal. With the leader's guidance and with the children assuming their share of the responsibility, everyone will enjoy most those experiences made more enriching through in-depth involvement.

EXERCISES FOR THE COLLEGE STUDENT

1. Select some material suitable for dramatization. Have in mind a particular group of children who will play it. Consider the following questions.
   a. What do you personally like about the material?
   b. How will the material serve the interests, needs, and concerns of the group of children who are to play it?

   c. What will be important for you to consider in presenting the material?

   d. What methods might you use to assist the children in understanding the material? Be specific.

   e. What considerations might be necessary for the group and/or for the material in playing it? Outline your plan for playing the material.

   f. What special effects might be used for the playing of the material?

2. Lead the children (or your classmates) in playing the above material. Analyze the effectiveness of your plan for playing. What changes might you make to improve your plan?

3. Select serious material. Practice reading it aloud, using your voice to convey the mood. Select music appropriate for the material. Rehearse the music with your reading until you can smoothly operate the phonograph as you read. Share this with your classmates.

4. Treat humorous material following the procedure suggested above.

5. Brainstorm with your classmates all the techniques the leader can use to increase psychological security and positive evaluation.

6

Designing Narrative Pantomime Activities

Thus far, all the materials suggested have been those suitable for narrative pantomime. The main reason for this is that pantomime materials are often easier for children to enact than dialogue materials. Pantomime is thus useful for beginning groups as well as for warmups with experienced groups. Also, in using the story materials, the children have been able to enact completed little dramas in pantomime from the very beginning. This can be very satisfying for both the children and the teacher.

In this chapter we will want to examine those materials more closely and consider the dramatic principles in them. Understanding and applying these principles should make it easier for the leader to design activities on his own. By designing we include selecting, editing, and adapting, as well as writing materials.*

Knowing how to select materials for narration makes it possible for the leader to use many materials he may already have at hand in such sources as basal readers, tradebooks, or magazines. Some of these materials can probably benefit from editing and adapting in order to make them suitable for dramatizing.

---

*It is a good practice for beginning leaders to write out their activities beforehand. As the leader becomes more experienced, he may simply outline his ideas for handy reference.

Knowing how to write materials is also an extremely useful skill. It can be helpful for sidecoaching all materials as well as for designing original narrated activities. The leader can also fill in details in sketchy storylines such as those found in folk and fairy tales, myths and legends, or in textbooks and tradebooks. Or, the leader may have information about a topic from his own personal interests and background and can make an interesting activity of it by placing it in a dramatic format.

EDITING ACTION

As we have said before, action will always be the central focus of narrative pantomime activities. Not all materials have sufficient action in them to use for creative dramatics. Sometimes it is possible simply to select the portions that have the most action. For example, in the poem, "Lines Written for Gene Kelly to Dance To" by Carl Sandburg (p. 60), we suggested using only the first section. These lines contain more straightforward action than does the rest of the poem. Incidentally, while sections of both poetry and prose can be edited, care should be taken not to omit lines or phrases of poetry if the rhyme or the rhythm would be destroyed.

Continuous Action

The action of the material should be as continuous as possible. Some literature has interruptions in the flow of the action for the interjection of reflective thinking, flashbacks, or additional information. If such interruptions are lengthy, they may require the players to pause and wait before they can continue the action. For example, a passage may read:

> His hand touched the doorknob and in that moment his mind raced back to a thousand memories. *It had been the same in other situations just like these. The time he opened the door to Old Man Henry's place on that fateful Halloween night. The guys had left him standing there. Ran off just as he was about to open the door. They had all decided to go in together and then everybody chickened out and left him standing there to hear Old Man Henry's voice bellow out at him.* He shook the thought from his mind, opened the door and stepped into the darkened interior.

By going back in time, the underlined passage keeps the players poised at the doorknob without moving. Through editing, the leader can tighten the action. In this case, the flashback can easily be omitted:

> His hand touched the doorknob. He thought for a moment about last Halloween. Then he opened the door and stepped into the darkened interior.

Sometimes a passage is interrupted with information:

> The little wooden guard doll was stationed at the gate of the toy village guarding and protecting it from any intruders. He marched in stony silence back and forth.
>
> Now there are some things you must know about this particular toy village. It was not ordinary; no, indeed! It belonged to a little girl named Becky and she had given specific directions to her grandfather on how she had wanted it built. At one end there was to be a park with a merry-go-round. There was also to be a hill for the children to go sliding down in winter. And a little toy pet shop was to be in the center of all the shops on Main street.
>
> But the one thing that neither Becky nor her grandfather had planned on or even knew about was that the entire village came to life once a year by some magical spell. Only the villagers knew about it.
>
> Tonight, as the little wooden guard doll marched back and forth he had a very worried look on his painted face. Something was wrong. . . .

Even though the guard doll can continue to march back and forth throughout the passage that follows, the information section gives the player very little additional action to perform or even to react to.

In both of the above examples, the information is probably important to the material. When that is the case, it may be included in the leader's introduction to the material before it is played.

Word Order

The cues for the action should always follow chronologically. If they do not, the players may be misled. For example:

> She left the apartment and went down to the first floor. When she got off the elevator and entered the lobby, she. . . .

Players who are following this narration might *walk down steps* rather than riding an elevator since this information is not specified until the second sentence. Changing the wording around, the following line is easier to enact:

> She left the apartment and got on the elevator. She went down to the first floor, got off the elevator and entered the lobby. . . .

Immediacy of Action

As much as possible, the action should be condensed into one time period rather than separated by gaps in time. When action is spread out over a period of time, it tends to lose its dramatic impact. For example:

The men worked, eagerly packing their gear for the adventure. After two weeks they were ready to start off. They left full of energy and with high hopes that they would be successful.

Three months later they were weary and disappointed. Almost everyone in the exploring party was ready to turn back.

Some literature focuses on interesting action, but skips ahead or even bounces back and forth in time. For example:

That day he decided to go for a swim. Two days later he was in the same spot again. Only that day it rained. By the end of summer, he had enjoyed boating, water-skiing, and swimming – but it was the swimming he enjoyed the most.

While there is plenty of action suggested in the above passage, it would be frustrating to try to pantomime it as written. Editing or rewording is required.

Present Tense and "You"

A sense of immediacy is sometimes helped by the use of the present tense and the wording "you."

Now you run your hand along the bark of the old tree, lean forward and smell the mossy dampness. . . .

This wording makes the action and the direction compelling and involving. Some children respond more easily to this direct wording since they can feel that the action is happening now and to them. It seems more logical to follow this kind of narration.

Robert McCloskey has incorporated this wording in his book, *Time of Wonder* (p. 129), but it is not a style of writing frequently used by authors. Although the leader may not want to change literature into this wording style, much of his original material and sidecoaching can easily be worded in this way.

CREATING ACTION

Many materials can be made more dramatically appealing by adding action to them. The leader may also select an idea that appeals to him and allows his imagination and knowledge to magnify it and fill it in with detail. The action he adds may be purely physical or it may also emphasize sensory awareness or emotional reactions. All of these are dramatic features and are helpful in making material more interesting and exciting to play.

For example, a line might read:

The farmer had many chores to do that kept him busy all day long.

The leader may choose to elaborate on that line and continue with additional action:

He had to gather the eggs; milk the cows; hoe the garden; feed the pigs; and rake the hay.

Sensory Action

The leader may also choose to add sensory detail. In the story of "Goldilocks and the Three Bears," for example, the scene of eating the porridge might be elaborated. In most versions of the story, Goldilocks tastes one bowl that is too hot and one that is too cold. The third she eats up because it is just right.

In the following example, the leader imaginatively elaborates on the porridge's texture, smell, and specific tastes:

T: You see three bowls of porridge and you are so very hungry . . . So you taste the porridge in Papa Bear's bowl. Oh! That's too hot! It burned your tongue!! Oh dear, well, nevertheless, you are still hungry and maybe the porridge in the middle-sized bowl will be better. You pick up the middle-sized spoon and scoop up a big spoonful from Mama Bear's bowl. You take a big bite and . . . oh no! That one is too cold. And LUMPY!. . . . Well, there's one bowl left. This time you take a tiny spoonful of porridge and carefully you taste it. Ahhh, this is perfect. What good porridge, not too hot, not too cold. The cream in the porridge is sweet . . . and you think you detect the flavor of butter and just the tiniest pinch of salt. Wonderful! Someone really knows how to make good porridge. And you eat and eat and eat . . . until there is just one spoonful left . . . and you eat that one slowly and savor the last bite . . . Ummmmmm . . . good!

In the following example the teacher elaborates on the first sentence with additional information he has about the subject.

T: As the door to his Bastille cell slammed shut, the new prisoner surveyed his miserable surroundings. There was one small window in the thick wall crossed with iron gratings. He tried to look out, but the opening was too small to permit a view. Besides, foul odors rose from the ditch below the walls and choked his breathing.

He examined the sparse furnishings. There was a worn, filthy mattress, musty and moldy. He picked it up on one corner. The chair and small table were broken pieces. The bowl on the table was cracked. . . .

One helpful point to keep in mind is that not all sensory material encourages an equal amount of action. Tasting and touching, for example, usually produce more active involvement because they encourage direct contact. The following examples are related to experiences based on the topic of Mexico.

(Tasting)   Pretend you're eating a tortilla sprinkled with a bit of hot chili.

Imagine you're eating a sweet, juicy mango.

(Touching) Stroke the burro's soft, warm muzzle.

Lift the wooden yoke with its filled water cans and place it over your shoulders.

The distant senses of seeing, smelling, and hearing can sometimes lack active involvement. For example, the following passage may not produce much pantomimic movement:

He gazed at the beautiful, multi-colored sunset. He heard the distant evening-time church bells. He smelled the familiar fragrance of blooming bougainvillaea.

Notice the difference in the detail encouraged by the two following lists. The second list invites more action.

SEEING

You see the chameleon.	You gently reach for the chameleon.

SMELLING

You smell the smoke from the farmer's brush fire.	You smell the smoke from the farmer's brush fire and cover your nose with your bandana.

LISTENING

You listen to the sound of an egg just beginning to hatch.	You lean over the nest and put your head close to the egg and listen to the tiny scratching sounds.

Language that is descriptive is exciting and encourages imagination. Language that is perfunctory may produce only limited results. When the leader's language helps to paint the mental images of seeing, touching, hearing, smelling, and tasting, it can artfully compel the children to be aware of the environment and to respond to the experience. The generous use of descriptive language invites involvement.

Emotion

Material that focuses on emotions may be written in different ways. Sometimes the emotion itself is mentioned:

a. The little rabbit was *afraid.*
b. The young girl was *happy.*

In these lines the mood is given but the children must fill in their own action in order to interpret it. To enact being *happy,* for instance, a child may smile, clap his hands, shiver with delight or whatever he thinks is appropriate to that mood.

Sometimes the material describes the specific action the person performs in expressing the mood:

a. The Captain stood quietly, feeling relief sweep over him.
b. He was so bewildered he could only stand and stare.
c. The merrymakers felt so happy and laughed so hard, they soon fell asleep.

In some cases the author describes the behaviors of a character and makes the reader infer the emotion. This kind of writing is often more subtle and may require editing or discussion in order for the children to understand it. For example, rather than saying the character is sad, the description might read:

He slowly walked away from the window. He sat down, sighing as he did so. He tried to hold back the feeling, but tears began to well up in his eyes.

Other examples might be:

The corners of his mouth turned up ever so slightly.

The woman suddenly stopped her work; she tilted her head in the direction of the sound she heard and waited, her body frozen in a statue-like pose.

In writing his own material, the imaginative teacher can capitalize on the emotions that certain ideas and situations create for him. For example, a single statement in a social studies text, "The pioneers suffered a harsh first winter," might trigger the teacher's imagination to envision many images and feelings. He may feel the wind rushing through the cracks in the cabin walls; see the family huddled around a table with little food; people ill, clad in rough, inadequate clothes; mothers feeling helpless; fathers depressed after an unsuccessful hunt; children solemn and quiet, robbed of carefree childhood. From these mental images the teacher may develop a story line about the harsh winter.

The following is an example of the elaboration of an emotional feeling one teacher created from a single statement about Daniel Boone climbing a hill and viewing Cumberland Gap for the first time. The leader added his own perceptions and speculations about the moment, interpreted what Daniel Boone might have done and how he might have felt, and then wrote:

T: Pretend to be Daniel Boone when he sees the hills of Kentucky for the first time.

You are on your horse and you've just come to a tiny stream. You get down and allow the horse to get a drink of water. . . . You stretch your legs; your back feels stiff. You've been traveling quite a while. The territory of Kentucky should be close by.

You decide to climb that small hill in front of you. It looks steep, but the thought of seeing Kentucky excites you and it seems worth the physical energy. You begin climbing. It *is* steep and you lean forward to keep your balance and clutch at rocks and saplings to aid your progress . . . You *are* tired, but you're almost to the top and then you can look about. You can see for long distances, and in front of you are the hills of Kentucky! How beautiful they are! A dream has come true! You've accomplished what you have been trying to do for a long time. A feeling of pride sweeps over you. You begin thinking of what this means to a lot of other people who have given you their dream. New Land! New frontiers to develop! New homes! New ways to live! . . .

You sit down and begin to relax. You breathe deeply and become conscious of another kind of feeling . . . one you hadn't noticed in your initial excitement . . . The view fills you with a sense of peace. You close your eyes and rest. Soon it will be time to make the dream a reality.

Fantasy/Reality

One other consideration involves the use of reality and fantasy. Often subjects such as animals and flowers have been personified and given human senses and feelings. There can be charm in such stories. It is humorous to read a story about a crayfish who needs an oil can to unstick a stubborn feeler.

But there can also be charm in scientifically accurate writing as well. Writers like Jean George and Holling C. Holling have created nature stories that are very imaginative yet accurate in their information. The leader should keep in mind both possibilities in his selecting and creating of materials.

Omitting Dialogue

When looking for materials suitable for narrative pantomime, one should generally avoid those with a lot of dialogue in them. When people talk at great length to each other in literature, they often stop performing actions. This means that the children have to stand for long periods of time looking at one another while the leader reads the dialogue. They can only feel foolish when this happens and will probably lose interest and involvement in the playing.

There are some materials that have a lot of exciting action in them in addition to the dialogue. Such materials may be made suitable for narrative pantomime if the dialogue is condensed or omitted.

Sometimes action can be substituted for the dialogue. This is true in the classic tale of "The Three Billy Goats Gruff." It is a delightful story to play, but the dialogue might be difficult for some children. With the teacher's narration, it can easily be played in pantomime. Following is one passage that might occur in an adapted-for-pantomime version:

> T: . . . The Little Billy Goat Gruff looked down under the bridge and begged the Troll not to eat him up. He was so scared when he saw the mean-looking Troll that he shook all over.
>
> The Troll stamped his feet and pulled at his beard. He told the Little Billy Goat Gruff to go on over the bridge. Then he sat down angrily and pouted while the Little Billy Goat Gruff skipped across the bridge to the meadow on the other side. . . .

Inanimate Objects

The leader should be sure that materials using personified inanimate objects have enough action to make them interesting for dramatization. For example, Virginia Lee Burton's charming story, *The Little House* (Houghton Mifflin, 1942), tells of the many reactions of a deserted house to its lonely situation, but there is very little if any action the house can perform. Another similar kind of story is Rachel Field's *Hitty* (Macmillan, 1959). This is the fascinating story of a doll to whom many things happen. But since she cannot move by herself, the experiences are all passive ones.

The leader may choose to create activities with inanimate objects if he gives them enough action and involvement in the story to make them interesting to play. Consider the following example:

> T: Today we're going to pretend to be a recliner chair. And this is what a morning in our life might be like.
>
> Here you are all ready for the day to begin. You can hear the family getting up for the day. Here comes Mom to open up the curtains and let in the morning sunshine. Swish! . . . Yikes, that sun's bright . . . It makes your button eyes blink! Now she goes out in the kitchen to fix breakfast and here comes the kids and the dog. You hope they don't jump on you this morning . . . but they do! Zingo! All of them, all at once . . . they stretch you out flat in your reclining position. Ooh, for so early in the morning that's hard to take! Now Mom is calling them to breakfast . . .

Good . . . Zingo! . . . you flip back into your upright position and now you ache all over. You just weren't built for that sort of thing. . . .

Now breakfast's over and the older kids and Dad have gone and here comes Mom to sit down for the extra cup of coffee and the newspaper. Oh, you really love to read the newspaper. Mom gets all comfy and reclines you and opens up the paper. You have to read over her shoulder . . . there's your favorite comic, "Peanuts." Oh darn, she turned the page . . . and there's a furniture sale. Oh, boy, if there's anything that makes you nervous it's an ad for a furniture sale. Your stuffing gets tight and your nap stands right on end. Good, now she's turned the page again . . . And that's the end of the morning paper. She gets up and you pop upright again.

Now Mom's getting ready to clean. Here comes the vacuum cleaner and she's . . . oh, no! . . . She's going to clean you today. Oh, gosh, it tickles so . . . up at the top . . . and then your back . . . your face . . . arms . . . footrest . . . oh, oh, oh, it makes you giggle so . . . Ah, now she stops and goes on with the rest of the cleaning. . . .

Now here comes Bobby the four-year-old to watch his favorite T.V. shows. Hey, Mom, look at that jelly all over him . . . he's coming toward you and Mom doesn't even see him . . . Yuck, jelly all over your arms . . . how uncomfortable . . . Now Bobby turns on the TV set and watches a cartoon of a cat chasing a mouse. . . . Bobby starts to jump up and down on you. . . . He pounds your arms and kicks at your legs . . . ouch . . . ouch. . . .

Oh, boy, here comes Mom to chase him off you. There he goes and here she comes with some cleaner for you. She sprays the foam where Bobby put the jelly . . . It makes you want to cough or sneeze or something. . . . And you do and again . . . Oh boy, that's all you need . . . Now Mom finishes cleaning up the jelly. She takes Bobby upstairs with her and you are left for a little peace and quiet so you try to catch a little shut-eye while you can. Ah . . . how nice . . . sleep tight.

Additional topics might be: the journey of an egg from an egg ranch through a modern day processing plant; the recycling of glass or cans; the adventure of a tomato from the vine to the soup can.

COMPLETED ACTION

Action is enhanced by a sense of completeness. Usually it is best if the activity focuses on a specified experience and follows it through to a conclusion of some sort. One's own feeling about completeness will be the best guide; what feels complete for one person may not be so for another. However, there are some clues the leader can look for in selecting material and can use in his original activities.

Word Order

One clue is the sense of progression or chronological order. This may be noted in wording such as, "First . . . and then . . . finally."

> **T**: In order to be sure his clothes are easy to get into at a moment's notice, the fireman first places his boots by his bed. Then he places his trousers over the tops of the boots so that he can step into his boots quickly and put his trousers on at the same time.

By using this wording in writing original activities, the leader can help create a completed feeling for the action.

> **T**: All the marionettes' strings are breaking one by one. There goes the string on the right arm — now on the left — now the right leg — then the left — and finally their heads droop and they are as limp as the rag dolls on the shelf above them.

A completed feeling is often found in material in which the characters perform a task; set a goal and accomplish it; or go on a journey and return home. There is one episode in Jane Wagner's book, *J.T.* (107), for example, when J.T. makes a house out of junk for a stray cat. Another example is Dantes' escape from prison in Dumas's *The Count of Monte Cristo* (80).

The story might involve the process of a day's work as in "Dippy's Day by Moonlight" (p. 50). Or, it may be a part of a life cycle as it is for the mole cricket in Jean Craighead George's *All Upon a Stone* (p. 58). The following is part of a story about the life cycle of a dragonfly.

> **T**: You wiggle and squirm through the crack in your old skin. It's hard work, but this will be the last time you will have to shed it. You push and push until you are freed. Your slim new body is still stiff, and your old shell clings to the stalk below you like a ghost.
> The sun is warm and your four wings start to unfold slowly. . .

Suspense and Conflict

Often an activity can simply be based on an interesting experience. It may be a pleasant experience as in Yashima's *The Village Tree* (p. 63). Or, it may be informative as in *Mousekin's Family* (p. 61), where we learn about the habits of mice.

Some experiences, however, have a conflict in them. Conflict causes events to happen; it sets action in motion. Suspense is usually created over the outcome. When the problem is resolved, the story comes to a satisfying ending.

Children usually enjoy and want plenty of exciting action and conflict in their activities. Sometimes they will add it even when the teacher has not included it in the narration. The line says to smell a flower; they do and a bee stings them. Or the line says, "He walked carefully so he would not slip"; they walk carefully but slip too! For some children there can never be too much excitement in their stories. The leader should be familiar with the various ways to include conflict in materials.

There are many kinds of conflict. Strong conflict is obvious in fights, chases, or meeting of an enemy face to face. Peter Rabbit's encounter with Mr. McGregor is one example; Little Miss Muffet and the spider is another.

Conflict is also present in natural phenomena. A threatening storm begins slowly. Then the winds blow and waves billow while thunder crashes and lightning strikes until a dramatic climax is reached. When the storm subsides, resolution of the conflict of nature occurs. Not only is the topic dramatic and intense, it also incorporates strong physical movement with restful conclusion. George Maxim Ross's *The Pine Tree* (p. 61) demonstrates the drama in nature.

Conflict can be in the daily struggle for survival. Even if a task is a rather methodical one, its importance is increased if it is crucial to continued living. Perhaps each step along the way has its own particular importance in reaching the final outcome. For example, Karana in *Island of the Blue Dolphins* (p. 128) must build a house to protect herself from the wild dogs.

Sometimes conflict and suspense can be additionally implied in the words used. If an action is being described as "carefully" or if a line reads, "He held his breath as he lifted the cargo . . ." an imminent problem is presented.

Often conflict generates more energized and hurried action. For example, we must swim fast to escape a shark. Meeting some sort of deadline also creates hurried action. Cleaning house before company comes; shopping before a store closes; getting the game ended or the picnic dinner eaten before it rains; or getting to work on time are all examples.

> T: Here it is Christmas Eve and you haven't done any of your shopping yet. The stores will close in two hours and you have to finish in that time. You've got six things to get in six different departments, so here we go: First over to the cologne counter to get cologne for Aunt Mary. But there's a big crowd there so maybe you better go up to the third floor first and pick up the cologne on the way out. Let's hurry, there's an elevator going up . . . People are blocking your way . . . Watch out for that lady's packages . . . She's going to lose control of them . . . There they go . . . better help her pick them up . . . Going up! You missed the elevator . . . how about the escalator . . . Hurry . . . Hurry. . .

Unusual adventures also create intrigue and suspense. For example, children may enjoy the dramatic conflict of a science fiction approach to selected subject matter. The following is an example of an exploration in the study of the parts of a flower.

T: Today we're going to look at the construction of a flower, but we're going to do it a little differently. We're going to pretend that it is the year 3001 and scientists have developed some new ways to conduct scientific explorations. You are a special consultant who has been called in for this mission in the exploration of flowers. But it is a secret mission so you do not know your instructions as yet. You will be given the instructions at special points along the way. Let me know when you are ready for your mission by standing at attention, saluting, and reporting for duty. (Children respond.)

You've waited all week for this assignment! In a few minutes you're going to be taking this secret and very unusual scientific mission. Check your equipment. Notice that you've been issued a very tiny notepad, a very small pencil and very tiny (handle them carefully!) special pollen-resistant goggles. There is also a capsule, but it is unmarked. Everything is encased in plastic to keep it clean.

The impersonal voice on the intercom instructs you to enter the green house. Inside you will be given additional equipment. As soon as you open the door you sense the cool, damp atmosphere. It makes you shiver slightly with eager apprehension. This assignment will challenge your best efforts. Look alert! In front of you there is a small box on the table. The voice tells you to add it to your equipment.

The voice now tells you the nature of your mission. In a moment you are to drink the contents of the vial, which will make you small enough to explore the flower from the inside. Before you do, however, you are to select your first flower specimen. You survey the room and spy your favorite lily-of-the-valley, but its long stem will make climbing difficult. You look about until you find the roses. They would be the perfect scientific environment. Since a rose is a complete and perfect flower you can sketch all the parts and proceed to others from there. Its spiky stem will also help your entry into the flower proper.

Now the voice tells you to drink the contents of the vial. You do and notice that it is a tasteless, clear liquid. Very quickly and painlessly your body shrinks. Your clothing shrinks with you. Your head swims, and you feel the slightest bit of nausea. The noises shake you and the fragrances of the flowers seem to bombard your every cell. You look around and calculate that you must be about one inch high; the perfect size for this assignment, although you will have to use gentle caution with the delicate hepatica.

The voice instructs you to open the box and inside you find a small laboratory coat, just your size. You are asked to remove any jewelry and any sharp protrusions or rough textures. You must leave the scientific environment exactly as you have found it: no marks, no tell-tale signs of human intrusion. Inside the box you also find a pair of soft cloth slippers and the voice instructs you to remove your shoes and put the slippers on. You put on the goggles, check that you have the notepad and pencil, and you are ready to begin. . .

Other explorations may cover subjects such as the bee hive, the workings of a watch, the inside of a tree or human eye. For pair work a corpuscle may guide an expedition through the blood stream, or dirt could give a guided tour through an anti-pollution device that he will one day go through.

Beginnings and Endings

As important as the activity itself is the beginning and the ending. The beginning of an activity should be like the slow warmup of an airplane for takeoff. The ending should include similar precautions for making a smooth landing.

Usually it is particularly helpful if the beginning and the ending are a bit slower and quieter than the middle portion. The children can begin in a quieted position and can become calmed down again for the ending. This is helpful both to them and to the teacher.

When the leader begins an activity on a quiet moment, the children can be in their places, poised and waiting for the signal to begin. A quiet ending is similarly helpful. It calms and relaxes, giving everyone a chance to absorb his experience. It also allows the teacher a contemplative moment and an opportunity to prepare for the next activity.

When an entire poem or story is used, there is often a smooth beginning and ending built in. For example, an animal may be lying in quiet wait for a prey. After he catches it and eats, he often rests.

Often there is awakening from sleep, working at a daily task, and then returning to bed at night. In some cases, the awakening may be magical. For example, the broom in the "Sorcerer's Apprentice" (p. 62) is immobile, but comes to life when magic words are spoken. When other magic words are said, the broom returns to its immobile state once again.

The leader can create quieted beginnings and endings in adapting or in writing original materials. For example, in Ezra Jack Keats' *Snowy Day* (p. 62), the leader may prefer to end the story when Peter goes to bed rather than playing the story as it is with Peter waking up the next day and going outside to play again. The ending line might be:

And Peter went to sleep, knowing tomorrow would bring another day for him to play in the snow.

Other relaxing or quieting endings might include:

Drinking a cup of hot cocoa after skiing.
Lying on the beach in the warm sun after swimming.
Sitting under a cool shade tree after working hard at chores.

While it is fun to have a happy ending or a mission accomplished, the ventures may not always be successful ones. Sometimes there is the suggestion that there will be another chance at another time. Perhaps the person is satisfied that he did the best he could. Or, a task may turn out to be an impossible one, and the realization may be one of those "sadder but wiser experiences."

> **T:** Sara took one last long look . . . the house would be sold now and she would never be able to return again. But she would imprint this last look in her mind . . . the view from the window . . . the quiet ticking of the grandfather clock in the hallway . . . She quietly closed the door, smiling as she did so, as if that gesture would seal this moment in time forever.

FURTHER CONSIDERATIONS FOR STORY IDEAS

Creating original materials need not be a difficult experience. Many ideas are readily available. They may come from literature.

We are told in one sentence, for example, that A. A. Milne's Winnie-the-Pooh (147) does "Stoutness Exercises." All we are told is that he reaches up and then down to try to touch his toes. A simple conflict is implied because we know that Winnie has a protruding tummy that makes bending over a bit of a problem. It would also make other exercises difficult.

Elaborating on this idea, the leader might decide to write an activity focusing mainly on movement, going through an entire fitness program, doing all sorts of body-building activities. There might be some jogging, lifting weights, doing pushups, and hitting a punching bag. The sense of completeness is the exercise program itself — starting and finishing it. The beginning might be slow, warmup exercising with just the paws. (After all, Winnie wouldn't want to overexert himself!) As the activities progress in intensity and difficulty, Pooh Bear will no doubt become tired and worn out and would finally need a rest — with the reward of a bit of honey perhaps.

The activity could be enacted individually. Or, it could be played in pairs. Since Pooh Bear does his exercises in front of a mirror, a partner could play Pooh's mirror image.

Research

Through research, one can also find innumerable possibilities for activities. Information can be woven into interesting storylines.

In the following story, an unusual spider works hard to live. He struggles to build his home under water. He exerts effort to keep the captured air bubbles anchored; he struggles to pull himself with his guide-lines; and he is alert to the vibrations and aware of his need to secure food. The story ends with the satisfying completion of a project and a deserved rest.

T: We're going to pretend to be a very unusual species of spider called "Argyroneta aquatic." This spider lives underwater by building air-filled homes.

You're in the process of building your web for the air bubbles you will soon capture. You move from one plant stem to another, throwing from your spinnerets silken web strands. . . .

Deftly your legs secure the threads to the plants . . . and you carefully move back and forth from stem to stem until you have a finely meshed web. This web will become your summer bell home; later you'll build another for winter.

Now for the air bubbles . . . You swim to the top of the water . . . Once there, you turn over and with your back legs you grab a bubble of air, pulling it gently toward you so that it covers the breathing pores around your abdomen . . . Now your legs search for the silken guide-lines you set earlier . . . There you are! . . . and holding securely to the line, you begin to pull yourself down to the new web. It's a difficult feat . . . for the air bubble is heavy and would rise to the surface if you didn't pull . . . At the web you release your air bubble . . . and it rises into the web — captured!

You take more trips to the surface for air . . . and soon your home contains several bubbles and is completed. Now it is time for a rest . . . You carefully enter your air-filled home . . . and hang head downward . . . As you rest the water house sways to the rhythm of the moving water . . . Its vibrations can communicate that danger or a potential meal is near . . . It's vibrating!

Your eight eyes signal food . . . You emerge from your bell, carefully carrying an air supply with you . . . A tiny fish swims near . . . You lunge . . . Grab . . . Sting with your poison . . . and carry the dead fish into your new home. You'll eat it in a while . . . but now you'll rest. It's been a busy day.

Personal Experiences

One of the best sources for narrative pantomime is the leader's own personal experience. For our student teachers, their summer and part-time jobs have been a rich source. Grocery checkout cashier, construction work, camp counselor, dental assistant, and tour guide at a cereal factory are just some of the many possibilities.

Sports have been another popular topic for pantomime stories including skiing, sky diving, scuba diving, and hiking. Pets such as hamsters, turtles, and guinea pigs have also had stories told about them that children have played.

Geographical areas and personal background lend possibilities also. Stories have been written about maple-sugaring in Vermont; selecting and cutting down a Christmas tree in Washington; being taken on a personal tour of the family's farm; or visiting a local junkyard. Vacation trips are another source.

The detail and realism students can bring to these activities are a direct result of their own involvement in them. Usually the students also feel comfortable with these topics as well as enthusiastic about them. All of this adds to the playing experience.

Space

As in all previous work the leader also considers the use of space. If the leader wants to work only with the desk area, he may design his material to fit that area specifically. The desk itself, for example, may be the box for a Jack-in-the-Box, which pops up on specific words in a brief story. Or, it may be the frying pan or popper in which kernels of corn heat up and puff out into popcorn.

Or, as in the following example, the desk may become several things.

> **T:** Let's pretend we're going shopping. First we drive our car, which will be your desk. Get out your key, put it in the ignition, give it some gas, and we're off. Back out of the driveway . . . carefully . . . look to be sure you're not going to hit anything . . . now stop, put it in "Drive" and we head for town.
>
> (Here one could include as much detail about traffic, safety, or the sights as he wishes.)
>
> Now you're at the department store. Get out of the car. (At the side of the desk.) Go through the revolving door. Now up the escalator. Up to the second floor where we are going to shop for a bicycle. Ah, here's a nice looking one. Try that one out. Oh, oh, I see some snowmobiles. Try one of those out. . . .

The leader may want to use the technique of assigning various parts but in limited space:

> **T:** For our story about the storm, Row 1 is the thunder, which vibrates; Row 2 is the lightning, which sends its jagged strikes through the sky; Row 3 is the rain; and Row 4 is the swirling wind. As Zeus, I will tell you when you leave the heavens and report to earth. Here is the story. . . .

Or, the children may be allowed to determine their own use of space:

> **T:** You may use all the space you need in the following story about the molecules. You must remember, however, that your actions will change as certain things happen to you. When I read the word "hot," you must move faster through space. If I say the word "solid," you must remain in position and move like vibrating jello. On the word "liquid," you will move past each other with floating movements. And on the word "gas,"

you move, hit an imaginary molecule, and bounce off. Finally, on the word "heavy," you will move slowly. Here is the story. . . .

Pairs and Groups

The leader may also write materials for pairs and groups. The following is an elaboration of the nursery rhyme "Little Miss Muffet" designed for pairs.

> Once upon a time there was a little girl named Little Miss Muffet. Although she didn't know it, there was a spider who lived in her house too. He was tucked way back in a corner, and she had never seen him.
>
> One day, Little Miss Muffet decided to clean her house. The spider was asleep in his corner and didn't know what Miss Muffet was planning. As he slept peacefully, Miss Muffet got out all her cleaning equipment – the broom, the scrub bucket. She filled the bucket with water and some cleaning detergent and started to clean. Just about this time the spider thought he heard something and opened one eye to look. Then he opened the other eye. He yawned and stretched his eight legs, but that's as far as he got. Miss Muffet poured water on the floor to scrub it and the water sloshed around the spider and swept him into a crack in the floorboard. As spiders do when they're wet, he curled up into a very tiny ball while Miss Muffet scrubbed and scrubbed away. And, ooh! was he mad!
>
> Miss Muffet soon finished the floor and put away all her cleaning equipment, the broom, the bucket. She was hungry and thought she'd eat some of the curds and whey she had in the refrigerator. She went to get them. The spider, in the meantime, was slowly drying out. One leg, then another was able to uncoil. He watched Miss Muffet get the curds and whey and go outdoors to sit on a tuffet to eat them. Then he decided he'd get even with Miss Muffet for disturbing his sleep. Very slowly he crawled out to where she sat, eating. She didn't see him at all, and he was able to crawl very near to her. The spider, knowing that people are often afraid of them, knew he'd only have to sit there and when she would see him she'd be frightened quick enough. Miss Muffet looked around just then, saw the spider, dropped her spoon and bowl, and ran in the house quick as a wink. She shut the door and flopped down in a chair to calm herself after such a fright. The spider, pleased with himself, just stayed out in the warm sun and finished his nap in peace.

Or, one may focus on tasks that require more than one person. For example, dentist and technician; pilot and copilot; an operating team; elves in charge of certain tasks in toymaking; group expeditions based on Thor Heyerdahl's *Kon Tiki* adventure.

The leader can also narrate an activity for groups. In the following example, based on a scene from Washington Irving's "The Legend of the Moor's Legacy" (p. 246), there are parts for four children: Peregil, the Moor, and the two enchanted men.

Here you stand at the entrance of the cave, waiting for the Moor to arrive. It is chilly this evening, and you shiver and wrap your cloak a little more tightly around you. As you wait, you think about your unhappy lot — being so poor with so many mouths to feed. And a wife who nags you all the time. Even now you can hear her scolding you and you cringe and cover your ears in the hopes of drowning out her shrill voice. "Peregil, you lazy good for nothing lout! I wish I had never married you! You can barely support me in the manner to which I have been accustomed!" Her voice fades away now and you realize you are again alone.

And now you examine for the hundredth time the sandalwood box left to you by the Moor. Perhaps it will indeed bring you good fortune. You look at it carefully, thinking to yourself how it could be the only lucky thing that has ever happened to you. You wonder if the Moor's words are true, that the box does hold secrets. You open it up and carefully take out the small candle and the fragile piece of paper with the strange Arabic writing on it. You look at the words, but they mean nothing to you. You begin to become impatient for the Moor to arrive, and you look around to see if you can see him through the dark shadows. A form can be seen through the trees in the distance. Is it the Moor? What if it should be a robber — you hadn't even thought of that possibility. Perhaps you should hide. Ah, it is the Moor — you can see him now. Thanks be to God that he has arrived.

You greet each other silently, and now you must hurry quickly to test the power of the box. You light the candle and hold it while the Moor reads the incantation on the scroll. The perfumes from the candle send a sweet odor through the damp air. You almost become drowsy with the droning of the Moor's voice and the sweet smell. Then suddenly there is a distant rumbling like thunder. As it becomes louder you become frightened. Suddenly the cave entrance opens and reveals a long winding stairway. You and the Moor huddle together as you decend below. You must be sure to shield the candle light, for if it goes out, you will be entombed forever in the cave. As you reach the bottom of the steps you see a large trunk with huge bands of steel encasing it. At each end of the trunk you see two men — enchanted they are — and their eyes stare ahead. They are motionless. Such a sight is very mysterious to you and you are very cautious.

Around the trunk there are many treasures, and you and the Moor slowly realize that you have indeed found wealth. But perhaps it is just a vision. Is there really such treasure before you? You slowly and cautiously go to examine it — to pick up a coin, to try on a bracelet, to examine a precious stone. Yes, it is real. And it is yours. Each of you takes as much as your pockets can hold. There is more than enough and you are not the greedy sort — but this wealth can take you out of your state of poverty. You must hurry because the candle is small and may burn out if you wait too long. You finish, and both of you climb back up the long stairs to the darkness outside.

You and the Moor take one more look at the enchanted men guarding the chest. You wonder if they saw what you did. They have such a knowing look about them. But you must hurry, there is no time to waste.

You blow the candle out, and the cave entrance closes. You, Peregil, keep the paper, and the Moor takes the candle. You part, each — for the moment at least — happy and wealthier than you have ever been in your whole life. You silently part — each into the shadows of the night.

Playing a Role

It often adds to the fun of the playing when the leader plays a role. Generally the character is an authority figure or one who can legitimately give orders. His character than can logically direct and guide the actions of the children.

For example, in the Winnie the Pooh exercise activity mentioned earlier, the leader might have referred to himself as Christopher Robin and said:

T: Now Pooh Bear, I know you have good intentions, but sometimes you need a little help. It's time for your exercise, and I shall watch to see that you do them. In fact, I'll even count for you. We'll begin with the first one. . .

Other roles might be as a "Control Tower" for an activity about an airplane flight; Zeus who gives the cues for the thunderstorms; an inventor who designed and is now testing out robots; the captain of an expedition; the oldest and wisest member of a tribe; or a tour guide. For example:

T: Ladies and gentlemen, now that you are settled in your two-man outboard motor boats, let me introduce myself. I'm John Tiesman, your guide for the study of sea lions off the coast of Alaska. This tour will have its splendors and there may be times when my trained senses will discover various sights which I shall quietly call to your attention. I trust our attempts to explore and study the life of this magnificent animal will be successful. Bon Voyage!

Often the children get more enjoyment out of following the character's rules and comply with them more willingly. For example, if they are Pooh Bear following Christopher Robin's directions, "Listen carefully, Pooh Bear . . ." they are responding to a concerned master rather than the teacher.

Because the role is an authority figure, it usually brings with it its own control and discipline. If necessary, the leader can use the role to make and enforce rules when they are needed along the way.

T: As your tour director, I must ask you not to touch any of the stalactites and stalagmites in the cave. They have been growing for centuries, and one careless move from a tourist could cause inestimable damage. From this point on, you must walk through the passageways with extreme caution. Anyone who cannot abide by the rules will be asked to return to the entrance – with no refund of admission charge, I might add. Are we ready?

Although it isn't necessary to change one's voice or mannerisms in order to play a role, some teachers do enjoy doing this. They may even give themselves a prop or two. A tourist guide might have a special hat or a badge or ribbon. A control tower operator might use a chalk eraser as a microphone.

A PLANE RIDE

T: Today we're going to pretend to be Amelia Earhart or Charles Lindbergh flying our planes. The desks will be the airplanes. You'll be in partners. One partner will be the pilot; the other will be a student who is learning to fly. We'll play twice so each person will have the chance to play both parts. Choose a partner and decide between you who will be the pilot first. (Pause for organization.)

Now in our plane, the Stearman bi-plane, the pilot sits behind the passenger-student. So arrange yourself accordingly. (Pause again.)

We are going to take a ride across the mountains and land on the other side. This is going to be a dangerous trip because of the bad weather through the mountains, and the landing will be very difficult due to the rugged mountains surrounding the landing field. Because this is a dangerous trip, you will have to listen to directions carefully.

The Stearman bi-plane needs its propeller twirled to help the pilot start the engine. Student, you need to learn this, so you stand at the side of the plane by the propeller. Now, pilot, fasten your seat belt and shoulder harness. Make sure they're on tight. We'll have to take our signal from the control tower. I'm operating the control tower and you will get your signal from me. Put on your earphones so you can make contact with the control tower and make sure everything is all set for takeoff. (Children pantomime earphones. Teacher holds hand to mouth to make a rather muffled sound as if speaking over the radio transmitter.) "Bi-plane NC 211, cleared for takeoff."

OK, pilot, adjust your engine controls. Student, spin the prop to start the engine. Whoops. Guess the old plane will need several spins to get started. You'll have to try again. (Pause) There! The engine throbs to life. Pilot, apply the brakes. Student, pull out the wheel chocks. Now climb aboard. Fasten your seat belt and harness.

Student, listen carefully, in front of you is a stick that controls the plane's directions. It is connected to the pilot's control stick. By placing your hands lightly, I repeat, lightly, around it, you will be able to follow the pilot's sensitive contol. In this way, you can get the "feel" of controlling the plane.

Both of you be sure your goggles are in place. Now let up on the brake and taxi down the end of the runway. You'll have to zig-zag so that you can see beyond the nose of the plane.

We're almost at the end of the runway now, so quickly pull the stick toward you. Remember, student, when the stick is forward, it makes the plane go down and when the stick is pulled toward you, the plane goes up. Now the plane is rising off the ground. Up we go! Check your compass to make sure we're going North toward the mountains. Look down below you. The airport is small and far away.

We're going through the mountains now. It looks like we're going into a storm. Be sure to bank the plane so the wings don't tip too much one way. They should be kept level with the body of the plane. It's starting to rain hard now. Reach up to the top of your control panel and press the blue button on the right to start the windshield wipers.

If you look over to the left you'll see the flash of lightning. Don't look too long. Keep your eyes on the altimeter to be sure you stay well above the mountains.

Keep watching for the mountain tops so we can be sure to pass over them. Careful! There's a peak right in our course. Quickly bank the plane or we'll hit it. Whew! That was a close call.

It looks like we're passing through the storm safely. We're almost on the other side of the mountains now and the landing field is coming up on the right. Pick up your radios and let's make contact with the control tower and let them know we're coming in for a landing. (Teacher as control tower.) "Flight NC 211. Cleared for approach to landing. Approach from the Southeast." Now check your seat belts and prepare to circle the landing field until we can come in for a safe landing.

Now let's bring the plane down easy. We have to go slow because the fog is thick and we might miss the field. There it is! We're right on course. Stand by for a landing. Check the air pressure meter next to the lever control. Now get ready to pull back the brake lever when we touch ground. We're down. That was a good landing. Pull back on the brake lever and let's bring it to a stop. A perfect three-point landing! Congratulations.

FLEXIBLE NARRATION

When the leader grows in confidence and experience, he will be able to be more flexible in narrating. As he narrates, he ad-libs, expands, or condenses the material according to the children's responses.

The amount of detail the children include in their playing will vary considerably. Some children will be able to elaborate on ideas more easily than others. For example, a line may read:

They prepared their equipment for the camping trip . . .

One child may be observed packing numerous items and making considerable preparations while another child quickly finishes only one idea. The leader makes the narration as detailed, descriptive, and compelling as the majority of children need in order to have an understandable and involving experience.

Sometimes the leader's narration is too specific for the group and may interrupt or hold up the children's own ideas. In this case, the leader might do well to condense his narration and allow the children to fill in their own details.

The experienced leader may be able to create a narrative experience incorporating the children's ideas as he guides them in the playing.

> **T:** ... It looks as if most of the families have finished packing their covered wagons. Now before we roll out, there may be some crucial questions we need to answer. Let's gather by the fire here, and those few who are still packing, join us as soon as you can. (They all sit.) Now, do we have sufficient medical supplies?
>
> **C:** We have some brandy and some bandages in our wagon.
>
> **C:** Don't worry, Mary and John and I have already checked the medical supplies.
>
> **C:** I have a question. I want to know how many days it will take us to get to Nebraska.
>
> **T:** Well, we'll be lucky to make twenty miles a day. How long will that be? (The group takes a few seconds to compute the time.) Are there any other questions? All right, we've got a long journey ahead of us. Let's get started. Which family did we decide would lead? Bring your wagon over here, and the rest will line up behind ...

With most groups, the leader must bear the responsibility for planning the various events, conflicts, and satisfying conclusion to the activity. He must also keep the group organized in their discussion and in their playing in order to keep the dramatic excitement strong. And he can, as he gains experience, develop his own variations of the narrative.

EXERCISES FOR THE COLLEGE STUDENT

1. Write a 300-word narrative pantomime on any of the following subjects. Underline the action words once, the sensory words twice, and the emotion words three times. Label the conflict. Make the story as interesting as possible. Consider appropriate beginnings and endings to the story.
   a. Select a nursery rhyme and write it as a narrative pantomime.
   b. Select a biographical character, historical character, animal, or insect or any other curricular topic suitable for narration.
   c. Select a personal experience you have had that you can describe realistically and in detail.

d. Choose an inanimate object that could be personified.

e. Choose a narrative poem and adapt it into a narrative pantomime.

f. Write a story specifically designed for pairs or groups.

g. Write a story specifically designed for the desk area.

2. Practice flexible narration. Outline or write in detail a 300-word story on a curricular topic you will share with your classmates. Before the activity, introduce any necessary information about the topic. As you lead the activity, concentrate on expanding or condensing the story according to your classmates' degree of elaboration.

LONGER MATERIALS FOR NARRATION

The following materials are suitable for narrative pantomime but will need to be adapted or edited. In some cases dialogue will need to be omitted. The materials are arranged alphabetically. The following symbols are used to indicate the age level the material might be best suited for:

Y   young children in kindergarten, first, and second grades

M   middle-grade children in third and fourth grades

O   older children in fifth and sixth grades

M–O   *The Black Pearl,* Scott O'Dell. Houghton Mifflin, 1967.
Ramon tells of his adventures with Manta Diablo, a fearsome fish, and of the search for a black pearl in Mexican waters.

M   *The Blind Colt,* Glen Rounds. Holiday, 1941.
A blind colt must learn of the world, its joys and its dangers.

M   *Brighty of the Grand Canyon,* Marguerite Henry. Rand McNally, 1953.
The story of a burro who spends his winters at the bottom of the Canyon where it is warm and his summers on the North Rim where it is cool.

Y–M   *Burt Dow, Deep-Water Man,* Robert McCloskey. Viking, 1963.
A fisherman and his giggling seagull pet have a unique adventure with whales.

M–O   *Call It Courage,* Armstrong Sperry. Macmillan, 1940.
A South-Sea island boy, son of a tribal chief, has many fears of the sea and sets out to conquer them.

Y–M   *Children of the Sea,* Wilfrid S. Bronson. Harcourt, Brace, 1940.
The tale of a dolphin who makes friends with a boy living on Nassau.

Y–M   *Emilio's Summer Day,* Miriam Anne Bourne. Harper & Row, 1966.
Emilio tries to amuse himself on a hot summer day in the city.

Y–M   *Evan's Corner,* Elizabeth Starr Hill. Holt, Rinehart & Winston, 1967.
Evan wants a place to be lonely in, a place to waste time in his own way. He fixes up a corner in his crowded apartment for himself and then

learns that helping his brother fix his corner is also a rewarding experience.

Y   *Flip the Flying Possum,* Nolla Young. Grolier, 1968.
The tree Flip lives in is chopped down, and he must find a new home.

Y-M   *Fox and the Fire,* Miska Miles. Little, Brown, 1966.
A young red fox searches for food and is interrupted by a barn fire.

M-O   *Island of the Blue Dolphins,* Scott O'Dell. Houghton Mifflin, 1960.
An Indian girl is left alone on an island in the Pacific and manages to survive.

M-O   *John Muir,* Charles Norman. Julian Messner, 1957.
The story of a famous naturalist and founder of the American national park system.

M   *Jonathan Livingston Seagull,* Richard Bach. Macmillan, 1970.
The struggles of a seagull who dares to perfect his flying skills into an art.

Y-M   *Josephina February,* Evaline Ness. Scribner's, 1963.
A little Haitian girl trades her pet burro for a pair of shoes for her grandfather.

O   *Julie of the Wolves,* Jean Craighead George. Harper & Row, 1972.
An Eskimo girl must choose between the world of her ancestors and the world of the modern white man.

Y-M   *The Little Old Woman Who Used Her Head,* Hope Newell. Thomas Nelson, 1935.
A little old woman lives alone and is very poor but is always able to solve her problems, even though in unconventional ways.

Y-M   *Lone Muskrat,* Glen Rounds. Holiday, 1953.
An old muskrat survives a forest fire and makes a new home for himself. His preparations for winter and his encounters with an owl, eagle and other dangers make a dramatic nature study.

M   *Lone Seal Pup,* Arthur Catherall. Dutton, 1965.
A seal pup loses his mother and must fend for himself.

M   *The Moon of the Winter Bird,* Jean George. Crowell, 1970.
The dramatic experiences of a sparrow trying to survive in northern winter weather.

Y-M   *The Mouse and the Motorcycle,* Beverly Cleary. Morrow, 1965.
A mouse has interesting adventures with a toy motorcycle.

M   *The Mousewife,* Rumer Godden. Viking, 1951.
A sensitive story of the friendship of an unusually curious mousewife and an imprisoned dove.

M-O   *My Side of the Mountain,* Jean George. Dutton, 1959.
The various adventures of a young boy who tries his hand at living by himself in the Catskill Mountains.

Y-M   *Nobody's Cat,* Miska Miles. Atlantic-Little, Brown, 1969.
The adventures of an alley cat in the city and his struggles.

Y-M   *Paddlewings: The Penguin of the Galapagos,* Wilfrid S. Bronson. Macmillan, 1931.
The growing-up process of a penguin.

Y–M *Paddy the Penguin,* Paul Galdone. Crowell, 1959.
Paddy the Penguin gets to fly with the help of an airplane and a parachute.

Y–M *Pagoo,* Holling C. Holling. Houghton Mifflin, 1957.
The growing and adventuring of a hermit crab.

  O *Robinson Crusoe,* Daniel DeFoe. Many editions.
A man is shipwrecked and lives for years on a lonely island.

Y–M *Rocky Billy: The Story of a Rocky Mountain Goat,* Holling C. Holling. Macmillan, 1928.
A mountain goat learns of the demands of his environment.

Y–M *The Secret River,* Marjorie Kinnan Rawlings. Scribner's, 1955.
With Mother Albertha's directions, Calpurnia finds a secret river filled with fish for her friends and family. Mysteriously, she can never find the river again.

  M *Sound of Sunshine, Sound of Rain,* Florence Parry Heide. Parents' Magazine Press, 1970.
A young boy's experiences in a sightless world.

  O *The Swiss Family Robinson,* Johann Wyss. Many editions.
The improbable story of a shipwrecked family on a desert island.

  M *The Tale of Mr. Tod,* Beatrix Potter. Warne, 1939.
Disagreeable Tommy Brock steals the baby rabbits but meets his match when he encounters the equally disagreeable Mr. Tod.

M–O *Tiktaliktak,* James Houston. Harcourt, Brace & World, 1965.
An Eskimo boy is trapped on a rocky island and must make it back to food and safety.

Y–M *Time of Wonder,* Robert McCloskey. Viking, 1957.
A sensitive description of a summer's experiences in Maine.

M–O *"To Build a Fire,"* Jack London: Laidlaw Reader, *Courage and Adventure.*
A man in the Yukon, after a brave struggle, loses his battle against the 75° below zero temperature.

Y–M *Vulpes, the Red Fox,* John and Jean George. Dutton, 1948.
The descriptive and sensitive story of the life cycle of a fox.

M–O *Wolf Run: A Caribou Eskimo Tale,* James Houston. Harcourt Brace Jovanovich, 1971.
Rather than face certain starvation, a young Eskimo boy sets off to find caribou against almost hopeless odds.

  M *Zeee,* Elizabeth Enright. Harcourt, Brace & World, 1965.
A little fairy hates people because they tear down her house and never notice her. One day a child saves her life and Zeee changes her attitude about people.

7

Designing
Creative
Pantomime
Activities

In the previous chapters we have focused mainly on narrative materials. The teacher selects, adapts, or writes the ideas for the children to interpret creatively. The teacher also encourages the children's own ideas. In this chapter we will discuss additional techniques for designing creative activities.

Creative activities encourage the children to discover their uniqueness and to develop positive self-concepts. The children have the opportunity to learn of their capabilities for producing ideas on their own. Creative activities give the teacher the opportunity for insight into the individuality of children.

Many children can create with ease. The teacher can toss out an idea and observe the children's self-confident responses. Some individual children and some classes, however, need encouragement. This chapter is devoted to the specific assistance the teacher can give.

In encouraging creative work, the leader's major role is to stimulate the children to formulate their own ideas for playing and to appreciate all sincere ideas. Guidance is also important. Making children feel comfortable and successful in discussing and playing their ideas is essential for their confident participation.

Overview

In creative pantomime activities the children must be able to think of ways to interpret the ideas through movement; there can be no pantomime without it.

"I can pretend to be two animals in one."

In addition to the physical action the children invent, "doing" may also include sensory response to environment or emotional reaction to situations.

Creative pantomime activities can be based on a variety of topics. A favorite story:

> **T:** Let's pretend that you are the "Gingerbread Boy" and you've just come to life in the oven. The door is still closed and you're waiting to get out. I'll be the Old Woman and when I open the door, you jump out and do *one* thing you think the Gingerbread Boy would do. Ready . . . (Opens "door").

A topic in social studies:

> **T:** The authors in our text have explained "norms of behavior." In your small groups, decide on one norm of behavior for this classroom that you all feel is very important. Then decide on a particular situation that would demonstrate that behavior in action. When all the groups have their ideas, we'll do them.

A piece of music:

> **T:** Listen to this electronic song from *The In Sound From Way Out!** Think about what could be happening to you . . . what you are doing.

*Recorded by Perrey-Kingsley on the album, *The In Sound from Way Out!* Vanguard Recordings for the Connoisseur.

A topic related to emotions:

> **T**: People react to situations in different ways. What people do often depends on how they feel about the situation. I'm going to describe some situations and you imagine that they are happening to you. Take a moment to consider how you would feel and then respond.
>
> The Principal has come into the room to announce the names of people selected for Safety Patrol. He calls your name. Everyone looks at you. How do you feel? What do you do? . . .
>
> You're in the middle of an argument with a good friend. Suddenly the friend stops yelling at you, sits down, and looks very sad. How do you feel? What do you do? . . .
>
> The teacher has just asked for quiet. The person next to you asks a question; you turn to look at him, but you don't say a word. At that moment the teacher calls your name and says in an irritated voice, "I just asked you not to speak. Please don't say another word!" How does this make you feel? What do you do? . . .

Creative pantomimes may be played individually, in pairs, and in groups. This may depend not only on the inventiveness of the children but on their social maturity as well. Many ideas can be played individually first and then as pair and group work in replayings. Pairs and groups working together will need to discuss and make cooperative decisions. Many young children will simply not be ready to do group planning on their own, although some may be able to make simple decisions with assistance.

The playing time of the activities will vary according to the number of ideas the children have. At first the leader may want to keep activities as short and as simple as possible in order to help the children feel comfortable. Children are usually willing to try inventing with one or two ideas.

> **T**: Imagine that the naturalist Euell Gibbons has asked *you* to go "Stalking Wild Food on a Desert Isle."* The magazine article describes the various foods the small party gathered as well as the various reactions to them. Some of the children did not enjoy eating nature's wild food. Some did.
>
> Imagine that it is lunch time, your first meal on this island. Gather one of the foods you think you would like; prepare it if you have to and eat it. I wonder what you'll choose and how well you'll like it.

As children grow in capabilities and confidence, activities may encourage more invention.

*Euell Gibbons, "Stalking Wild Food on a Desert Isle," *National Geographic,* July 1972, p. 46.

T: According to our studies of Columbus, it seems that this man had great determination. One early historian, who talked with some of the great men on that famous voyage, recorded that it was Christopher Columbus who persuaded the captains of the *Pinta* and *Nina* to continue sailing for three more days. At the end of three days, Columbus said he would turn back if land were not sighted. The day this promise was made was approximately October 9th; land was sighted on October 12!

We know that mutiny was always a real possibility. Yet Columbus kept the sails at full spread even though his men were afraid of the strong gales. We know that he offered rewards for sighting land. We also know that Columbus felt he had divine guidance.

In view of what we do know, let's imagine that you are Christopher Columbus. Put yourself back in time to the evening of October 11, a few hours away from the moment land was sighted. You'll be playing this experience by yourself; if there are any people with you, they will be imagined. Where do you think Columbus would be during those hours? What is he thinking and feeling? What are some of the things he would do?

At first the children should play their ideas in unison. The ideas should be for their own satisfaction, enjoyment, and self-evaluation rather than for audience evaluation. Later, children will probably enjoy sharing and evaluating each other's work.

It may also be important in beginning attempts to keep the work anonymous, with private responses. In order to do this the children can play a brief idea and then freeze. While they are frozen, the leader can move around to a few children quickly and quietly and ask them to whisper their ideas to him, *if they wish*. This gives him an indication of their readiness to experiment with creative work.

Usually it is fun to try two or three ideas in this way in succession. Then the leader may quickly check on the ideas of five or six children. For example, the ideas may be based on a well-known story such as "Cinderella."

T: Okay, here's the first one. You are Cinderella and you are cleaning the house. Your stepmother says, "Get to work, Cinderella!" What will you do? One . . . two . . . etc. Freeze. I'll just come around to a few people and you whisper what you are doing at this moment if you care to. (Teacher moves around to five children).

Here's the second one. You are one of the stepsisters getting ready to go to the Ball. You think you are very beautiful and elegant, but you have to work hard to make yourself even presentable. One . . . etc. Freeze. (Again talks quickly with a few children.)

And here's the third idea. You are someone attending the Ball, and there are so many marvelous things to do and see. Think about who you are. I wonder what you will do. One. . . . etc.

"My idea is . . ."

As the leader listens to the ideas, he encourages and appreciates without making judgments. For example, he might say simply, "That's interesting," "Yes," or "I see." Or, he may respond nonverbally with smiling and nodding his head.

After he has heard their responses, he may share some of the answers with the entire group, making certain he does not identify children with their responses.

> **T:** Some stepsisters were putting on lipstick getting ready for the Ball. Someone was putting on a corset. And one poor man said he couldn't find his false teeth, and he didn't know if he would be able to make it to the Ball at all! And someone was crying because her false eyelash kept sticking her in the eye.

When the leader repeats the responses, he is accomplishing two things. By stating them aloud, the leader shows acceptance of them, no matter how ordinary they may be. If there are a variety of responses, the children hear different ideas. They may want to try some of these new ideas in repeated playings.

It is important that the leader convey interest in the children's ideas. For some children he may even need to be enthusiastic. The leader should set the tone that the experience is an enjoyable one. His attitude and response should relax everyone.

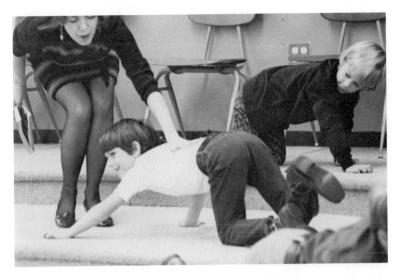

The teacher can appreciate nonverbally.

DEGREE OF ELABORATION

Initial Material

In beginning creative work it is helpful to use stimulus material that contains some specific ideas. The more ideas that the stimulus provides, the more ideas there will be for the children to try out first or to fall back on if their own imagination just can't get going. The ideas contained in the material help "prime the pump" of creative thinking and can also be helpful to the leader in sidecoaching.

For example, in Mary Ann Hoberman's poem, "The Folk Who Live in Backward Town" (34), everyone does things backward. The people walk on the ceiling, wear their hats inside their heads, eat apple peelings, and sleep under their beds.

The children could play the ideas mentioned in the poem. And, they may elaborate further on the idea of backward living, adding such notions as: driving their car backward, reading the newspaper upside down, and turning the lights on before they get into bed.

Some materials suggest paired playing. For example, a poem called "Clay" (32) states that there are many things one can make with clay. One child could be the molder and the other child could be the clay. A little book called *I Need a Friend* (Putnam's, 1971) tells of all the things one can do by oneself but says that friends are needed for doing other things. For example, one can pack a picnic basket by himself, but it is nice to have someone with you on a picnic. The partners could play the first half of the idea solo and the second half together, alternating just as the book does. The popular song, "I'd Like To Teach The World To Sing"* also offers possibilities for pair work. Children could teach each other how to grow apple trees and honey bees and a house furnished with love. Or, in the book *These Were the Sioux†* by Mari Sandoz, a "heyoka" or "Contrary" is explained. This was a particular societal role played by certain persons whose function it was to perform the actions of others backwards. The children might like to play such an idea in pairs — one performing the actions in the normal way and the other playing the role of the "heyoka."

Activities That Require Elaboration

Some activities will require more elaboration from the children and perhaps more guidance from the teacher. For example, the teacher might suggest the idea of being mischievous little elves who delight in irritating human beings. The teacher may have to help the children think of all the things the little elves could do, why they would do them, and who they would want to irritate.

Or, the leader may guide the children to invent and elaborate on the further adventures of selected characters. For example, the teacher might read the first few episodes of Jean George's *My Side of the Mountain* (p. 128). He reads the part describing Sam's first morning at the mountain, his growing hunger, and his attempts to get a decent meal. After he has eaten, Sam begins to explore his new surroundings. At this point, the leader might stop and ask the children to pretend they are Sam and think about where they would go next and what they would do.

The following are additional examples of activities that require the children's elaboration for pantomime:

A. INTERESTING WORDS

T: We've been talking about connotations of words, and I thought you might enjoy acting out some of them. For example, if I said the word "adventure" and you were to act out your idea of that word, what would you act out? (Other words might be: *discovery, sacrifice, freedom, dream, happiness, invention, serendipity*).

B. POEM

T: The girl in the poem "Carolyn" (42) sticks her tongue out at people. The last line says that she won't win many friends that way. Let's pretend

---

*Words and music by B. Backer, B. Davis, R. Cook and R. Greenaway. Several recordings available, including one by The New Seekers on the album, *We'd Like to Teach the World to Sing,* Elektra Records.

†Mari Sandoz, *These Were the Sioux* (New York: Hastings House, 1961).

to be Carolyn and do all of the things she could do to upset other people. Then we'll pretend to do all of the things she could do to win friends. What different ideas do you have for the Carolyn who upsets people?

C. STORY

T: The story *Horton Hatches the Egg* (p. 245) doesn't tell us, but I wonder what Maizie-Bird does all day long before she manages to convince Horton to sit on her egg. Let's pretend we're Maizie. What kinds of things would you have around your nest that might help you pass the time away? What are some of the things you could do to help you forget that you're bored and tired and have kinks in your legs?

D. PROP

T: Look at this ordinary rope I brought from home. While it looks perfectly common, I can assure you that it has helped me on innumerable occasions. Think about a situation in which you might need a rope. What would you do with it?

FURTHER TECHNIQUES FOR STIMULATING CREATIVE THOUGHT

For children who need further assistance in elaboration, it may be necessary for the teacher to set up the questions very carefully, discuss them thoroughly, and even sidecoach the playing as well. Following are a number of techniques the leader may use.

Discussion

The leader may guide a full classroom discussion. This allows him the opportunity to assess the children's readiness for ideas. Through discussion the children have the opportunity to hear the ideas of others and to modify and expand their own ideas. The teacher can also participate in discussion, adding suggestions to help children visualize their own ideas more fully.

A.

T: We've been studying about ecology. I found a poem that seems to deal with that subject. It's called "Vacant Lot" (50). The poet wants to change the vacant lot by planting a lovely garden. That's one idea; maybe you have others. What other things might one do with a vacant lot?

We'll be playing out our ideas of what we can do, first by ourselves. Then we'll be planning and playing in groups. But let's just brainstorm a few minutes about what other things one might do with a vacant lot.

C: How about making a recycling center?

C: I'd build a playground for kids.

C: I'd make a park like the one the Jaycees put on Fifth Street.

B.

T: Now that we've heard the song, "Come Saturday Morning,"* what would you and a friend do on a morning that you would remember for a long time?

C: I'd like to take a trip on my bicycle . . . somewhere . . . I guess.

T: On some Saturday mornings my friends and I used to bicycle to the limestone caves and eat lunch.

C: Oh yeah! I forgot. Randy and I always used to go searching for butterflies around there. I'd like to do that.

The leader should speculate on the possible responses his group may have and consider his own answers to the questions. Often when a student teacher has difficulties and is asked, "What answers did you expect to receive?" he responds, "Oh, I hadn't thought about it. I just thought the children would have better ideas than they did. I thought kids were supposed to be creative!"

The wording of discussion questions can also encourage creativity. For example, the words "if," "maybe," "perhaps" should be a conspicuous part of the leader's vocabulary in stimulating ideas. These words connote a conditional state; they imply possibilities, not absolutes. They suggest that a child can consider an idea but he is under no obligation to use it. The wording also keeps additional possibilities open and leaves room for one to change his mind. Conditional wording also indicates that the leader does not have some preconceived answer he expects the child to guess.

Brainstorming

In stimulating creative thinking another technique is to brainstorm. Brainstorming may be done in discussion or in the playing of the ideas. With brainstorming the children are encouraged to think of as many ideas as they can, as quickly as they can. The emphasis should be on getting the ideas out with no time to worry about them.

No evaluation is made of the ideas as to which is best. The children have a full reservoir of ideas waiting to be tapped; early evaluation can squelch the flow of the ideas. For example:

T: Today let's explore the idea of "Feelin' Groovy." What are some of the things you do when you're feeling groovy?

*Words and music by Fred Carlin and Dory Previn. Available on several recordings, including one by The Sandpipers, A & M Records.

The children's answers might include: eating, sleeping, playing baseball, reading, playing the guitar, baking, and so forth.

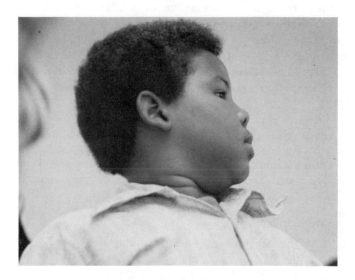

"I'm a proud king."

Particularly with familiar topics, the leader may dispense with discussion and go immediately to a brainstorm playing. For example:

> **T:** There are probably a lot of things we all like to do. For a few minutes we'll do some thinking about what we like, but instead of talking about them, we'll do them.
>
> We'll just play at the sides of our desks. Whenever I say, "Try another idea," you change what you're doing and try something else. If you get stuck for an idea, don't worry. You may want to repeat an earlier idea you had.
>
> As you play the ideas of things you like to do, I'll play Paul Simon's "Feelin' Groovy" to help us get in the mood.

Some of a child's ideas will probably be better than others. After brainstorming, the leader may have the children select their *best* idea. In replayings they can work on and play their best idea in depth.

For example:

> **T:** Now that we've played a number of things you like to do, pick one you'd like to do the most. Let's just focus on that one idea for our next activity. Think about all the things you have to do in order to experience this activity. Or, perhaps you should think about all the things you might see during this activity and all your feelings about it. . . .

Sidecoaching

Sidecoaching may still be necessary for creative work. Through sidecoaching the leader gives suggestions for action, or he adds to the description of the environment, or he suggests emotional feelings and attitudes. He may sidecoach by reminding the children of the different ideas they mentioned in discussion or by noting the ideas he sees other children doing. In the latter case, the leader's comments should be as objective as possible, avoiding reference to specific children. The following example is based on Lindsay's poem, "The Potatoes' Dance" (1).

> T: The potatoes are all so busy getting ready for the dance; I see some sweeping the floor. And I believe some are hanging some decorations from the ceiling. There seems to be a lot of cooking going on too; I see some stirring I think. . . .

The amount of sidecoaching the leader gives will depend on how much help with ideas the children need. Usually the leader waits for a moment to see how many ideas the children have as they begin to play.

Even if the majority of children in a group are highly creative, sidecoaching may still be necessary for those children who are unsure. Generally the children who have their own ideas will not be distracted by the teacher's sidecoaching. The children who need help are the ones who listen for it.

Sidecoaching can also fill in what might be awkward silences. Just the sound of the teacher's voice can give security to those children who need it and can guide and encourage through moments of hesitation. When it is enthusiastically delivered, sidecoaching can sell the children on the idea of becoming involved. Frequently a group's lukewarm response to an idea changes to excited involvement with expert sidecoaching from the enthusiastic leader.

CONTROL AND ORGANIZATION IN CREATIVE WORK

In the narrative materials the children had to listen to the narration of the teacher in order to know what do do. Control and organization was thus built into the material. In the creative activities, the leader will need to establish the organization and control.

In initial work, the beginning and ending of the activities usually must be carefully defined. The signals can simply be "Begin" and "Freeze." Or, if music is used the leader may say, "When the record begins, you may move. When the music stops, you stop."

The leader may be more inventive with the signals if he wishes. Often the material itself can provide the idea. In the earlier example of the "Gingerbread Boy" (p. 131), the leader pretended to be the old woman in the story and gave the signal, "When I open the oven door. . . . In the musical selection "Danse Macabre," by Saint-Saens, skeletons rise from their graves and dance until dawn. The leader may say,

> When the lights go off, it will be midnight, and the skeletons will rise up and perform their dance. When the lights come on again, it will be the approach of dawn, when you must return to your resting place once again.

The leader might want the children to time their own length of playing. Some may participate for a short moment; those who need or wish another moment may have it. However, the leader must still set instructions. The children may be instructed to freeze when they have finished and wait quietly until all the other players have finished their moment. To help sustain everyone's involvement and thinking about the moment, the leader may ask those who have finished to close their eyes or put their heads down on their desks. This also helps the teacher assess who is finished and who is still playing.

Another control may be the space the children are given to play in. As with all previous materials, the activities should be in limited space first, utilizing more space later. In some cases the children may even be asked to plant their feet firmly on the floor and move the rest of their bodies without taking a step. This is a challenge to one's sense of balance and coordination. Usually the children think of it as a game rather than a limit.

Mechanical Movement

Another technique for control is to use mechanical movement. It is orderly, predictable, and organized. The leader can be the operator of the machines and can control the beginning and ending of the activity with an "on" and "off" switch.

For individual playing, the children may be robots with the leader as the inventor in control of them.

> **T**: Robots, when I sound the buzzer, you will prepare yourselves for your work. First, you will be self-cleaning and self-oiling. Here we go . . .
> Now, robots, you do your work . . .

In pairs the children may create a machine with accompanying sounds. The children have to plan together which movement will go with which sound. The sounds may initiate the movements of the machine, or vice versa.

For group work, the various parts of the machine might be created. For example:

> **T**: In the story from *Homer Price* called "The Doughnut Machine" (99), the doughnut machine plays a very important part. If we were to create

that doughnut machine, we'd have to understand what different parts it has and how they each work. Once we have that all figured out, perhaps we can create more than one doughnut machine. Let's start with the first question: What are the parts and how do they work?

The children will probably mention the "part that squeezes out the dough," "the flipper to turn the doughnuts over," "the paddle that keeps pushing the doughnuts along," "the chute they come out of." Usually the parts the children mention are the parts they would like to play.

After the various parts are mentioned, perhaps some of them are demonstrated so that everyone understands. Then, perhaps a preview of one machine is given. Perhaps six children become the machine, and several may go through the machine as the doughnuts. Appropriate music may be played. After a few minutes of preview, the entire class may be divided into groups to create their own doughnut machines. On replays they can switch parts. If it should happen that there are only two or three parts of the machine that are of interest, only those parts need be played. And, if only one part of the machine is intriguing or if the children cannot handle group work, the leader might suggest that each child be the entire machine, acting out as many parts of it as he wishes.

Imaginary machines can also be invented. The children might have ideas for creating machines that will solve all sorts of problems, from doing their homework to changing personalities.

Setting the Picture in Motion

Another orderly, structured format might be called, "Setting the Picture in Motion." A picture comes to life and then returns to a still picture once again. These experiences may be played individually or in pairs and groups. Some possible ideas might be:

A.

T: We've studied in our science book that there are various ways animals prepare for winter. Some lay eggs and die; some hibernate; some change their color; people put up storm windows. In your small groups, decide who will be what animal. Each animal will do one specific thing to prepare for winter. After you've had a few moments to plan, you will hear the wind blowing and very slowly each animal will prepare for winter, and when the wind dies away, each animal will become very still.

B.

T: When the music begins, your idea of a "slithy tove" will come to life and "gyre and gimble in the wabe." When the music stops, the still picture of the Jabberwocky's (4) home will return.

C.

T: In this short poem, "The Shopgirls" (36), there is the idea presented that when the shopgirls leave the stores and the working day is over, certain things in the store come to life. What might some of these things be and how do they move?

D.

T: This picture shows five people in a crucial moment. There seems to have been an accident of some sort. In your groups decide how the situation might have begun and what events led up to this moment. Think of another still picture to begin with; then you'll act out the moments leading up to this picture and freeze.

(Left) "I'm a mighty warrior." (Right) "I'm riding my Honda in a fast race."

Another way to set a picture in motion in quite a dramatic way is to do it in sequence. Each child in the group is assigned a number. After they have all decided what part they are to play and what they are to do, they all take their places and freeze into position. Then the leader calls out "1" and all the 1's begin moving. The leader calls "2" and all the 2's move along with the 1's. When everyone is moving, the action is reversed until everyone has stopped moving and is frozen again.

This organization may be used for various subjects. For example, the children are studying early railroad-building in the United States. The leader divides the children into groups of six. In each group there will be men who lay the ties or "sleepers," men ("shakers") who hold the spikes, men who hammer, men who carry the water, and one foreman. The teacher assigns numbers:

#1, the men working the "sleepers"
#2, the "shakers"
#3, the "hammerers"
#4, the water carriers
#5, the foremen

After a few moments of planning, the groups take their place, and as the leader calls the numbers, the children begin the action they had planned.

A variation of this might be to have a variety of "pictures" of railroad life: a group of men scouting ahead, a "gandy dancer's" ball, etc. The leader may think of other variations for this orderly structure.

Completed Action

Guiding the children to think of an ending to their ideas aids organization. Usually it is helpful if the ideas have a framework of completed action: the accomplishment of a task, a day's work, an adventure, and so forth. Again, it is helpful if the beginning and ending are slower and quieter than the main action.

A.

T: We've studied that in the early 1800's the cowboy was very instrumental in making the Great Plains a cattle country. He had many jobs and responsibilities.

If you were a cowboy during this time, out on a drive, what are some of the specific jobs you would do? What jobs cause you some concern? When the day is done, what will you do?

We're going to pretend we are cowboys driving cattle on the open range. When you hear the clanging of pots, you'll know the cook's signaling for the new day. You'll work hard the entire day, and you'll know the day is ending when you hear the soft strums of the guitar.

B.

T: This poem called "Chant of the Awakening Bulldozers" (7), tells about bulldozers who want to be set free. If you were a bulldozer who could be set free for a little while, what would you want to do? Where would you like to go? What interesting experiences or adventures would you have before you had to return to the construction yard?

C.

T: After Hansel and Gretel hear their parents talking about leaving them in the forest, Hansel has a plan to save them from their fate. He must get some shiny stones to mark their path. Let's think about every step Hansel must make in leaving the house and in returning again without being discovered. We'll have to think about what the house and the forest outside are like. And we need also to think about how Hansel must have felt throughout his experience, remembering that he was trying to save his life.

Let's just try this once without discussing it. I'll play some music from Humperdinck's opera while you work. When you hear the old owl softly give his night call, that will be your signal that Hansel has gathered the stones and must quickly slip back into the house and into bed before his mother and father discover what he is doing.

LEADER'S PARTICIPATION

The leader's participation can be very helpful. It can help set and sustain a mood and highlight the dramatic situation. The leader may want to play a character who could be logically related to the situations the children are working on. His character can describe the situation or present the conflict. Then he pretends to leave the scene, allowing the children to react to the moment in their own way.

By describing the situation and by communicating the mood of the situation, the leader gives the children something to respond to emotionally. It helps avoid the awkwardness and difficulty of "feeling" the situation. And the character is infinitely more interesting than the teacher's verbal signal, "Now begin."

For example, there is a strong moment in the story "Knights of the Silver Shield" (60). Sir Roland, a young knight, is told by his commander to guard an isolated castle. He wants very much to fight, and he is bitterly disappointed over the assignment. It is this dilemma that creates an interesting emotional moment. Although he obeys his commander, the temptation to leave his post is ever present.

The leader might initiate the experience by pretending to be Sir Roland's commander, who gives him his orders.

> **T:** Sir Roland, being the youngest knight here, you have been chosen to stay behind and guard the castle. You must not allow anyone to enter until the battle is over and we all return. We are leaving, Sir Roland. Report to duty.

After saying this to the children the leader could then turn away as if he, the commander, were going off to battle. Sir Roland is left alone to wait, to guard, to pass the time, and to think about his feelings in that moment. The leader may end the experience by narrating a sentence about the return of the wounded knight.

The leader may also invent a role. For example, the experience may focus on Miles Standish and a party making the first trip to the shore of their new land. The children may be divided into several small exploring groups. His role is that of one of the Pilgrim fathers who stay behind on the *Mayflower*.

T: Goodman Standish and friends, be at rest about those of us who remain on board ship. We will be safe. But good brothers, be vigilant. The shore looks peaceful but dangers would lurk. Do not tarry.

A teacher may observe the children during these experiences and sidecoach. It is important to speak in the mood of the experience in order to be most effective.

Sometimes the teacher chooses to play along with the children. After speaking the words of his character, the leader can turn around again and become a character along with the children. This technique is helpful when children are bothered by the teacher's observation or need assistance in feeling that they are truly alone in their experience. By playing with the children, the teacher is also demonstrating his willingness to accept the challenge the activity presents.

In the following example, the leader plays the part of a Chief, and continues that role in the discussion that follows. Notice also how the mood of the moment is built.

T: We've learned that a guardian spirit, a "Wyakin,"* was very important to a number of Indian tribes. It was important to have a supernatural force that had power to protect. For the Nez Perce Indian his spirit could appear in a number of shapes, and each shape had a particular meaning. A grizzly meant power. A deer brought speed. We're going to imagine that you are all Indian youths involved in the sacred search for your Wyakin. Listen to my questions; think about them.

If you were an Indian youth, where would you go for your sacred experience? In your mind, carefully observe the area. It will be important to note what's around you, for something in that environment may be your guardian spirit.

The Nez Perce's custom was to build a pile of stones and wait for the sign. What will you do to prepare for your spirit? What will you do as you wait for the spirit to appear? What thoughts and feelings might go through your mind as you wait? In what form will your Wyakin appear? What power will he bring?

When you have thought about these questions and have some idea in your mind, come over here and we'll sit on the floor in a circle. (The children do.)

I'm not certain what ritual preceded the young Indian's search, but let's imagine that it is time for you to begin your search. I'll pretend to be the Indian Chief giving you your final instructions. Are you ready?

(The teacher stands, walks slowly around the circle, softly and rhythmically clicking two hard sticks together. He sits.) My children, your moment has come when you must seek your guardian spirits. Go search for the

*Adrien Stoutenberg, *People in Twilight: Vanishing & Changing Cultures* (New York: Doubleday, 1971).

place where your spirit will come to you. Prepare for him. Follow the customs, keep your vigil. You will know when the Wyakin appears ... When he does, return home ănd speak to me of your spirit. (The children leave the circle each at his own pace, prepares for and discovers his Wyakin, returns and describes his Wyakin to the "Chief.").

CREATING FIGHTS AND BATTLES

Creating fights and battle scenes needs a special word. Sometimes the description of the fights is brief and requires the creative imagination of the leader and the group to develop it. Since fights involve exciting action and physical contact, the leader must "stage" them as, in fact, they are handled in movies, in the theatre, and on TV.

Children are usually intrigued and impressed with the fact that the "realistic" fights they see in dramas are really artful pretense. They like to learn, the way actors and stuntmen do, how to throw a punch without making actual physical contact with the partner. They like the challenge of pretending to receive a blow in a convincing manner.

For the first step in staging the children should probably work alone, imagining their foe. They must practice and perfect their skill in stopping the blow at the precise moment before contact. The point of contact they aim at may be imagined. Or, the children may want to aim at a wall, their desk or the palm of one hand.

Next, they pretend to receive the blow. Again the foe could be imagined. It is a good idea to direct the punches by counting or beating on a drum. The teacher may say, "You will hit (or be hit) three times. Ready? 1 ... 2 ... 3." The teacher may want to say *where* the hits will be. "The first will make contact on the left shoulder; the second in the stomach; and the third on the chin."

The teacher may be the imagined foe, if he wishes, and then can respond to the punches or pretend to throw them.

(Receiving) "Ya got me there ... Ooh! ... Ugghh! Whew! I've had enough!"

(Giving) "Take that! ... And that ... Zingo! That'll teach ya, ya ornery varmint!"

When the leader is assured that the children do understand the staging of fights, he can allow them to work in pairs if they want to. He may even leave the planning up to them. They must decide who throws punches and who receives. It would probably be wise to limit them to five blows for the first time. Again, the leader can control it by counting or drumming the beats as above. The leader should go slowly with the counting, quickly assessing what is happening before proceeding further. The speed is increased only when the children exhibit skill and sensitivity to each other. If any children find it too difficult to control themselves in pairs, they may need to work solo for a while longer. If problems occur, the activity must be stopped immediately, or else children should be separated.

Further help is given when the leader reinforces the challenge of skilled, artful pretense.

> **T**: All of you could actually hit someone, but it will take skill and concentration to come close and *not* touch.

When the children have shown real skill and care in their work, they may want to try some scenes of fights and combat from different materials — social studies, science, or literature. The fights may be between men or animals. Along with these dramas might be valuable discussions on historic weapons or animal armor.

Here are two examples:

A.

> **T**: Now that we've read the Robin Hood episode with the Miller (46), let's divide into groups of five and pretend to be the Miller, Robin, and some of his men. We'll just do the part beginning with the Miller opening his bag as he pretends to search for the money, continuing with the blows he gives the flour-covered men, and ending the scene when Robin gives three blasts on his horn. I'll give those blasts. Get into your groups now and plan who will play what part; how Robin and his men react when the joke they have planned backfires. Also, you need to plan who will get hit first, second, etc.

A lively instrumental tune played during this episode of a would-be joke can help keep the brawl lighthearted.

B.

> **T**: Now that we've learned a little about the African Nuba tribe's ancient and traditional ceremonial wrestling ritual,* let's pretend that we are a part of that ritual.
>
> The first wrestling rank involves practicing the rules and movements of this ritual. We don't really know what those rules and movements are, although the pictures from this book give us some idea. Let's talk about what rules and specific movements we think could be a part of this ritual. (The children and teacher discuss.)
>
> Let's pretend that you are the young boys and I am the master wrestling teacher, guiding you through your practice. Apparently in this first

*Basil Davidson, *African Kingdoms* (New York: Time, Inc., 1966).

wrestling rank the young men do not wrestle each other, so all of you will practice these movements alone. Pretend now that you are asleep, and as the dawn comes up I'll arouse you with the sound of the gong. One beat means you should arise and begin your practice. I'll come around and observe your progress. Two beats on the gong mean that the practice and the pretending is over. Remember the importance of this wrestling ritual to the entire village and the esteem this ritual brings to the boy, his family, and his tribe. (The children experience this first ritual.)

Now let's pretend that we are preparing for the second wrestling rank. You'll need to be in pairs for this. (The children find partners.) Between you, decide who will be the young boy and who will be his father. Plan together now what specific things the father does to decorate his son. You might want to look at the pictures again; they show you how his face and body were painted. When you are ready for this experience, raise your hands. We'll use the gong as a signal again. One gong for the beginning of this solemn rite; two for the end. Remember that this is a crucial occasion for both father and son. (The gong strikes.)

For the third and most important ritualistic wrestling rank, you need to be in groups. You five can be together, you five, etc. In each group one of you will be the youth who is about to have his first serious match, and four of you will be the older male guests who come to the youth to comically demonstrate the "finer" points of wrestling.

Let's talk about why you think the older men would come to be funny in such a serious time and what you think they did; let's also consider the youth's attitude and feelings during this part of the ritual and what he did while they were performing. (There is a discussion.) Now each group find an area where you can have some space. When the gong strikes once, the older men have just arrived to perform for the youth, and when the gong strikes twice, the ritual will be finished.

Spend a few minutes practicing the comical wrestling holds. Concentrate on making them funny and *appearing* as if you were wrestling. But there should be no real wrestling contact. Does everyone understand?

EXCERCISES FOR THE COLLEGE STUDENT

1. Collect interesting props. Design a creative pantomime on one of the props you find most intriguing.
2. Make a list of ten popular and classical records that could be used to stimulate creative pantomimes. From this list, choose five and briefly describe the pantomimes the music could stimulate. Lead your classmates in a creative pantomime activity based on one of your selected records.
3. Make a list of poetry especially suitable for stimulating creative pantomimes. Design a creative pantomime activity on one of these poems.
4. Practice giving encouragement during creative pantomimes. Select a story and

design three creative pantomimes. Lead your classmates in these three pantomimes. After each pantomime encourage a few of them to whisper their ideas to you. Verbally and/or nonverbally appreciate these ideas. Discuss with your classmates the positive techniques you used and the effectiveness of them.

5. Select an interesting literary character. Design a creative pantomime activity on the character's "further adventures."

6. Design a creative pantomime using the brainstorming technique. Lead your classmates in this activity. After the experience guide them to select their best ideas and in a replay, encourage them to explore their best ideas more fully.

7. Design a creative pantomime activity using the "Mechanical Movement" or "Setting the Picture in Motion" format. Base the activity on a curricular topic. Specify the signals for beginning and ending the activity.

8. Design a creative pantomime in which you will play a role to stimulate the children's involvement. Select a curricular topic and a topic based on literature.

9. Outline a plan for staging a fight or battle scene. These may be from literature (e.g., *The Tale of Mr. Tod* by Beatrix Potter; *Brighty of the Grand Canyon* by Marguerite Henry, or *Wind in the Willows* by Kenneth Grahame) or they may be based on historical events or science (e.g., animals and insects).

8

Creative
Pantomime
Stories

In the last chapter we discussed various ways the leader could initiate and develop creative activities. In this chapter we will discuss ways the leader can guide children to create and play dramatic stories on their own. In addition to the techniques for creative work already covered, the dramatic element of conflict will be emphasized as an important part of dramatic story-building.

Individuals, Pairs, and Groups

As in all previous work, each child can create his own pantomime drama, or pairs and groups can work together. For example:

INDIVIDUAL PLAYING

T: You are Man whom Prometheus has just fashioned out of clay. This is your first day of living. When you awake you will be moving for the first time. The things you see and experience through your senses will be for the first time ever. The feelings you have will be new and perhaps strange to you. What will your first day be like? How will you live it? What problems will you have and how will you solve them?

PAIRED PLAYING

T: Decide between you who will be the shadow and who will be the person the shadow is following and imitating. You'll have to decide who the person might be, what he does, where he goes, what kind of job or work he does, and some of the experiences you think he might have. What problems might the shadow have? How might they be solved?

SMALL GROUPS

T: Each of you will become a part of your group's printing press. What parts of the press will each of you choose to represent? What is your job? How do you operate? As I play the music for you to work to, there will be a part where the music changes and the machine experiences some sort of problem. Decide what that problem will be and what changes it makes for you. And, then, how will your story end?

Space

The use of space may also vary. The desk area continues to be useful for beginning work.

T: You're going to play your story drama about an exciting day in the life of a South American gaucho right at your desk area. The desk will be your horse, the Pampas, the campsite, or whatever else you will need in your drama. . . .

The area for playing can be expanded whenever the children are ready; often this expansion is possible in replayings.

T: You will be a Pilgrim guarding your land and crops at night from the many dangers — wolves being attracted by the scent of decaying fish, and such. You will be playing by yourself, but you may pretend that the entire room is your plot of land. If you need to move around to survey it all, you may.

Unison/Sharing

For beginning work and for first playings the dramas may be played in unison. When the children are pleased with what they have created, they will enjoy sharing their stories with each other.

Stimulus Material

For initial experiences in story-building, the leader may want to guide the children to build the dramas on materials that already have a strong story line. If the children have a difficult time creating their own original plot, they have the initial story line to fall back on.

The following is an example of how one teacher guided a class of second-graders through a creative pantomime drama based on Mary Norton's book *The Borrowers* (71).

The children were not familiar with the book, so the teacher told them briefly about the tiny people who live under the floorboards of the house and who search around the house for things to use in their own miniature world. The book's illustrations were shown so that the children could see a number of ordinary objects such as postage stamps, thimbles, and pins being used in unique ways.

Each child was to pretend to be a Borrower who would go searching for new objects to use in redecorating his own little house. To stimulate new ideas about what could be used, the teacher brought three objects to class to discuss: a small, gold pillbox; a fancy beaded ballpoint pen; and a small decorative mirror. What might they be used for? Where would the little Borrowers find them? How could they get these objects down from tables or out of drawers left ajar? Since the children are to be tiny people working in a giant world, what equipment might they need in order to get and transport the objects back to their home under the floorboards?

The children discussed using string and safety pins to hook various objects and pull them to where they were needed. They also thought of the possibility of hooking the pin in a drape and climbing up the string. The pillbox they thought of using for a baby bed; the pen could be used for a decorative column; and the mirror, they thought, would make a neat skating rink.

The leader also focused on the problems the Borrowers might meet in an ordinary-sized house. The children commented on the problems posed by household pets; the dangers of getting too near a bathtub filled with water; and the difficulty of walking on shag carpeting.

The discussion of all these ideas took about 25 minutes. The first playing was done individually, and the children were allowed to find their own space to work in. The lights were dimmed to indicate nighttime — the working day for Borrowers.

The children settled in their working spaces and were to pretend that they were listening to be sure when all the household had retired. Their cue to begin playing their story would be the "clock" striking one o'clock. For this signal, the leader hit a stick on a metal platter. The children knew they had to be as silent in their work as possible since discovery by the homeowners would mean great trouble.

With the accompaniment of the somewhat mysterious "Arabian Dance" from Tschaikowsky's *Nutcracker Suite,* the children began their borrowing. As the selection neared its completion, the second signal of six bongs to indicate six o'clock was given. The children knew they would have to return quickly home again since the household awakened at that hour. While the clock was striking, the children hurried to finish their story and made their way home safely. Then, because they had worked so hard all night long, the leader sidecoached by saying, "You fall exhausted into bed," as the music faded out and the lights were turned on again. After telling their experiences, the children were given a few moments to plan a second borrowing episode with a partner.

The following is a written account of one child's experiences:

> . . . My partner, Don, and I pretended to be borrowers. We waited until 1:00 A.M. We crawled through a tunnel. We met face to face with a cat that cut me two times and rolled over on Don. The clock started to ring 6:00 A.M., and we heard someone getting up. So we got out of there! Don forgot to take something back so he tore back, put the things right outside our tunnel, and tore back just as somebody went by our tunnel. (Jim, Age 8)

Some stimulus ideas may be more abstract and require more inventiveness. For example, sometimes creative stories can be stimulated by the use of numerous interesting props. Some props might include a cape, a feather, a jewelry box, ornate key, crown, treasure map, or anything else that could stimulate the imagination.

The leader poses some general questions about the props, such as: Who would own this? Where is the treasure buried according to this map? What does the key unlock? etc. Then the children may be divided into groups. The teacher selects three or four props for each group, and the children make up a story involving their props. For example, a scarf, candlestick, pocketwatch, and mallet might suggest this story to a group:

An elderly woman (wearing the scarf) and her husband (carrying the pocketwatch) are robbed. The only clue is the candlestick which was dropped by the thief. A courtroom scene evolves with the mallet as the judge's gavel. The thief, the butler in disguise, is apprehended when his fingerprints are found on the candlestick.

Props can stimulate story ideas.

"Who's got an idea about this prop? Where did it come from? What was it used for? Who owned it?"

We think and think . . . new ideas sometimes take time . . .

"Ooh! I've got an idea!"

"We think some more . . ."

"Now, what sort of story might be made up out of three props together?"

More ideas come now . . .

We divide into groups . . . we talk and plan . . .

We decide who's going to be who . . .

And who's going to wear what . . .

"I'm ready but nobody else is!"

The girls have a story about ladies shopping.

"Oh boy, it's our turn!"   *"And everybody dies but me!"*

PLANNING THE IDEAS

Although the dramas the children invent to play may be fairly simple or quite complex, the basic structure for the experience is as follows:

1. Introduction of the topic or stimulus material.
2. Discussion of drama questions to generate the story idea.
3. Possible preview playing.
4. Organization for playing.
5. Playing.
6. Possible further discussion.
7. Possible replaying, sometimes with variations.

The leader's primary method of guidance will be through a discussion of drama questions about action, environment, emotion, character, and conflict. The children may also create the beginnings and endings for their dramas.

The specific questions asked to stimulate story dramas, however, will depend on the topic selected. The following list contains some general questions for each drama element.

ACTION
What jobs do you perform?
What is your occupation?
What sort of mission are you on?

What are some things that happen to you?

What is your primary method of exploring the area?

How do you move or operate?

What sort of adventure are you planning to have?

What do you do during a typical day?

ENVIRONMENT

Where do you explore?

What are some of the things you find or notice?

What are some of the interesting sights you see? (things you touch, hear, taste, smell?)

Where do you live?

What sort of shelter do you live in?

What sort of nest or house do you make for yourself?

Where do you hunt for food?

What tools or weapons do you use for hunting food?

What kind of equipment and supplies do you have?

What kind of transportation will you use to get around?

What kind of special clothing do you wear?

What sort of artifacts might you collect to bring back with you?

CHARACTER

Will you be yourself or someone else?

Who will you be?

Describe yourself.

What kind of personality do you have?

EMOTION

How do you feel about the adventure?

What feelings do you have about your occupation? (environment?)

What are your emotional attitudes about the situation?

What kind of emotional changes might you have?

What situations motivate your feelings?

What do you like to do the most?

Conflict

Essential to the dramatic story will be the conflict. The story may be based entirely on a conflict. For example, an experience could be centered on the problem of capturing — alive — a wild tiger!

> **T:** Imagine that you are a member of a conservation crew who has the responsibility for capturing a tiger. This is a dangerous job and it requires much skill. . .

Or, there may be subtle conflict, as in an old knight's lifelong search for his "Eldorado" (37).

> **T:** In Poe's poem the knight searches for his "Eldorado." If you were that old knight, what would be an Eldorado for you? . . . Would you ever find yours? And what problems would your search lead you to or cause?

Conflict may also be *added* to an idea. For example, beginning with the idea of being robots, a story drama might be created around these questions:

> **T:** Imagine you are a robot designed for a particular job. What sort of work would you like your robot to do? How are you constructed? How do you move? In a typical day, what are some things you might do?

To add the possibility of conflict to this experience, the questions might be:

> **T:** Let's suppose you got one of your wires crossed right in the middle of the day. What sorts of problems would this create for you?
>
> **C:** I'm a postal robot that sorts mail and I start putting mail in the wrong baskets and nobody gets the mail he should get.
>
> **C:** I'm a dishwasher and I break all the dishes.
>
> **C:** I speed up so much that I burn out everything inside me.

Other general conflict questions might be:

> What problems might you have? How will you solve them?
>
> What might happen to your equipment? What if some of your equipment breaks down or won't function?
>
> What if you ran out of supplies?
>
> What if the inhabitants of the land were unfriendly to you?
>
> Who are some of your enemies that you must look out for?
>
> What will happen if you don't meet your deadline?

Beginnings and Endings

In previous work we have used a framework for our stories. The stories had a sense of completeness and a beginning and an ending. These included life cycles, adventures, tasks, a day's work, coming to life, and returning to your original state. These formats are also helpful to use in guiding the children to create story experiences. Some general questions might be:

> How does your adventure begin? end?
>
> What is the first thing that happens in your day? What is the last?

What happens to make your character come to life? Why does he return to his original self?

How do you begin your job?

What do you set out to do? What is your goal? Do you think you will accomplish it?

It is important to ask only those questions that apply directly to the experience that will be played. Children usually do not want to talk about ideas if they are not essential to the story. For example, if the subject is about astronauts exploring the moon, there is probably no point in questioning about what the astronauts do when they are at the Houston space center. Or, if the children are going to be Jack in the Giant's castle, there is no need to talk about how they would play the part of the Giant.

Planning for Control

If the leader feels it is necessary, control can be built into the story idea. In order to lend credibility to the rule that they must be as quiet as possible, for example, the children might create stories about secret agent undercover work. Or, they may be museum statues, which come to life when all is dim and quiet. They may be elves secretly doing good deeds or slyly making mischief; or they may be wild animals stalking prey. They may also be a character who is left alone for a while and cannot let anyone discover what he is doing.

Thinking Through the Experience

Before the teacher introduces an idea for story dramas to the children, it is wise to speculate on the ideas he thinks the children may have. The inexperienced teacher will find this technique especially useful for organizing the activity and for having a reserve of ideas when or if the children need some suggestions.

As an example, let us analyze with the teacher as he plans an experience based on the brief poem, "Imaginings" (23). In this poem the reader is invited to imagine a red door that leads under a hill. It mentions a door knocker, a shoe scraper, and a carved key. The poem takes the reader to the point where he is opening the door, and then it ends, leaving the reader to wonder where the door leads.

Encouraging the children to think of their own dramatic stories with this red door might lead to numerous stories. Some children may want a quaint, pleasant experience. Some may see themselves involved in an exciting adventure. Others may have an experience that will convince them never to open another curious door again!

Thinking about the possibilities hinted at in the poem, we would probably first want to explore what one would see upon opening the door. Is there a fantasy land behind it? Are there treasures stored behind the door? Or, is the door a tempting trick and a plot to make you think something nice is behind the door when in actuality there is a trap behind it. Asking the question, "What will you see when you open the door?" might garner a wide variety of ideas.

But, so far, the children have been encouraged only to talk about what they *see* behind the door. There is *action* implied in the poem, but to be as helpful as possible, the leader should focus a question on it. "What do you *do* after you open the door?" "What do you *do* if you don't open the door?" Some may choose to go inside and explore, discovering all sorts of adventures. Some may decide they would rather report the incident to the authorities and then go off to look for the culprit who planted the trap.

If the story or experience the children see themselves having already has *conflict* in it, the leader may ask them how they plan to solve their problems. If conflict has not yet entered into their thinking, he may decide to introduce this possibility by asking, "What problems might you have behind that door? What will you *do* about them?"

In order to guide the children to have the satisfying experience of building a story line with a *beginning* and *ending* he might ask, "How do you *discover* the door in the first place? What were you *doing* when you noticed it?" And for an ending he might question, "Once a person is finished with his adventure behind the curious door, how does he get back? Does he return to the door? Do you think you will get home safely?" For those who decided not to open the door he may ask, "What happens to the door? Do you leave it there? Is it possible to get rid of it so that it won't tempt others to fall into the trap?"

DISCUSSION

The length of time spent discussing the questions will vary. It should continue only as long as it motivates and helps children formulate their ideas. Some groups enjoy discussion immensely, while others prefer to proceed to the playing as soon as possible. With experience the leader will be able to calculate when discussions are continuing to be profitable and when they are beginning to bore.

It is not necessary to try to ask questions of every child. What is most exciting about the discussions is the evolving of numerous ideas, the cross-fertilization of thinking, and the expanding and elaboration of ideas. During discussions children may hear ideas they particularly enjoy; some they may like even better than their own. They may decide to put several ideas together in their stories — their own ideas as well as those of others. Discussions are most valuable when they encourage this kind of creative process.

Discussions are also useful to the leader. They help forecast the ideas and plans the children have for their stories. With this information, he can better organize the playing. For example, some children may comment on possibilities for fierce combat in their adventure. The leader may then decide to arrange for individual playing, to preview the fight scenes, or to control space, so that the ideas can be played safely and successfully.

Discussions also help the leader recognize what is happening in the playing. Because a child mentions in discussion that his balloon ship will develop a leak, the leader can more readily understand why the child is swirling and sinking as he plays. He also knows what to look for in the playing to use for positive feedback in discussions later.

There may be times when the leader prefers to have the children discuss their ideas with each other rather than in the large classroom grouping. This can be helpful for shy children who may feel reluctant to express their ideas in front of the entire group. They may feel more comfortable talking to a friend or two.

Small, private discussions are also possible when the leader is confident that the children need little assistance or guidance from him. The children may be a very creative group who seem to have ideas about everything. As soon as the leader asks the first questions, there may be a buzz of excitement from them and excited waving of hands. He may proceed in one of several ways.

The children may discuss among themselves:

T: Talk to your neighbor about your ideas and when you're ready to play, raise your hand.

He may limit the length of general discussion:

T: Let's just take a moment to run through our usual questions. . . .

He may telescope the questions and merely announce them for private consideration:

T: If you have your ideas about what you will be investigating on the moon's surface, what kind of equipment you have, the problems you will encounter, and how your trip begins and ends, raise your hand. Maybe we can go ahead without discussing. Do you need to talk about your ideas?

And, he might even forgo a discussion and say simply:

T: I can see that you have a lot of ideas; why don't we go right ahead and play them?

Particularly when children are excited about their own ideas, it may be more important to let them carry them out rather than waiting to listen to the ideas of other children. Children are often more interested in talking about their stories after they have played them.

"Is this group almost ready?"

During discussion a child may hear an idea expressed that he prefers over the one he mentioned. Also, as children play they will often see additional possibilities they can improvise and add to their original thoughts. In fact, they may be inspired at the last minute to do something different. Sometimes children feel as if they are obliged to play the idea they said they would do and feel that they cannot throw in a new idea. It may, therefore, be helpful to tell the children that their ideas will and can change, and that it is not necessary (especially if the children are working individually) to stay with the ideas discussed. To encourage flexibility in playing, the leader may say,

> **T**: As you play your idea, you may find some of your original ideas changing. You don't need to stay exactly with the idea you have now.

Preview Playing.

As a helpful measure, the leader may want to have the children preview a part of their ideas before playing the entire drama. For example, in a poem called "The Doze," James Reeves (38) has created a fantastical creature who wanders aimlessly through the woods. It may be helpful to "try on" the physical characteristics of this animal, as each child perceives him, before enacting the story about him.

Or, before a story drama is created on sky diving, the leader may want the children to check out the procedures and maneuvers a diver goes through in order to have a safe fall. For example, he may want the children to practice the "stable" fall with both arms and legs apart. Such maneuvers must be understood and learned so that they become automatic for the sky diver. Practicing before enacting the story thus simulates actual conditions.

PLAYING

As we mentioned earlier, the length of playing time for these dramas can vary. For initial experiences the children may be able to create only short stories; gradually they will be able to increase their playing time to several minutes.

Even though the children have thought about their own beginnings and endings for the stories, it may still be necessary for the leader to give signals for the beginning and ending. In other words, the children think about *how* they want their stories to begin and end; the leader gives them the signal *when* to enact them. This is particularly important for first playings or for groups who have trouble sustaining involvement. Whenever the leader observes that the involvement is decreasing, he may give his signal for the stories to end.

> **T**: Start bringing your story to its end. . . .

When the children have had some experience, the leader may want to let them finish their stories at their own rate of time. Some children may continue to play, while others may be finished. The advantage to this is that not all children will have the same involvement in their story nor as many details to experience in playing it.

If the leader is concerned that those children who have finished early may somehow distract the children who are still involved in playing, he may remind them of the appropriate audience behaviors.

> **T**: When you finish your story, please sit and wait quietly until everyone has finished. You may have some work you could quietly do at your desk.

Even when the children are experiencing their stories at their own rate of time, the leader should continue to give some sort of signal to indicate that children should begin pretending. This signal lets everyone know that the moment to dramatize has come. Without such a signal some children are pretending, while others are making last minute preparation. The appropriate mood and atmosphere necessary for involvement is difficult to establish.

The signals the leader gives to children may be as simple as "Begin . . . Bring your story to its end"; and the playing time can be as brief as a 30-second musical interlude. Or, the leader may wish to be more descriptive and contribute to signals in more imaginative ways.

A.

T: If you have your adventure for your magical broom thought out, find a place to work in. I'll play some music (Paul Dukas' "Sorcerer's Apprentice"), which will weave the magic spell and cause you to slowly come to life. Your adventure will begin! When the music starts to fade, the magic will begin to disappear, and you will slowly return to your broom state once again.

B.

T: When you and your partner have planned your photography hunting expedition into the backtrails of Yellowstone, raise your hand. The signal to begin your expedition will be the early morning call of the Blue Jay. . . .

The leader may also choose to give his signals through a role. Frequently his role lends mood and atmosphere to the children's dramas; sometimes it strengthens the conflict. The following is an example. The children are creating dramas about child labor in the dangerous and unhealthy factories of the 1900's. The class has decided that everyone's story would begin during the early morning hours at the factory. The leader plays the role of a foreman.

T: All right, you ragamuffins, get to work! And make no mistakes! There'll be no pay for the sloppy and lazy. Get started and be quick about it!

In another example, groups of children are creating story dramas based on the idea of race car driving. They are in groups that include the drivers and crews. The leader through his role lends an air of excitement and authenticity when he takes on the role of the official announcer.

T: It's a great day for the races, ladies and gentlemen. The cars are lined up for the beginning of this day-long race. The excitement here is great – the atmosphere is tense. The engines are roaring, and the race is about to begin. At the wave of the flag, gentlemen, each team is on his own. Good luck! . . .

Sidecoaching can help these experiences also. In addition to the encouragement of ideas, sidecoaching may also include commentary to help children concentrate. Even though the suggestions for concentration may be discussed prior to playing, sidecoaching may be helpful in continuing it.

That's right, keep your eyes closed while you are imagining what it is like to enter the fifth dimension. . .

Remember you're alone on this exploration. No one else is with you unless you imagine them. . .

Remember you're not fourth-graders any more but an ant colony. . .

Second Discussions

The leader may or may not choose to have a discussion after the first playing. In some instances the enacting of the idea is so physically and mentally complete that the children do not seem to care to discuss it a second time. Some groups of children simply want to do it again, and with little or no variation, they repeat the playing. Some groups want to share their dramas.

There are times, however, when a second discussion is desirable. As in the first discussion there may be a general discussion, or smaller groups may discuss. Those children who did not care to exchange ideas in the first discussion can have the opportunity now. Those who did discuss earlier may relate more details of their experience.

Discussions at the end of the playing can become lengthy with children who are highly verbal and who have a tendency to monopolize conversation. In order to give more children the opportunity to tell about their ideas, he may again use pupil-to-pupil discussions.

> **T:** Tell your neighbor what you did and what happened to you, and he'll tell you his story.

If the teacher wants to hear some of the ideas himself, he can move around the classroom and listen in.

If, for some reason, he wishes to conduct a large group discussion, he may need to limit the answers. He might specify:

> Who was the *most interesting* person you met on your adventure into the time machine?
> *Describe in one word* what it felt like going through the tesseract.
> What was your *most serious* problem?
> What was the *most unusual* thing you saw?

Often children will begin to think of such limitations as a game, and they enjoy focusing in on their best thoughts and ideas. Often they also become more articulate in the process.

With a little planning it is possible to blend a second discussion into the total dramatization, so that while the children are still pretending, they can discuss the experiences they have just had. For example, the sky divers could rendezvous at a "picnic spot" near their diving area and discuss their falls. Or, after a journey to the bottom of the sea, the children could plan to meet on some coral reef and discuss their experiences in the wondrous watery world.

Often these discussions are stimulating, because the children are still in the mood and spirit of the experience. The leader may want to be a part of this discussion; if so, then he too must enter into the spirit of the play. He might take on a role and become, for example, the "cook" in charge of refreshments at

"Watch out, Sarah!"

Sarah's picture about her story.

the picnic area; or a "water spirit," who listens to the discussion on the coral reef.

For the teacher, the second discussion can clarify what some of the children were enacting and give him the opportunity to comment. He can indicate his awareness and understanding of the children's ideas:

Oh, that's what you were seeing when you looked so surprised.

Yes, I saw that horrible monster you were. I would hate to have to meet you unarmed!

What was happening when your arms were moving this way, Tom? (demonstrates) Oh, I see, you became the *propeller* of your plane.

In a second discussion the leader can also encourage self-evaluation.

If you were to play this idea again, what would you do that would be different from the first time?

Were you involved in your idea, or would it help your involvement if we rearranged the room or changed the music? What do you think?

Verbalizing

Often in working with group pantomime skits, children will see verbalizing possibilities. If they are not reticent, they may ask, "Can we talk?" When the question is stated in that way, it usually means they are ready to add dialogue to their skits, and they may be allowed to do so.

On the other hand, some children may ask anxiously, "Do we have to talk when we play our skits?" These children probably are hoping that they will not be required to use dialogue and would be uncomfortable doing so. They should not be required to use dialogue even if other groups are.

Usually the teacher can simply say, "Those of you who want to talk while you are playing your stories may do so; if you want to do your story in pantomime, that's all right too." There is no premium placed on either method. In fact, there may be some stories in which only one or two children speak, and the others remain silent. This, too, is allowable. Guiding specifically for verbal interaction will be discussed later.

EXERCISES FOR THE COLLEGE STUDENT

1. Outline a plan for stimulating a creative pantomime story. Include the following considerations:
   a. stimulus material.
   b. individual, pair, or group playing.
   c. amount of space needed.
   d. discussion questions (label).
   e. conflict question.
   f. story framework; beginning and ending.
   g. special effects.

  h. leader's character role.
2. Keep a file of materials that can stimulate pantomime stories. Be sure to include curricular ideas as well as literary ideas. You might want to take special consideration of the following: newspaper clippings, pictures, props and costumes, music, slides, and films.

9

Pantomime for Audience Feedback

In the previous chapters, the methods of playing were designed primarily for private communication. The children played their ideas mainly for their own satisfaction. As often as possible, all the children played in unison so that no audience was created. In fact, they were sometimes encouraged to close their eyes so that they would not be distracted by anyone else around them. There were opportunities for voluntarily sharing experiences with each other, but there were no obligations on the part of the children to present their dramatizations to their classmates.

Even though there was no intent earlier for public communication to be the goal, anyone watching the playing would probably have been able to understand what many of the children were doing and "saying." In fact, the leader has been translating nonverbal ideas when he comments in sidecoaching.

> **T:** I see some happy people.
> Something very dangerous must be happening to some people.
> I can tell by your movements that some of the animals in our zoo are very big and some are very small.

In order to encourage children's abilities to send and receive nonverbal messages, the leader can involve the children in pantomime games. In pantomime,* the players enact ideas while the audience watches and guesses. They base their guesses on the players' actions and facial expressions.

There are benefits enjoyed from audience situations for both player and observer. The audience gains practice in watching and interpreting as accurately as possible the ideas of others. The player has the opportunity to communicate his ideas to an audience. For some children, having their classmates watch what they are doing is an incentive for them to concentrate and become involved. It seems to give them a goal or a purpose for their activity. Often the player is stimulated and challenged to communicate as clearly as possible and to polish and refine the expression of his ideas so that they can be more clearly understood.

The audience becomes an important part of the communication process because it evaluates the effectiveness of the communication. It is this performer/audience situation that will require some considerations in order to make the learning situation as valuable as possible.

Although it is a usual procedure to have one child at a time pantomime an idea in front of an entire class, we prefer to avoid it. It places undue pressure on the performer, which is usually unjustifiable. And, if the plan is to have everyone in the class perform a pantomime by himself, the audience may become bored and tired before the ordeal is ended. There are a number of other methods we find preferable.

Team Pantomime

One kind of pantomime activity is based on a popular children's game called by the various names, "New Orleans," "Trades," or "Lemonade." Two teams line up and face each other. Team 1 decides on an occupation to pantomime for Team 2. They walk to a designated line near Team 2 and chant the following:

Team 1: Here we come.
Team 2: Where ya from?
Team 1: New Orleans.
Team 2: What's your trade?
Team 1: Lemonade.
Team 2: Show us if you're not afraid.

Team 1 then pantomimes the trade or occupation they have decided on. Team 2 calls out its guesses, and when they guess correctly, Team 1 must run back to

---

*It should be pointed out that pantomime can be a highly skilled art form as practiced by an artist like Marcel Marceau. It is not our aim to have children learn to pantomime in this stylized manner.

their original place without being tagged by anyone from Team 2, who chases them. Tagged members must join the opposite team.

This game can be played acting out topics other than "occupations." It may also be played by more than one group at the same time. The chanting and chasing are optional.

An observant audience can give constructive feedback.

Sequence Game

Another method, a popular one with children who can read, is called "sequence game." For this game, pantomime activities are written on cards. Since the pantomimes are to be played in sequence, the cue is also written on the card. The cards are distributed at random to the children. There should be enough so that each child has at least one card. Each player's pantomime has to be interpreted correctly before the next player can participate. Suspense is created in the quiet and careful watching and waiting for one's cue to his pantomime.

The first card might say:

> *You* begin the game. Pretend to mount a Harley-Davidson 750. Rev it up and cruise around the room once. Then sit down in your seat.

Another player will have the card that reads:

> Cue: Someone pretends to ride a motorcycle around the room and then sits.
> *You:* Turn off the lights and then go back to your seat and sit.

The next player will have the card:

> Cue: Someone turns off the lights. Sits.
> *You:* Stand and clap five times. Then sit.

It is helpful to the children to write the cues in a different color than that used for the directions for the pantomime. For example, the cue may be in red and the pantomime in green. Having the children stand to pantomime and then sit down helps also.

The individual pantomimes in the game may be totally unrelated to each other as they have been in the above example. Or, they may tell a simple story or include concepts in certain curricular topics. The following is an example of a modern Eskimo seal hunt.

> *You:* Stand and pretend to put bundles of heavy clothes, sealskin boots, and boxes of food into the umiak in the middle of the circle. Sit.
> Cue: Someone pretends to put supplies in the umiak.
> *You:* Go to the center of circle and pretend to step carefully into the umiak. Then sit in the umiak.
> Cue: Someone sits carefully in the umiak.
> *You:* Join him, sitting behind.
> Cue: Two people sit in the umiak.
> *You:* Pretend to start the small motor that propels the boat. After a few moments, pretend that the motor catches and then sit down, ready to steer the boat, etc.

A master sheet, which contains all of the pantomimes in their proper sequence, is helpful in case the group gets lost. For example, during a moment when children seem uncertain, the leader can refer to the master sheet:

> T: Now, someone has just turned around twice. What's that the cue for? (He pauses to see if anyone can pick up on this. If no one does, he might say,) The sheet says that someone is to stand and bow next ... does someone have that card?

In order to involve as many children as possible and as frequently as possible, the leader can make three sets of each sequence game and three master sheets and divide the class into thirds to play simultaneously. A child from each group can follow the master sheet.

Continuous Pantomime

This next game is played similarly to the sequence game. As before, one player's nonverbal message must be understood before another player can participate. In this game, each child invents his pantomime to fit the topic.

The activity begins with one person pantomiming an idea while the audience tries to guess *silently* what is being pantomimed. When someone guesses, he is allowed to join the first player and assist him.

For example, one child may pretend to cook dinner. The second player may decide to set the table, another may make a salad, etc. The players may add on to the pantomime until a specified number, perhaps 12, has been reached. Until the children have some skill in pantomiming, it may be helpful for the teacher to check with the first player so that he knows what topic the initiator intends to do. Then, to be sure all the additional players will be contributing to that same idea, he may need to check with them before they play.

Small Group Pantomimes

For another way to pantomime, the leader may divide the class into several groups of five. In each group three members try to pantomime ideas for the other two members to guess. For example, the instructions might be,

T: Pantomime all the words you can think of that begin with the letter "R."

"And one bandit bit the dust!"

The three players need not confer with each other; each player may think of his own ideas and pantomime as many of them as he can. The two guessers try to guess as quickly as possible. It is a good idea to impose a time limit; for example, two minutes may be sufficient for each pantomime topic.

The children might write down the pantomimes they guess. However, the leader should avoid the tendency to introduce competition. There is no need to count the number of words in each group's list, but the group might like to discuss the pantomimes that were the most humorous, most difficult to guess, and so forth.

Count-Freeze Pantomimes

Another method is to select six or eight volunteers to pantomime simultaneously in front of the rest of the group. They may pantomime individually, in pairs, or in small groups. This method is useful when the space is limited or when the teacher wants only a few children to play at a time.

This method has the largest audience watching. Therefore, the playing time should be kept moving along as quickly as possible. The leader may have the children pantomime their ideas while he counts to five or ten. He may count as slowly or as quickly as he feels is necessary. Sometimes when the performers are having a difficult time, a fast count can make them and the audience feel more comfortable. If the players are truly involved in their pantomimes, and the audience is interested in watching, the counting can be slowed.

The counting can be partially silent with the leader saying, "One . . . two . . . three . . . (pausing for a few moments and then finishing) eight . . . nine . . . ten." Usually it is helpful to say "Hold," or "Freeze" until the guessing is completed. The players may sit down when they are guessed.

GUIDING FOR NONVERBAL COMMUNICATION

As we have said before, for audience/performer situations the leader must do everything he can to encourage appropriate audience behaviors. In addition, whenever the children perform for an audience to guess, it becomes important to emphasize the goal of conveying and interpreting messages as accurately as possible. In order to achieve these ends, the leader should keep several points in mind.

Limited Guessing

There is usually little justification for allowing more than three guesses for each pantomime idea. When the children know that the guessing will be limited, they are challenged to perform and guess more carefully. In beginning work, the leader may even want to limit the guessing to only one guess. If the idea cannot be guessed, the child should simply state what he was doing.

> **T**: We can't guess your idea, George; would you like to tell us what it was?

"You stand and pretend to be a patriot sneaking on board the ship to dump the tea."

If the leader allows guessing to go past three guesses, he will inevitably run into problems. Some children can perform interminably:

> One little second-grader was performing something extremely elaborate. The directions were for the children to continue to pantomime until their idea was guessed. The little boy went on and on, saying "no" to each guess. Yet, he continued pantomiming interesting actions.
>
> Finally the teacher asked, "I guess you'll have to tell us what your idea was Billy." Billy thought for a moment and then answered somewhat sheepishly, "I forgot."

Sometimes children enjoy the audience's attention, and they keep their actions vague in an attempt to trick the guessers. Limiting the guessing can help avoid this problem.

Sometimes children also become upset with the audience when their idea is guessed. They think they have failed to trick the audience. To reinforce the goal of communication the leader might say,

> **T:** You pantomimed your idea so well we were able to guess it right away.

Sometimes children do not realize that their idea cannot always be guessed with total accuracy, and they hold out for specific guesses.

Audience: You're a lion.
Player: No.
Audience: You're a tiger.
Player: No.
Audience: You're a panther.
Player: No. I'm a *lioness with green eyes.*

Evaluation.

The leader may reinforce the goal of communication through his verbal feedback to the performers.

> **T:** Sandy, I knew immediately that you were a tiny spring in the clock. You stretched, and then relaxed and jiggled. And each time you did exactly the same movement.
>
> I can tell you have really been studying that book on armor. All five of you were pantomiming so believably I could practically feel the weight of each article of clothing you put on.

It is helpful to discuss particularly careful pantomimes, pointing to the details that help the audience accurately receive the messages. For example,

> **T:** What do you suppose Cliff was doing when he moved his hands like this? (He demonstrates.)
> **C:** Taking the cap off a tube of toothpaste.
> **T:** How did you know it was toothpaste? Couldn't it have been hair cream? Or first-aid cream?
> **C:** No! He squeezed it on his toothbrush and brushed his teeth!
> **C:** Cliff used a special kind of toothbrush, didn't he? What kind was it?
> **C:** Electric.
> **T:** How do you know?
> **C:** Cause he plugged it in and jiggled.
> **T:** What was Orlando doing?
> **C:** That's easy. Peeling an onion.
> **T:** How could you tell?
> **C:** Because he peeled it and cried.
> **T:** Cliff and Orlando were very careful in their actions. They added details that helped us know what they were doing.

The leader should, of course, be careful about implying that a child is unsuccessful in his pantomime. Some children *will* be more successful than others, but it is important to encourage continued work. The more the children have the opportunity to play pantomimes, the more skilled they will become.

Through his questions, the leader can directly influence children's evaluations. He may ask them to respond to questions such as:

> As you watched the performers, what was the most believable moment and what did the player do that made the pantomime so convincing?
>
> You looked as if you were enjoying watching the first group enact their ideas of transportation during pioneer days. Who can name the five or six different forms of transportation Group 1 pantomimed?

Questions should be worded to solicit a *positive* response. Those questions that make it possible to answer negatively should be avoided. For example, the following questions could easily elicit an emphatic "No!"

> Didn't you like the way Tom pantomimed his mean pirate with a wooden leg?
>
> Did you like the kerosene lamp Andy pretended to carry into the old house?

More positive responses would come from statements worded like the following:

> What did you see that you enjoyed because they were pantomimed particularly well?
>
> As you watch this next group, watch for those moments when things are done so carefully that they practically exist before your eyes.

To stress the importance of close observation, the teacher might ask the viewers to try to guess silently what each person is doing and then write it down on paper. After the pantomiming is over, the teacher can call on one volunteer to guess everyone's ideas while the other members of the audience check their lists for accuracy.

The children may be challenged to see if they can guess and *remember* each person's idea without writing the answers on paper. This method can give them an exercise in recalling details.

Sometimes it may be necessary to remind the children of the supportive behaviors an audience observing creative dramatics must demonstrate.

> **T:** I noticed that when this group was sharing its idea with the rest of us, the audience didn't seem to be giving its full attention. Remember that if you want others to watch you, then you must treat them with the same consideration.

The discussion should not be allowed to become boring or overly critical. Again, the greatest improvements will come about through practice and through doing rather than through the extended evaluation of others.

SIMPLE ACTIVITIES

The following subjects are suggestions for pantomimes. They may be used with any of the methods discussed in this chapter.

1. *Who Am I (Are We)?* Players choose someone from history, literature, science, etc. to pantomime.

2. *What Am I (Are We)?* Children can pantomime certain animals, inanimate objects, machinery, toys, flowers, etc.

3. *What Am I (Are We) Doing?* (or seeing, hearing, tasting, eating, smelling, touching). Players concentrate on receiving a message from one of their senses.

4. *What's the Weather?* Players enact clues for audience to guess the climatic conditions.

5. *What Am I (Are We) Feeling?* Children act out emotions. May use whole body or limit the children to using only their hands, feet, face, back.

6. *Creating an Object.* Players become parts of an object. For example, if the object is a clock, one player may become the hands, another might form the face, while another may become the alarm. Other parts might be the second hand, legs, knobs, gears, springs, etc.

7. *This Is What I (We) Saw.* Children pantomime what they notice on

the way to school	television
a field trip	a walk through a woods

8. *Sight Seeing.* Children pantomime specific things they might see or do if they were taking various excursions. They can visit

a museum	a fantastical place	a geographical location
a hospital	a painter's studio	an historical location

9. *Let's Get Ready to Go.* Children pretend to pack a suitcase or load equipment for traveling and transporting. Children pretend they are

going on a fishing trip	loading a covered wagon
preparing for a hike	equipping an explorer's ship

10. *Transportation.* Players pretend to journey on various modes of transportation: modern, historical, fantastical.

11. *Family Portrait.* Children are members of a family, preparing for and getting their portrait taken.

historical family	animal family	pompous family
famous family	absent minded family	fictional literature family

12. *Dress Up.* Players pretend to be certain kinds of people or characters dressing in their appropriate garb.

a witch	desert nomad	Roman soldier
astronaut	seal hunter	Egyptian priest
Viking warrior	steel worker	Spanish bullfighter

13. *Foods.* Pretend to grow, harvest, shop, or prepare familiar and foreign foods.

lobster	spaghetti	pineapples

coconut	avocados	hot peppers
wild rice	candied apples	grapes
corn	coffee beans	

14. *Occupations.* Children can pretend to do daily tasks.

doctor	botanist	ballet master
speleologist	truck driver	delivery person
forester	teacher	hair stylist
orchestra leader	crane operator	chauffeur

Pantomimes can also focus on the occupations of

| grandparents | other countries |
| pioneer days | the year 2050 |

15. *Tools.* This activity is similar to "Occupations," but the emphasis is on the various tools man has used or now uses to perform certain occupations or tasks.

16. *Building a Place.* This is a variation of Viola Spolin's "Where" exercises in *Improvisation for the Theatre* (Northwestern University Press, 1963). Children pretend to equip a designated area with necessary and appropriate furnishings. The players bring one object at a time into the specified area. The object is to create a complete, imaginary environment; therefore, the players must remember where each item is placed so that they do not walk over or through it. Children can build:

a modern living room	a cliff dweller's home
an igloo	an Indian longhouse
a one-room log cabin	a castle
an Egyptian tomb	a scientist's laboratory

Literary homes might include:

Bob Cratchit's home in Dickens' *A Christmas Carol*
Onion John's house in the book by Joseph Krumgold
Grandfather's hut in the Alps in *Heidi* by Johanna Spyri

An added challenge is requiring the children to use the previous item in some way after bringing in each new item. Example: bring in test tubes in the scientist's laboratory and then light the Bunsen burner brought in immediately before.

17. *Sports and Seasonal Activities.* Children can pretend to participate in various activities as themselves or famous athletes.

| tennis | ping pong | horseshoes |
| hockey | basketball | weightlifting |

18. *Biography.* Children can pretend to be various famous or historical people, pantomiming typical activities.

Mary McLeod Bethune	Hannibal	Gordon Parks
George Foreman	Margaret Mead	Leonard Bernstein
Rachel Carson	Cesar Chavez	Frederick Douglass
Thomas Edison	Susan B. Anthony	Matthew Henson
Maria Tallchief	Pearl Buck	Shirley Chisholm

Clippings from magazines can stimulate story ideas.

19. *Making Sounds.* Children pantomime making a vocal sound by using their faces and body but not their voices. Fun to do in slow motion.

cough	chuckle	pant
sneeze	hum	gasp
growl	gulp	sigh
shout	sputter	cry

20. *Word Pantomimes.* Several games can be played using categories of words or parts of speech. For example, in an *Opposite Game* the leader might inform the players they are to act out the word "hot." The audience must guess the opposite word, "cold."

Adjectives, adverbs, and verbs can also be acted out.

PANTOMIME SKITS AND STORIES

More elaborate pantomimes can also be done. The children, individually or in pairs or groups, can plan and play lengthier activities that may develop into complete story lines. For some of the activities listed, the children may want to add dialogue, although it is not required.

As the children become skilled in pantomime, it should not be necessary to have to guess each detail of the story, although evaluation of the communicative effectiveness is still important:

What was the most understandable moment?

When did you have difficulty following the story?

Were the characters clearly delineated?

Were the character's feelings understandably motivated?

Was there a satisfying ending?

ACTIVITIES

1. *Proverbs.* Children are asked to develop a skit to illustrate a proverb.
   "Make hay while the sun shines."
   "A stitch in time saves nine."
   "A friend in need is a friend indeed."
2. *Without Saying a Word.* In groups the children must *plan* and *play* a nursery rhyme or fairy tale *without* saying a word the entire time.
3. *News Story of the Week!* In groups, children illustrate a news event. Having a newspaper at hand for this activity can stimulate interest in reading further about the events as well as providing the ideas for the skits.
4. *Television Shows.* Children can act out favorite television shows.

soap operas	late night movies
situation comedies	

   They may combine TV shows with story commercials (those that can be pantomimed and do not require verbalizing).
5. *Your Hit Parade.* Some years ago there was a television show called "Your Hit Parade." Each week the top songs were sung and dramatized in simple fashion. A song that remained in the top listings for several weeks had to be dramatized in a variety of ways. Some songs had lyrics and some didn't. Select some songs that can be pantomimed in groups while the music is playing, and see how many varieties there are. Children will enjoy using popular music.
6. *Opening Lines.* Children can base skits on opening lines, such as the following:
   a. It seemed a perfect day for the event. Crowds were gathered for the momentous, historic occasion. One person in the crowd, however, seemed out of place.
   b. Silently and without warning it seemed to come upon them like a thief in the night. Not until the following morning were they aware of what had happened.
7. *You Are There.* Skits may be based on scenes of scientific or historical significance. Facts about the events may be listed on cards, or the children might do research work in preparation.
   Test drive of first automobile
   When the Wright Brothers flew their plane
   When penicillin was discovered

When land was opened in Oklahoma
Driving golden spike for Transcontinental Railroad
During first heart transplant
When Jane Addams opened Hull-House
Charles Lindbergh landing after trans-Atlantic solo flight
Alexander Graham Bell making first telephone call
When women were allowed to vote
Discovery of radium by Madame Curie
When the Mississippi River was discovered
When King Tut's tomb was found

8. *The Invention.* Children act out their version of the discovery of these inventions:

laughing gas	mirror	potato chips
suspenders	popcorn machine	snowshoes
rubber band	fireworks	bubble gum
fire	the wheel	

9. *Famous Last Words.* Create skits that focus on "last words" such as:

"I have an idea that will revolutionize mankind!"
"It's never going to work!"
"I know exactly what I'm doing!"
"Let *me* show you how to do it!"

10. *Superlatives.* Players pantomime skits based on topics such as:

A most embarrassing (frightening, awesome, happy) moment!
A strange (funny, scary, wonderful) dream!
An unbelievable (crazy, science fiction, incredible) event!

11. *Charades.* Players are given song, play, book, film, or television titles as well as common sayings to act out. Usually the words are acted out one at a time, although they need not be acted out in the order they appear in the title. Sometimes only one syllable at a time is acted out.

The pantomimers have several aids they can use:

(a) They may tell the guessing players, "This is a _____ (title or saying.) There are _____ words in it. I'm going to act out the _____ word."

(b) The player may say, "This is a short word." The guessers then simply call out as many short words as they can think of until the correct one is called. Words such as "a," "an," "the," or various pronouns and prepositions can be handled quickly in this manner.

(c) The pantomimer may act out a word that *sounds* like the original word if he thinks that would be easier to guess. The word "car," for example, might be easier to act out and guess than the word "far."

EXERCISES FOR THE COLLEGE STUDENT

1. Write a sequence game. Base it on a story or curricular topic.
2. Practice giving positive verbal teacher feedback. Organize your classmates for a pantomime game. Carefully observe their pantomimes, and after the activity positively evaluate their pantomimes.
3. Practice guiding an audience to positively evaluate player's nonverbal communication. Organize your classmates for a pantomime game, with half of the class as the audience. After the pantomimes, guide the audience to give positive feedback on what they observed.
4. Select one of the pantomime games and add your own ideas. Or, create your own pantomime games.

10

Verbal Activities

In the previous chapters we have discussed and emphasized pantomime. However, we have encouraged the teacher to allow verbalizing whenever it occurred spontaneously. The leader will also want to develop the children's skills in verbalizing. He will want them to grow in confidence and in the ability to express themselves and to interact with others.

Children vary in their readiness to verbalize. Some children feel free about talking and expressing ideas, opinions, and feelings as they play; other children are more reticent.

The teacher's goal in verbal interaction is to help all children talk their ideas and feelings in drama experiences. There will be many ways to do this, using many of the techniques and methods discussed previously, including: narration/sidecoaching, unison playing, double casting, discussion, leader participation, catalyst role, and preview playing.

BEGINNING ACTIVITIES

There are many simple verbal activities and games that can be played to help the children feel more comfortable with talking. At first the leader may want to begin with just sounds. The children do not have to use language, but can simply play with the voice, making sound effects.

Sound Effects

There are a number of stories and poems that focus on sounds. The leader can narrate sound effects materials just as he did with pantomime. For example, Eleanor Farjeon's poems "The Sounds in the Morning" and "The Sounds in the Evening" (17) give opportunities for making such sounds as dogs barking, wind whispering, cats mewing, and owls hooting. George Mendoza's story "The Devil's Pocket" (15) contains echo sounds.

Other materials might include: "The Bed" by Pura Belpre (56); "Hearing Things" by Aileen Fisher (51); "I Speak, I Say, I Talk" by Arnold L. Shapiro (8); *Noisy Nancy and Nick* by Lou Ann Gaeddert (Doubleday, 1970); *The Little Woman Wanted Noise* by Val Teal (Rand McNally, 1943); *The Noisy Book* by Margaret Wise Brown (Harper & Row, 1939); "Rhyme of Rain" by John Holmes (36); *Time of Wonder* by Robert McCloskey (Viking, 1957); and "Wind Song" by Lilian Moore (27).

The leader can also create his own materials to focus on sound effects. He may base activities on the seasons, holidays, nighttime, or storm sounds. The sounds might be in different locations or countries, such as a farm, the city, a busy seaport, or a jungle camp.

Certain sounds that younger children (and even older ones) have trouble pronouncing, such as "s," "sh," "th," "r," could be incorporated into a sound effect story or exercise. The "s" sound might, for example, be made by a rattlesnake getting ready to strike; "r" the sound of a motor; "th" air escaping from a leaky balloon; "sh" the sound of running water.

The sounds may be combined into a story:

A.

T: One dark night I was at home alone. I was reading a book in a chair by the window. Outside the wind was blowing softly. (Sound) The tree limbs were gently tapping on the roof and the windowpanes. (Sound) The tall clock in the corner ticked steadily. (Sound) Then it struck one o'clock. (Sound) Then strange sounds began ... (The story proceeds with scary sounds and builds to a climax of something being knocked over in another room. The narrator discovers a cat had wandered into the house and caused the accident; it wasn't a ghost or prowler after all!)

B.

T: Let's imagine it is the afternoon of April 9, 1865.

It's very quiet ...

All eyes are looking down the dusty road to the Court House.

A blue jay calls ...

An annoyed squirrel answers back ...

In the distance, young children shout and begin a game of tag ...

The muffled sound of horses is heard ...

And a gray figure riding a gray horse approaches ...

All sounds cease . . .

Slowly the gray horse, Traveller, passes the line of waiting Northern soldiers . . .

He stops at the gate of the McLean house . . .

General Lee's footsteps on the wooden stairs are clear and brisk. . .

Now another figure on horseback rides into view . . .

And while the watching men softly sing "Auld Lang Syne" . . .

General Grant disappears into the house

And the battle-weary country waits for peace.

"Follow the arrow to make the sound."

Controls

Often children enjoy making sound effects so much that they get carried away. To control the sounds, the leader should preview or rehearse some of them before narrating the entire story. In addition he may need to establish some special signals and control for the volume of the sound.

One leader taught her class three of the hand signals choral directors use. When her hand raised upward, the volume increased; when it descended, the volume decreased. A definite cutoff was a quick hand movement with a sudden stop midair.

Brian Way, in his book *Development Through Drama* (p. 18), suggests controlling sound with an "arrow." The teacher holds a pointer or "arrow" to signify a volume dial and uses it to indicate the directions for on and off and for varying degrees of volume.

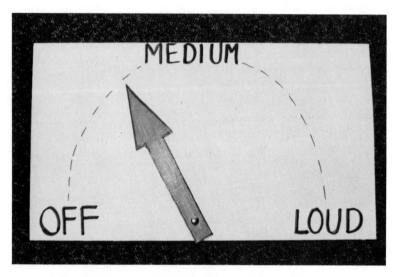

"The arrow tells us to lower the volume."

Whatever signal the leader uses, he will probably have to practice with the control until the children can follow it easily. Usually they are very responsive to the control when it is introduced in the spirit of fun and as a challenge:

> **T**: Now that you know the signals, we'll see if you can follow them. You'll have to keep your eye on the indicator. Let's just practice with the sound "oh" first. Ready? (They practice for a few tries.) So far so good. But maybe I'll be able to trick you this time and catch you off guard. You'll have to really watch this time because I'm pretty sly . . . (Again more practice until the leader is sure they can handle an entire story).

Sequence Game

As in "audience pantomimes" a sequence game can also be made for verbal activities. The children have an opportunity to talk, but they read the lines written for them rather than having to invent dialogue.

Again the cards are made up with a cue and a line to read (or perhaps a pantomime to perform.) The cards are distributed at random, with each child receiving at least one card. The first card might say,

> You begin the game. You stand and say, "Good morning, ladies and gentlemen. Welcome to the 4th Grade TV Personality Show!" Then bow and sit down.

Another player will have a card that reads,

> Cue: "Good morning, ladies and gentlemen. Welcome to the Fourth Grade Personality Show." Bows and sits.
>
> *You:* Stand and say, "Brought to you by 'Multi-colored Jelly Beans.'" Then sit.

The next card will read (there might be three of these cards)

> Cue: "Brought to you by 'Multi-colored Jelly Beans.'" Sit.
>
> *You:* Stand and clap and clap and clap. Then sit.

As before, it is helpful if the children stand in order to perform, and sit following their activity. Color coding of the cards is also helpful; for example, red print for the cue line and green print for what is spoken or pantomimed.

Sequence games may be based on riddles and jokes. They may also have a story line. Stories such as *"I Can't," Said the Ant* and *The Green Machine* by Polly Cameron (Coward-McCann, 1961 and 1969) or "Talk" (14) have been made into sequence games by placing the dialogue on cards and having the leader serve as the narrator.

Curriculum topics are also possible. The following is an example of a sixth-grade social studies lesson on exploration in The New World:

1. You begin the game. Stand and say, "The time is the late 1400's. The place is Europe. Curtain going up!" Then sit.
2. You stand, walk around the circle, and call out, "For sale, for sale, our latest shipment of spices, silks, perfumes, and gems! For sale, directly from the Indies. Come and get it while it lasts!" Return to your seat.
3. You stand and say, (shaking your head sadly) "Too bad we can't have more." Sit.
4. You jump up and say excitedly. "Ah, but we could if we had a sailing route to the Indies." Sit.
5. You stand, clap your hands as if you're trying to get someone's attention, and say, "Children – recite today's geography lesson." After 2 people recite, you sit.
6, 7. (Two cards) You and another person will stand and recite together: "Roses are red – violets are blue. The earth is flat – and that's the truth." Then bow and sit.
8. You stand and say slowly, "Very interesting." Sit down slowly.
9. You stand and say, "But not true!" Sit.
10. You stand and say, "And it doesn't even rhyme." Sit.
11. You stand and say, "Mama Mia, Have I got an idea! I'll go west (point one way) to get to the east" (point the other way). (Wait to sit down until someone tells you to.)

12, 13. (Two cards) You stay seated and yell, "Noooo!"

14. You stand and say, "Sit down and be quiet you dingaling. Everybody knows the earth's flat as a pancake. And if you go too far, horrible sea monsters will get you." Then pretend to be a sea monster, growling and showing claws and teeth. Sit.

15. You walk slowly around the circle pretending to be very tired and say, "Poor Columbus left Italy and finally went to Spain — to King Ferdinand and Queen Isabella. They gave him three ships and a crew." Return to your seat.

16. You stand and rock back and forth on your feet and chant, "Sailing, sailing, over the ocean blue. And when we arrive — if we get there alive — it'll be 1492." Sit.

17. You stand, look around, put your hand up to your forehead as if you are shading your eyes and shout "Land, ho!" Sit.

18. You stand, pretend to be near death, and gasp out the words, "Thank goodness, I thought we'd never make it." Then stagger and fall down.

19. You stand, pretend to plant a flag in the soil, and say, "I name this island San Salvador and claim it for the King and Queen of Spain." Sit.

20, 21. (Two cards) You stay seated and cheer, whistle, clap hands, etc. (There will be two of you doing this.)

22. You stand and say, "Columbus and his crew stopped at other islands in the Caribbean Sea also." Sit.

23. You stand and say, "What do you know? We're the first ones to ever take a Caribbean Cruise! Think I'll go for a swim." Then pretend to dive into water. Sit.

24. You stand and say in a big, deep voice, "I have named this island Hispaniola and on it I have built a fort. Guard it well men! I'm going back home." Then walk around the circle and sit back down.

25, 26. (Two cards) You stand, salute, and say, "Aye, aye, Sir." Sit. (Two of you will do this.)

27. You stand and say, "Now it's 1513 and I'm Balboa. I have crossed the Isthmus of Panama and I claim this body of water for Spain. I name it the Pacific Ocean — meaning peaceful — (Yawn) — boy, it sure is . . . (then lie down and fall asleep and snore once).

28. You stand, pretend to ride a horse around the circle, and then say, "I'm Cortes. I've spent the last four years conquering Mexico in the name of Spain. We sure get around, don't we!" Sit.

29. You stand and say, "The year is 1532. Pizzaro's the name and exploring my game." (Then say in a loud whisper) "Listen! I've heard that there's lots of gold and silver down in South America. The King of Spain has agreed to help me get it. What do you say? (After DeSoto shakes your hand, you sit.)

30. You stand, go over to him, shake his hand, and say, "The name's DeSoto. I think we'd make a good team." Then return to your seat.

31. You stand and march to the center of the circle, and announce in a big voice, "They marched toward the heart of the Inca Empire." Then return to your seat.

32. You stand and say in a frightened voice, "Who are these men who steal from us?" Sit.

33. You stand and yell, "Our towns are burning! Run for your lives!" (Then pretend to be hit and fall dead.)

34. You stand and say, "The Emperor will save us!" (Then pretend to be hit and fall dead.)

35. You stand and raise your hands up as if asking for silence and calm and say slowly and in a big voice, "I am the Emperor. I am God. I have thirty thousand soldiers, and the Spaniards have only a few men. Why is everyone so afraid?"Then fold your arms across your chest and sit down slowly.

36. You stand, cup your hands to your mouth and call to the Emperor, "Hey, Emperor! How about dinner at our place?" (Then turn your head and laugh behind your hand.) Sit.

37. You stand and announce, "And so, the Emperor and five thousand unarmed Inca warriors went to a feast. The Emperor came in a golden chair carried by slaves. The warriors were killed by the Spaniards." Sit.

38. You stand and shout angrily, "Why do you do this terrible thing?" Sit.

39. You stand and shout "Gold! We want gold!" Sit.

40. You stand and say, "I will have this room filled with gold if you will let me go free." (Remain standing until you hear someone say "What do we do now? Kill him." Then fall dead — but do it in slow motion.)

41. You stand and say, "Gold and silver came from all parts of the Inca Empire. At first the Spaniards were glad. Then they worried about what to do with the Emperor." Sit.

42. You stand and say in a loud whisper, "What do we do now?" Sit.

43. You stand and say very seriously, "Kill him." Sit slowly.

44. You stand and say, "Thus ends a sad chapter in history. Land and wealth gained but at the cost of human suffering." Curtain going down! (Music)

One-Liners

For initial work with verbalizing, it may be easiest to begin with what might be called "one-liners." These are activities in which the children have to say or create only one line of talk. As the children become more inventive, the talk may go beyond one line. There are several kinds of activities that can serve this purpose.

The leader can make a list of familiar one-line introductions and have the children pretend to be announcers. They can experiment saying these introductions in ways that command attention and interest. Such familiar introductions might be:

"Ladies and gentlemen, the President of The United Sates."

"Heerrreee's Johnny!"

"The Edge of Night."

The children can also create their own introductions, basing them on a variety of situations. They might pretend to be a high-powered disc jockey introducing the latest hit; a circus Ring Master introducing a dangerous high wire act; a famous actor introducing the winner of a Hollywood Oscar.

One-liners can be combined with props. For this activity, the leader selects a simple but interesting prop. Volunteers demonstrate a use for it, saying one line of dialogue to accompany the prop's use. For example, a folding yardstick can be shaped into several things: a fishing pole, a letter Z or a triangle. One-liners that can accompany these uses might be:

"Shucks, been here over three hours and haven't had a nibble."

(Holding letter against chest) "Coach, I'm gonna get in there and win the game for old Zorro U."

(Holding triangle around face as a picture frame.) "The family doesn't know it but I can see everything that goes on around here!"

Variations of this activity might be:

a. One prop at a time can be selected for brainstorming ideas.

b. Several props might be set out on the desk, and the children can choose those they have an idea for.

c. If children have a lot of ideas, they might break into two groups so that more children can participate in the game.

Pictures can stimulate ideas for one-liners. For this activity, the leader selects pictures of people or animals in interesting poses with unusual facial expressions. He asks the children to think of what the person or animal might be saying if he could talk. They should try to say the line as they think the person or animal would say it.

Monologues

The leader may also want to have the children try activities that allow them to talk to themselves. This kind of activity can relieve them of the pressure of having to carry on a conversation with someone else. In addition, several or all may talk at the same time. These activities may be done with sound effects, with nonsense language, or with real language.

For example, the poem "Little Charlie Chipmunk" by Helen Cowles LeCron (4) tells about a chattering chipmunk who talks all the time. The chipmunk talk need not be an intelligible language; it can be fun just to make the sounds in whatever way the children want to interpret them. As the leader reads each line of the poem, he can pause and allow some chattering to occur.

Other opportunities for monologues are numerous. In the narrative story, *Gregory* (p. 59), by Robert Bright, for example, Granny talks to her hens to get them to lay eggs. The dialogue is not recorded, but we are told that her kind and gentle talking paid off. The leader might give the children a few moments to explore some of the things they might say in an imaginary, coaxing conversation with hens.

Storytelling

Storytelling can also give the children opportunities to verbalize. The children may create their own short stories or retell familiar ones. In initial experiences their stories will probably be a series of events or tales that have no endings. With repeated experiences, the children can become quite skillful.

Pictures might be used to stimulate storytelling. Unusual pictures work well, but the leader can make even an ordinary picture sound interesting. For example, a story based on a picture of a man on horseback might be started by the teacher, "Once upon a time there was a man who owned an enchanted horse that could take him anywhere he wanted to go."

As the children tell their stories, they may enjoy pretending to be certain characters: Eskimos of long ago sharing myths or stories of hunts during an Arctic night; hobos telling tales of dangerous railroad rides; or soothsayers reading signs and predicting the future.

There are literary sources that give specific examples of storytellers in action. The children may pretend to be the poet mouse who shares his supply of beautiful stories with his family in the story *Frederick* by Leo Lionni (Pantheon, 1967); or Mother Bear, who tells Little Bear stories about himself in the book *Little Bear* by Else Holmelund Minarik (Harper & Row, 1957); or Pa Ingalls, who entertains his children with short adventures from his past in Laura Ingalls Wilder's *The Little House in the Big Woods* (108).

Another way to begin storytelling is to have one child start the story with one sentence and pass it to others to add their sentences. An added challenge might be to include certain words (e.g. spelling words, vocabulary words, etc.) in the story.

As the children become more skilled in storytelling, the leader may need to establish a time limit for each person's contribution. There are various ways to do this. The leader may use the chiming of an oven timer or the flashing of the classroom lights. Whatever timing method the leader chooses, it is helpful if the child receives two signals: one to indicate that his story should be coming to a close, another to indicate that his story should be finished.

One student teacher uses a ball of knotted twine, which he passes to storytellers sitting in a circle. As a storyteller spins his tale, he unravels the ball. When he comes to one knot, he knows that his story should come to a close; by the time he unravels the twine to the second knot, his story should be finished. Then, he passes the ball to the next storyteller.

CUE: When someone says, "What time is it when the clock strikes 13?"

You stand and say, "Time to get the clock fixed!"

CUE: When someone says, "I'm a Hessian Soldier and I'm here to fight."

You stand and say, "Well, I'm a Minute Man, so look out!" (Then pretend to shoot.)

Sequence games based on riddles (top) and the American Revolution.

Simple Conversations

Sometimes it is fun to allow the children to work in pairs, carrying on an exploratory conversation. These conversations might be based on the ideas in some poetry such as "You'd Say It Was a Funeral," or "You'd Say It Was a Wedding," by James Reeves (59). These poems suggest that two people are talking together and in one case everything they say is sad; in the other, they are very gay. The poems give some ideas; the children may think of others. In essence, they are thinking of all the sad things or all the happy things they can.

Another poem, "Univac to Univac" (41), suggests that two computers talk about man. They have their doubts about him and question whether he will really be able to make a contribution to society or whether he is merely a passing fad. The voice of the computer in itself is interesting to speculate on.

If the children care to share their ideas with each other, it is probably best to keep them very short and to establish a time limit. Since they are exploratory, there may be no real end to them, and the leader may have to help the children stop them.

Commercials

Children enjoy creating simple commercials; they enjoy selling and demonstrating the use of real or fantastical products. For greater participation, there could be small groups with some children being the TV director who asks for "quiet on the set" and others being the cameramen who pantomime operating the TV equipment and request "lights, camera, action." In replayings the children can reverse roles.

ADDING DIALOGUE TO NARRATIVE PANTOMIME

As was mentioned previously, verbalizing flows more easily when children are interested in the material and are so involved in it that talking seems perfectly natural to include. For this reason, the leader may want to use some of the narrative pantomime stories mentioned earlier and encourage the children to think of possible verbal interaction that might be added.

The leader narrates the story, pausing for the moments when dialogue is suitable. The advantage of selecting the pantomime materials is that verbalizing is not essential to the story. The children are pantomiming and talking if they wish to. With pantomime materials they may feel more successful since they can still be involved in the playing, even if they are hesitant about verbalizing.

The stories may be played individually or in pairs and groups. For the individual (monologue) playing, the leader may also have the children remain at their desks for the security the area provides.

The playing is done in unison, which, as always, provides for psychological security. No pressure is on any one child, since several children are verbalizing simultaneously.* Each child may respond as he chooses. The verbal children can be as expressive as they wish; the more reticent children do not have to worry about being "on the spot" or about anyone focusing only on what *they* say.

First the leader reads the story and the children play it as a narrative pantomime so that they are familiar with it. Then, if the children like the story and want to add dialogue, the leader prepares for a replaying.

Discussion

Before replaying, the leader may wish to have a discussion of the dialogue possibilities in the story. The fewer actual dialogue lines there are in the story, the more the leader may have to help the children generate them. For example, in two earlier narrative stories the discussion might be:

A.

T: When the man who didn't wash his dishes (p. 61) sits and thinks about the predicament he is in, what do you suppose he might say to himself?

C: "Boy this place is sure a mess."

C: "Maybe I can get the guy next door to clean it up for me."

C: "I could just move out and start all over."

B.

T: In *The Three Poor Tailors* (p. 62), the innkeeper asks for payment but the tailors don't have any money. What are some things the innkeeper might say, and how might the tailors explain that they have no money?

C: The innkeeper would say, "You'd better pay up or I'll throw you in the klink!"

C: "Here's my credit card. You'll get paid at the end of the month."

C: They might tell the innkeeper that they had spent all their money at the market and maybe they could wash dishes to pay for their food.

Preview Playing

The leader may also choose to preview play with a group of verbal volunteers. They can sometimes give ideas to the rest of the children.

The leader should use several children for monologue preview; perhaps three pairs for pair playing; and two groups for group playing. In this way there is less pressure on any one child.

---

*As long as the children are relatively quiet in their speaking, the unison talk is not at all distracting to them.

Double Casting

In preview playing, it is also possible to double-cast for one scene. Double-casting means that more than one child plays a given role. What one child cannot think of to say, the other one usually can. They also can lend moral support to one another.

All the precautions for audience behavior in preview playing with pantomimes should be observed.

Flexible Narration

The leader should be flexible with his narration of the stories for this kind of playing. For one thing, the children will not all have an equal amount of talking to do. The length of the leader's pauses for dialogue will have to be played by ear. Secondly, by changing the narration, the leader can include dialogue wherever he and the children decide they want it.

Thirdly, the leader can also include prompting in the cues he gives. Rather than saying,

And so the Fox said to the Rooster. . .

it may be easier for the children to think of something to say if the leader's cue is:

Then the Fox tried to coax the Rooster to come down from his perch. . .

It will have to be explained to the children that their conversations may not be completed. The technique is designed mainly to stimulate talking in a number of different situations presented by the story but not necessarily to complete each conversation.

> **T**: As we play the story with dialogue, some of you may be able to think of things to say, others may not. Maybe you can think of something one time, but not another. And maybe some of you will have so much to say that you won't be able to finish it by the time I ring the bell to go on. But don't worry about that. We're just testing and experimenting to see if there are some places in our story that could have talking in them.

Control

Whenever the leader narrates, then pauses for dialogue, it may be difficult to get the attention again for the next line of narration or the next cue. This can be helped by flicking the lights so the children know when they are to stop talking and go on with the pantomiming. It is also possible to use some sort of bell to cue the talking.

Spontaneity

The leader encourages the children to speak spontaneously rather than try to remember or memorize dialogue. Because of traditional experiences with drama, however, some children find it difficult to understand that they may say the dialogue in their own words. Even though the leader explains that they may say what they feel is right for the situation, worried children may still ask, "What am I supposed to say?" or "I can't remember what comes next." It may take some time and patience until some children can feel comfortable with what may be a new experience.

Additional Materials

After trying some pantomime materials using this technique, the leader may wish to try some other stories in the same way. The leader should remember that the story should have as much pantomime in it as possible so that the children have that to fall back on. If it does not have pantomime, the leader may be able to add some of his own.

The following is an example of the old folk tale, "The Little House" by Valery Carrick (44). The children are divided into groups of five, and each child is pretending to be one of the animals who approaches the jar and carries on a brief conversation with the animal who lives inside. The leader is using his own wording in the narration and has added action as well.

> When the little mouse saw the jar, he scampered over to it. He sniffed around it and looked it over and decided it would make a very nice house for him to live in. So he peeked into the opening of the jar and asked if anyone was at home. (Pause.)
>
> But no one answered, so he went inside and found nobody there. He decided to make himself at home and live there himself. So he nested himself in the end of the jar.
>
> Then along came the frog. He hopped and hopped all around the jar and saw that it was quite nice for a house for himself. He asked politely if he could join the mouse. (Pause.) and the mouse agreed. (Pause.) And so the frog hopped very carefully into the jar, and the mouse and frog lived there together.
>
> By and by the rabbit. . .

Replaying

Once the children have been narrated through a story with dialogue, they may want to try it on their own. This may be done in simultaneous playing; usually, however, children want to share with each other. Additional techniques covered in Chapter 11 will be helpful if they have difficulties enacting their stories for each other.

VERBAL INTERACTION
IN CREATIVE PANTOMIME STORIES

Creative pantomime stories provide another good opportunity for beginning verbal interaction. Again, since the basic story line can be played in pantomime, the verbal interaction is considered additional to the experience. This can be comforting to everyone if the verbal interacting poses difficulties.

Leader Participation

One way to begin verbal interaction is for the leader to play one of the characters in the material or to invent a logical role of someone who can say a few words to the children as they play. He stimulates brief conversations with those individuals, partners, or groups who volunteer to talk to his character.

For example, in the story based on *The Borrowers,* discussed earlier, the leader might play a Borrower who lives in another part of the house and who is out borrowing for himself. He may only say a quiet "Hello" to some of the children; he may tell them of a good find; he might ask for their assistance in carrying something; or he might offer assistance to them.

Before the leader can go around to talk to the different individuals and groups, he must be sure that everyone is involved and occupied in their work. For this reason, it is usually best to play the experience first in pantomime and add the verbalizing on a replaying. Then the leader will have a better idea of how many ideas the children seem to have and how involved in them they can be.

While the children play, the leader quietly talks with them in his character role. Some conversations may be as brief as one question and one response.

The leader stimulates conversation by asking questions about the children's action, their environment, conflicts, feelings, or character-role. In general the questions could be:

What are you doing? Can you teach me how to do that?
What's it like around this place?
That *is* a problem. How are you going to solve it?
I have a problem. Can you help me?
How do you feel about that?

The leader's character should have a logical reason to talk and initiate conversation. Stock "interview" characters are particularly helpful. The leader might be a new neighbor, a biographer, census taker, tourist inspector, reporter, etc.

Problem Solving

Often it is fun if the leader has a problem to solve and needs the help of the characters the children are playing. For example, the children might be pretending to be a member of a community in France in the Middle Ages. The leader could pretend to be someone from the twentieth century who had to learn about their ways and customs in order to live. He would have a legitimate reason to question the children about means of transportation, the food they eat, their jobs, the style of clothing he should wear in order not to look out of place, or about what kind of work he could do in order to become an integral part of their community.

Forecasting Questions

Before the children play their experiences, it is helpful if the leader forecasts the questions that might be asked. This gives the children some time to think and to formulate their replies. If it seems necessary, there could be a brief discussion about what the children might answer if the question were posed to them.

> T: When I come visiting, I may ask you to describe the place you're in. I'll be new to the area and will want some information about it. What would you answer if I asked, "Do you have changes of seasons here?"

> T: As I journey around, I'll be making notes on the various activities in this community. I'll probably ask you to describe what you're doing. What would you answer if I asked you to tell me about the importance of your job to the community as a whole?

It is also helpful for the teacher to tell the children that if they do not feel like talking, they are free to remain silent. It is especially sensitive on his part to give them a legitimate reason for not speaking. Consider the following example:

> T: As you pretend to be an Eskimo on this life-giving seal hunt, I'll pretend to be the oldest and wisest hunter of your tribe and journey around to see how the hunt's progressing. I will ask you questions about the hunt. If you want, you may answer. Since I might approach your hunting area at a crucial moment when the seal is near, you might not be able to talk at that time. If talking would disturb your hunt, just shake your head and I will quietly leave.

The leader's conversation should not interrupt the story the children are dramatizing, but should be considered a complement to it. His role and his interaction can even help the involvement and the success of children who might be having difficulties creating their experience. Simply by asking a question such as "I don't understand what's happening here; can you explain it to me?" can help children sort out their thinking about what they are trying to do. (Further techniques for leader participation will be discussed in the next chapter.)

Children can work in pairs on simple verbal activities.

Meeting People

Another way to encourage verbal interaction in creative pantomime stories (in addition to allowing spontaneous dialogue) is for the leader to suggest to the children the possibility of meeting people in their adventure. Even in individual playing, the children could imagine the people they meet and converse in monologue. Note that the following activity, which could be played individually, in pairs, or in groups, encourages verbal interaction possibilities:

T: Imagine you could go back in history to a particular time and could spend one day there:

PANTOMIME QUESTIONS

What period and place would you choose?
What would you do during the time you had to spend there?
What difficulties might you encounter?
How do you get there and back?

VERBAL INTERACTION QUESTIONS

Who are some of the people you might meet there?
Will you be able to talk with them?

If so, what are some of the things you might talk about?

What questions would you ask them?

What do you think they will say to you?

A word of caution: It is possible that the children will see conflict with the people they meet. While this can produce an exciting story, it may be necessary to check out any plans for playing aggressive action as we have suggested before.

T: It sounds as if you might have a hostile reception from the natives. Remember how we worked that out last week? You'll need to do the same for this. Do you need to discuss and rehearse it a bit beforehand or shall we go ahead and you'll exercise caution?

EXERCISES FOR THE COLLEGE STUDENT

1. Collect stories and poems suitable for sound effect activities.
2. Create your own sound effect story. Base it on a curricular topic.
3. Practice telling or reading a story while using the control of an arrow. Select or write a story appropriate for this device. Decide where in the story the sound effects should occur. Decide on the appropriate volume for each sound effect. Practice operating the arrow while you rehearse the story.

   When you are prepared, present the story to your classmates. Ask them to make the sounds while following the arrow. Evaluate your presentation with your classmates.
4. Adapt a story for a sequence game.
5. Write a sequence game; base it on a curricular topic.
6. Collect interesting pictures, props, and one-liners useful for stimulating verbalization.
7. Select one of the narrative stories or poems suggested in Chapter 3. Choose two or three moments when verbal interaction could be encouraged. Decide on the questions you will use to encourage verbalizing. Practice telling the story and asking the questions. When you are prepared, lead your classmates in this activity.
8. Design a creative pantomime activity. Plan a role for yourself. List the broad and narrow questions you might ask. Lead your classmates in this activity. Tell them your role and forecast some of your questions. Remember to give them a legitimate reason for not verbalizing with you if they do not wish to. After the activity, discuss your guidance with your classmates.
9. Design a creative pantomime that offers the possibility of meeting and talking to others during the experience. List the pantomime and verbal interaction questions.

11

Creating Dialogue Scenes

Thus far, all the verbal activities have been fairly simple ones. It is also possible to create dialogue situations in which the children improvise their conversations on the spot. Dialogue scenes require the interaction of two or more people.

There are many sources for creating dialogue scenes. For example, children may enjoy experiencing verbal situations from literature. They may like to reenact the verbal guessing game between Rumpelstiltskin and the Queen when she reveals his secret name; or they may like to try Toad's fast talk in *Wind in the Willows* (146) when he tries to get himself out of many trouble spots.

Many stories revolve totally around a dialogue scene. Verbalizing becomes a necessary and integral part of it. The solving of a conflict through talk becomes crucial to the outcome of the story.

For instance, the Dr. Seuss story, "The Rabbit, the Bear, and the Zinniga-Zanniga" (p. 227), is an example of a story that is essentially a conflict dialogue scene. It is a "trickster" tale in which a Rabbit skillfully talks his way out of a touchy situation. A hungry Bear decides the Rabbit would be a tasty dinner and the Rabbit knows he must think of a trick to escape.

Dialogue scenes may also be created out of the imagination and resourcefulness of the group. They may enjoy creating the dialogue that might have occurred when Governor John Winthrop tried to convince the people of Massachusetts that the water was pure enough to drink. Or, they might create the dialogue that could occur between a reluctant plant and some scientists who are conducting experiments on the prevention of water evaporation.

What makes dialogue scenes intriguing and dramatic are the motivations behind them. Interesting interactions may involve people conversing for enjoyment, seeking information, or attempting to convince or persuade others. Convincing, persuading, and problem solving are often based on conflict situations.

For example, a scene might be created in which old prospectors sit around a campfire and have a *contest* to see who can tell the tallest tale; Benjamin Franklin, busily inventing, might experience increased annoyance while being interviewed by a *persistent* biographer. Or a scene might be derived from the tense moment in the story *Tomás Takes Charge* (140) when Tomás and Fernanda try to *convince* the landlady that their father has not left home and that the rent will be paid soon.

Some children can improvise dialogue readily and with little difficulty. They may be verbally sophisticated or experienced in creative dramatics. Or, the leader may have progressed the children to a point where they are ready to experiment with improvisation. The leader's supportive guidance of their previous efforts will play a great part in continuing their self-confidence and imagination.

Some children need much help and guidance from the leader. For these children the leader's own participation in the scene and careful planning and discussion may be crucial to their success in dialogue work.

PREPARING DIALOGUE SCENES

Dialogue in Literature

The amount of actual dialogue suggested in literary materials will vary. Sometimes a selection records exactly what the characters say. For example,

> "You shouldn't be afraid of getting wet," said the pansy to the daffodil. "After all, rain is good for you. And besides, your face is protected by your bonnet."
> "That's true," said the daffodil, "but I really would like to have a polka-dot umbrella. . . ."

Sometimes the conversation is implied but not recorded.

> Quietly Sid and Kim discussed their plan for escape. In the early morning Sid was to ring the bell as he always did. That would be the signal for Kim to release the heavy door latch. . . .

Or, some passages may not give much definition of character or dialogue.

Hardly anyone believed that a car could be a substitute for a horse.

Yet, any of these passages could form a basis for creating a dialogue scene.

Adding Dialogue in Storytelling

Children often listen very carefully to the dialogue in the stories that are told to them. Much of that dialogue is repeated in their playings. For this reason, many leaders like to add direct dialogue to stories they tell. For example, a line might read,

> As the young man went down the road he met an old woodcutter. He asked the old man if he knew the way to town. The old man told him to follow his nose.

Adding direct dialogue to the above passage:

> As the young man went down the road, he met an old woodcutter. He said to the old man, "Excuse me, sir, I wonder if you could tell me the way to town?"
> The old man answered, "Follow your nose; follow your nose. You can get to almost anywhere you want if you follow your nose!"

Inventing Dialogue Through Discussion

Dialogue possibilities can also be generated through discussion. For experienced groups the leader may set up a situation and let the groups plan on their own.

> **T**: We've learned that species evolve as they change to fit an environment. This evolution takes a long time. Imagine that it is millions of years from now, and for thousands of years man's only environment has been the lily pad. How would man's physical self have to change in order to survive in that environment? What problems does he have in this environment? Use the information we've studied to help you formulate your ideas.
> Divide into groups of four. Three of you will be the newly adapted man. One of you will be "man" as we know him. Somehow this twentieth-century man is in this future century. He must adjust to this environment, and he has many questions.
> Each group has many things to consider as they plan. You'll have to use your imaginations, but combine it with the information you have. How have your men changed? What do they do in this environment? What

specific questions will the twentieth-century man ask? Where is the entire group during these questions? What do they do as they converse?

When you have your ideas, let me know.

The leader may need to guide a full classroom discussion in stimulating ideas for dialogue. The discussion will center mainly on questions about what will be said. In addition, however, there may be questions about the personality of the characters and their motivation for saying what they say. There may also be some consideration of the environment of the scene (where it takes place); the action (what the characters might be doing as they are talking or listening); and emotions (how they might be feeling).

It is not necessary to ask all these questions in one discussion. Sometimes the dialogue questions are asked first; the scene is played once; then the additional questions are explored before a replaying. With several playings the questions can be interspersed among them. Here are some examples:

A.

T: Let's have a scene with Pooh and Christopher Robin and Rabbit (147). Pooh has just become stuck in Rabbit's house. Rabbit goes off to get Christopher Robin, and they've decided that Pooh will have to remain where he is until he loses weight. Pooh is upset about this, and Rabbit and Christopher try to make him feel better during his long wait.

What are some things Pooh might say that let us know he's unhappy?

What are some things Christopher Robin might say to comfort Pooh? We know he reads stories to Pooh; what else might he do to entertain him? (Action or speech possibilities.)

Rabbit is worried about his house, but he also cares about Pooh. What are some things he might say? What does Rabbit do while Christopher Robin entertains Pooh? (Action possibilities.)

B.

T: Let's reenact the moment when Kit Carson and Lieutenant Freemont try to keep their small expedition party in good spirits.

Why are the men's spirits low? Where are they? What are the environmental conditions?

What does the Indian visitor say that discourages the already discouraged men? The text says that not all of the men could understand his words, but they did understand his meaning. How was he communicating?

What is Eagle-That-Talks' attitude? What does he say and do?

Carson and Freemont seem to be undaunted. What might their real feelings be? Why don't they express their attitudes?

What do they say to keep the men optimistic that they will find a way through the Sierra Nevadas?

C.

T: If you were Mama in the story *Cricket in Times Square* (82), what would you say when you learned that your son, Mario, wanted to keep his cricket as a pet? What reasons would you give him for not keeping this cricket?

We know that Mario tells her that crickets are good luck and can help you estimate temperature. If you were Mario, what else could you tell Mama that might convince her to let you keep the pet?

We know that Papa tries to change the subject. If you were Papa, what would you say to change the subject? What would you say when your mind was made up that Mario could keep his pet?

Another way to stimulate ideas is for the leader to initiate conversation with some children as they sit in their seats. Rather than asking them what they would say, he becomes a character who talks with them for a moment or two.

T: I wonder what would happen if some of the Sneetches (40) were afraid or unsure about entering Sylvester McMonkey McBean's star-making machine. What would he say in order to convince them that everything would be all right?

Let's suppose I were a customer and you were Sylvester McMonkey McBean. Who thinks they could convince me? (Children volunteer and the leader walks over to one.)

T: (in character) Mr. McBean, I sure would like to have a star on my belly, but I'm afraid to go inside that machine. How can I be sure that it won't hurt me?

C: (in character) I'll go in first and you can see that I'm O.K. when I come out.

T: (in character) All right, I think I would try your machine. (Goes to another child.) I'm afraid of the dark, Mr. McBean, so I don't think I'd like to go inside that machine of yours. I'll bet it's awfully dark in there. Is it?

C: (in character) Naw. You see, the stars inside are shiny, and they make it bright enough to see.

T: (in character) Well, what do you know? I never thought of that. All right, I think I'll try your machine.

Accuracy of Dialogue

In creating a situation for dialogue, one point must always be considered: how much freedom and leeway of interpretation does the leader and the class want to allow? When children make up their own stories or situations as well as the people in them or when they elaborate on ideas, often they are at liberty to interpret the characters and the dialogue in a variety of ways. There may not be as much freedom possible when the characters are well defined in the literature or if the setting is to be an historically accurate one.

For example, sometimes it is fun to put historical people in a modern setting. Amusing scenes can develop if George Washington tries to converse with the Jackson Five, or if a cave man receives a call from a modern appliance salesman. Anachronisms by themselves provide humor, and some children enjoy these kinds of conversations. It is also an enjoyable way to make comparisons with different eras in terms of technology, language, and attitudes.

But with some materials, the leader and/or the class may prefer to be as accurate as possible, which may require some additional discussion.

For example, one group of children became upset with a child who pretended to ride on a motorcycle in a serious story set in medieval times. They knew the motorcycle was inappropriate to the setting. It was also an anachronism that introduced humor into a serious story. As a group they decided that motorcycles should not be allowed.

Sometimes frequent stereotyping of characters or a misunderstanding of the life style causes children to have difficulties in understanding the motivations of characters. One leader discovered this in a discussion prior to a story from *Tom Sawyer* (139). When she asked the question, "What kind of person is Aunt Polly and how does Tom feel about her?" she was deluged with responses such as, "She's a witch and rides a broom." One child, in all seriousness, said "Tom would like to take her out behind the barn and beat the ____ out of her." The interpretation was that Aunt Polly was sadistic and extremely cruel to Tom.

By examining the evidence in the book, the leader guided the children to see that Aunt Polly did care for Tom but often had difficulty accepting the very natural inclinations of boys his age, and that Aunt Polly also made comparisons between Tom and Sid, who was considered a sissy by most of the children but a model child by Aunt Polly's standards. The children came to realize that her demands of Tom were no more or less than those for many boys of his day. Tom knew and accepted Aunt Polly's demands, although he was not above trying to get around them whenever he thought he could get away with it.

There are times when there can be leeway for interpretations, or when understanding of character differs. For example, one leader, having told the story of "Little Red Riding Hood" to a group of children, asked, "How do you suppose Little Red Riding Hood felt as she skipped down the path on the way to Grandma's house for a visit?"

The leader expected the children to say that the little girl felt happy since the teacher's own choice of words and tone of voice indicated gaiety. However, one little girl doggedly replied, "Awful." When the teacher asked, "Why?" the little girl's understandable response was, "Because her mother made her go."

One six-year-old boy felt that the Little Billy Goat in "The Three Billy Goats Gruff" would run away rather than talk to the Troll. *"I'd* run away," he said, "I wouldn't stop to talk! I'd be too scared!" And as the leader narrated the story, this child played with his group in his way. The leader simply changed the line to:

One Billy Goat didn't stop to talk, but the others did and they said to the Troll. . . .

PLAYING THE SCENES

Usually the children want to share their dialogue scenes with the rest of the class. This may be done in two ways:

a. They may play the scenes improvisationally without any planning among themselves.

b. They may rehearse them in groups before playing.

Whatever procedure the teacher selects, it should be noted that any dialogue scene, no matter how much planning is used, will always be improvisational and spontaneously performed. Even when small groups plan, they cannot work out verbatim what they will say, although they do have a chance to experiment a bit first.

Playing dialogue scenes improvisationally is usually intriguing and fascinating to children. They usually listen intently to hear what their classmates are going to say next, even when they know the plot of the story. Some children even surprise themselves by what they can think of to say.

After the dialogue scene has been described and possibly discussed, the leader will ask for volunteers to dramatize the scene while their classmates watch. When this group has completed the scene, the leader will ask for another group of volunteers, until all the children who want to participate have the opportunity.

First Playing

Generally a first playing is somewhat like the preview playing referred to in pantomime. Those children who volunteer serve as demonstrators to generate ideas and as models for future playings. For this reason, it is a good idea to select the more verbal volunteers who can play the scene with ease.

In a dialogue scene, usually only one person speaks at a time. When the scene is played in front of an audience, everyone's attention is focused on the speaker. Any insecurities are viewed and heard by all. In order to minimize any discomfort, the leader may double cast and/or participate in the scene himself.

Double Casting

Double casting can be very helpful. Those children who feel confident can speak out. And generally, what one child can't think of to say, the other one can. Those who are more reticent can still be a part of the experience without having to bear the total responsibility for the verbal exchange. For example, two witty Rabbits together can help one another verbally distract a hungry Bear; or two small groups (rather than two individuals) of modern pioneers can more successfully debate together the safety of a newly colonized planet and the wisdom of remaining.

The following example of double casting is based on one of the adventures of Tyll Ulenspiegel, "A Portrait Which Suited Everyone and Pleased No One" (46). The nobleman commissions Tyll to paint an accurate portrait of his members of court. Yet each demands a flattering picture of himself.

Lady #1: Painter, when you look at us, what do you see?

Tyll #1: Well . . . I see two girls. . .

Lady #2: What do you mean?

Lady #1: You see two beautiful ladies with small feet, that's what you see.

Tyll #2: But if *I* were to describe your feet . . . I don't think I'd call them small.

Tyll #1: *I'd* call them downright *big.*

Lady #1: You'll call them *small* and that's the way you'll paint them or you'll hear from our husbands.

Lady #2: Come, Tilda, I think they've got the message. (They leave)

Tyll #2: Well, I guess if *you* say you have small feet . . .

LEADER PARTICIPATION

Earlier we discussed the procedure of the leader participating in the initiating of dialogue in the children's creative pantomime stories. He may also participate in improvisational scenes. He may cast himself along with the children, or he may step in and lend aid whenever it is needed. Usually the leader chooses the kind of roles mentioned earlier: the innocent bypasser, the reporter, or anyone who could legitimately participate in conversation.

For beginning groups, for younger children, or for first playings, the leader's participation may be crucial. Often it is helpful to select a story with a major character throughout whom the leader can play. Sara Cone Bryant's story, "The Cat and the Parrot" (3), is an example.

A synopsis of the story is as follows:

A parrot is the dinner guest in the home of a cat. A meager meal is served, but the parrot returns the invitation to the cat and serves a feast. The cat eats everything, including his host, and casually sets out for home. On the way he meets, one by one, an old woman; an old man with a cart and a donkey; a wedding procession including a newly married prince, his wife, his soldiers and many elephants walking two by two. The cat tells everyone he meets to get out of his way. When they refuse he eats them

Store owner (teacher) asks customers' assistance with a heavy bolt of cloth.

"slip! slop! gobble!" He finally eats two land crabs who pinch a hole in his stomach, and everyone escapes. The cat is left to sew up his coat.

Since the story has one main character who interacts with other characters throughout, the leader can play the main character himself. In this way he is in a legitimate position to progress the story line. His character may also be able to give orders and directions. He must, of course, carry the burden of the dialogue when it is necessary, and he may also have to carry the burden of making the story exciting and interesting by his own involvement in it.

The playing can begin when the cat leaves the parrot's house. The route the cat takes can be designated, and then all the characters can be situated along the "path" according to the order of their appearance in the scene.

To designate that they have been eaten, they may line up behind the leader and continue on the journey with the cat. After they escape from the cat's stomach, they can tiptoe back into their "homes" or seats.

Leader Responsibility

For beginning groups and for young children, the leader must often be prepared to assume the major responsibility for the verbal interchange. It is not uncommon for children to experience difficulty in expressing ideas during the playing. Even when children have ideas in discussion and volunteer to take part in verbal interaction, they may become insecure during the actual playing. Often a child likes to be in on the experience even though he is not an avid conversationalist. We have known many children to volunteer contentedly and happily time and time again for verbal experiences and then say very little.

Narrow and Broad Questions

The leader may find himself doing a great deal of the talking with the children. He should be aware that the kinds of questions he asks can be modified according to each child's readiness to talk.

For example, the leader may ask either narrow or broad questions. Narrow questions require only "yes" or "no" answers or choices between alternatives the leader poses.

Q: Do you like it here?
A: Yes.
Q: Is that difficult or easy to do?
A: Difficult.
Q: Are you going to stay for a long time or will you have to leave soon?
A: Leave soon.

Because these questions can be answered easily, the child is able to be more relaxed and is under minimum pressure.

Broad questions ask for more reflective thinking. They ask for opinions, reasoning, character motivations, and emotional attitudes. For example:

Q: How do you feel about your job?
Q: What kind of working conditions would you prefer to have?
Q: Why have you chosen to stay behind when others have journeyed elsewhere?

The following examples demonstrate the teacher's use of broad and narrow questions as he converses with children. He and the children are playing a dialogue scene based on the story, "The Peddler and His Caps" (46). The leader has asked groups of three children each to think of possible villagers they might be. He will be the Peddler, trying to sell them a hat. They are to think of all the different reasons they can for not buying one. Notice that the children in the following example are at ease in verbalizing.

T: Good morning, sirs. Isn't this a beautiful day?
C#1: Is it? I haven't noticed. I've been too busy.
T: Oh, what keeps you all so busy?
C#1: I'm an accountant and I have to add all the figures for the grocery store.
T: Oh, I'm sure you *are* very busy. And how about you?
C#2: We stack the shelves.
T: Well, I don't want to take much of your time. I have some fine hats and I wonder if you'd care to buy one?
C#1: Now what would I do with a hat?

T: Why, couldn't you wear it, sir?

C#1: I work all day long, from morning to night and I never leave this house and I don't wear a hat inside. It's bad luck.

T: Well, how about you, gentlemen?

C#3: No we don't want any either. It's bad luck.

These children have conversed with confidence, particularly child #1. The leader was able to ask him broad questions that encouraged him to use speech to reflect his thoughts. Not only was this child able to respond to the questions, he was capable of asking his own question: "Now what would I do with a hat?"

Another group of children in the same playing, however, were not as verbal. They gave limited responses, and the leader had to carry the scene. He used the narrow questions to continue the playing so that the children could still feel successful.

T: Good morning, ladies, isn't this a fine morning? (The three children giggle and only one responds.)

C#1: Yes.

T: What are you doing on this beautiful day?

C#1: Cleaning.

T: Ah, well, now, I have just the hat for you. It's the latest in dusting caps. Just the thing to wear when you're cleaning. Won't you buy one? (More giggling and finally:)

C#1: No.

T: Aw, shucks. Do you mind telling me why?

C#1: (Pause and then whispers) I don't know.

T: Would you like to look at any other hats I have here?

C#1: No. (The other two shake their heads.)

T: Well, thank you very much for your time. I guess I'll have to try someplace else. Goodbye.

All: Bye.

There are times when children do not immediately answer a question the leader poses. They may lack knowledge and understanding of the subject, or they may simply need time to think. After allowing sufficient time, the leader can reword the question or continue the dialogue as if the unanswered question were not important to their conversation. Otherwise, the children may feel that they have failed in verbalizing. This could be detrimental to their future attempts at verbal interaction.

Sometimes the children like to accompany the leader as he initiates conversation, double cast with him in his role. This plan works with both very verbal and not so very verbal children. For the verbal children, the leader can subtly urge them to ask the questions, make comments, and respond to each other. In this way, he encourages them to interact with each other and gradually relinquishes his role as the initiator. For the not-so-verbal children, it gives a stronger feeling of being part of the experience to accompany the leader and identify with his role.

As the children become more capable of participating in dialogue scenes, the leader's participation may not be as crucial. He can, however, continue to be an incidental player if both he and the children enjoy his participation.

Mediator

In some scenes, the leader may be a mediator between two groups. For example, in Roald Dahl's *Charlie and the Chocolate Factory* (76), Willy Wonka has difficulties with several children. One little girl, Violet, swells up like a blueberry and turns purple after disobeying orders not to chew the experimental gum. The Oompa-Loompas have to take her away to the juicing room. Willy is the owner of the factory and boss of the Oompa-Loompas. He is upset with Violet for disobeying his rules, but he would like to have her problem solved also. A scene might be built around Willy arbitrating between Violet and the Oompa-Loompas. The situation might be:

> **T**: Oompa-Loompas, what will happen to Violet in the juicing room? Have you perfected your methods yet? What sorts of machines and equipment do you have in there?
>
> Violet, we are still in the experimental stage in our work in the juicing room. I can't guarantee what will happen to you. What do you think you want to do?

A similar arbitration scene might be played between the Pilgrims and the crew of the *Mayflower* based on Wilma Hays' book (79). The Captain wants to help the Pilgrims get settled before leaving them to fend for themselves in a new country. But he is also worried about his crew. They are anxious to get home because the time is December and the sailing will be difficult. Each day they are becoming more hostile. Both the crew and the Captain had wanted to be home for Christmas, but it is now impossible.

The leader might play the Captain and suggest that the two groups try to settle their grievances. They must think of their character, their feelings, and their reasons for their side of the argument.

Participating to Aid Dialogue

The leader should always remain ready to step into the scene if he is needed. He may lend aid as a character already established in the scene, or he may invent a new role. Sometimes in lending aid, he may simply become a passer-by who is legitimately unsure of what is going on and can ask questions to get things back on the track again.

In the following example, the children are playing the story, "The Three Wishes" (46). They are in groups of four, with two playing the wife and two playing the husband. They have begun the argument over the sausage on the wife's nose, and they are having trouble getting to the solution and the third wish — to have everything back to normal as before. The leader can narrate them out of the predicament:

> **T:** And so, the man and the wife began to wonder why they were shouting so much, why they were arguing. They stopped to think a moment. No one spoke, and they silently thought to themselves, "Isn't this ridiculous?" There really is only one wish to make — just to have ourselves back to normal — the way we were." The man was the first to speak. . .

Or the leader could step into the scene in a character role:

> **T:** (as a neighbor) Hello, hello? I came to borrow a cup of sugar and I . . . what in the world happened to you? What is that thing on your nose? . . . (the children explain the situation). What are you going to do now?
>
> **C:** We don't know.
>
> **T:** I can see it would be a difficult decision to make. But if I were you, I sure wouldn't want to go through life with a sausage on my nose. It wouldn't do much good to have fine clothes and a fancy house with a sausage hanging on your face. Of course, it's your life. Well, I'll not bother you with a cup of sugar at a time like this. Good luck.

In this instance, the leader reminded them of the solution presented in the story, in case they had forgotten it. Usually, this kind of assistance helps the story along. Sometimes the children begin talking to the leader in his role, and he can sense that they want him to remain in the playing with them. Interestingly, too, children often begin to see the new character as another person they can cast in the next playing.

Participation for Control

Even though the leader may feel that his participation will not be necessary, he should remain alert to those moments when he can help the children with any difficulties. In the following example the leader, in a quickly assumed character role, briefly steps in to keep the dialogue scene progressing. The children are dramatizing their ideas of the "Word Market" from the story *The Phantom Tollbooth* (117). Five of them are improvisationally creating the scene in which Milo and Tock visit different word booths and listen to the salesman try to convince them that they want to buy their words. The children have been instructed that the two who are playing Milo and Tuck will visit each booth, and the sellers will do their best to persuade them to buy.

As the children play, the leader observes that Milo and Tock have lingered an exceedingly long time talking to the salesman in the first booth, while the other two children are restlessly waiting their turn. In his quickly invented character, the leader approaches this group and speaks to them in a low voice.

> **T**: Hey buddies, you're bargaining at a pretty sharp booth, all right, but before you buy, you'd better check the action in the other booths. This character here is a high-class salesman, but the word's out that this entire place is jiving.

The leader could also have entered this playing through narration. Rather than assuming a character, he could have assumed a commanding voice and guided Milo and Tock to proceed to the other booths.

> **T**: And so after much deliberation at the first extremely interesting word booth, Milo and Tock decide they had better take a look at the other booths, for this entire Word Market seemed very exciting. . .

The following is an account of a leader's participation with a class of third-graders in the story "Taper Tom" or "The Princess Who Couldn't Laugh" (46). While the leader chose to play the major character, the Princess, in the first experience, she relinquished this role to a child in the second playing. However, she continued to participate through an invented character, the Queen. Through this role, the leader was able to influence behavior in one particular instance.

> After she told the story, the leader focused on the situation where numerous contestants offered to try their skills in attempting to make the Princess laugh. Initially the leader felt that the group would want to be the contestants. She would be the Princess and through this role help carry the conversations when necessary as well as the organization of the various entertainments.
>
> In the role of the Princess, she established that each contestant would announce himself to the court and bow upon entering and leaving the courtroom. (In character) "State your name, my good man and bow before the court."
>
> The children had suggested a variety of antics to make the Princess laugh, but when the ideas were enacted, they were all variations on the theme of pratfalls. During the first playing these ideas were

accepted by the teacher. For the second playing, however, the leader suggested that they think of new ideas, omitting any falls.

For the replaying, the children suggested adding several Princesses, servants, and a guard. The leader continued to feel that her participation might be necessary for organization, and she created the authority role of Queen.

During this experience the children's ideas for making the Princess laugh included tickling feet, telling jokes, flipping pancakes, playing in a musical band, dancing, and acrobatics. The Queen actually had very little to do this time. The children duplicated much of what she had established in her role as Princess. The children easily carried conversations, and the "Princesses" were particularly adept at keeping the entertainment progressing from one act to another. "Servants, give this man some money for his show; but we're still not laughing! Next!"

The teacher's leadership was necessary, however, when pretended liquor drinking occurred with the musicians. The leader initially chose to ignore the drinking, but when other children chose to imitate it, the "Queen" told a servant that there would be "no drinking on the job." With no rancor, the servant obeyed, and the scene proceeded smoothly.

OTHER TECHNIQUES
FOR ORGANIZING DIALOGUE SCENES

When the leader does not participate in the playing, he may use other techniques to help the children organize their scenes. For example, each child might be given a number. The teacher may have the numbers placed on cards, and he holds up a number when that person is to continue the conversation. The children must watch for their number and speak only when their number is held up. If the teacher holds up two numbers, those two people speak to each other until new numbers are held up.

Another technique is to write ideas for conversations on cards or the chalkboard. For example, the dialogue scene might center on sayings or cliches, such as "It's a small world"; "It's raining cats and dogs." When children need ideas for their conversation, they may look at the listing or refer to stacked cards. Whenever a child needs an idea, he can go over to the stack and draw one.

Sometimes it is fun and also helpful to freeze a scene and have other children enter and continue it; or, create other characters to see what they might contribute to the situation. This procedure demonstrates different ideas and ways of handling a situation.

"Be sure to include an ending for your story."

It is helpful to suggest to the children that as they plan, they should work out an ending to their scene. This is necessary so that they will all know when they have reached the point when their scene is over. Even so, they may forget to do this. What happens then is that a scene can reach an argumentative stage, and fisticuffs and wrestling seem to be the only way out. And often they cannot even bring that to an end.

In these cases, the leader may walk over to the group and ask quietly, "Do you have an ending?" If they do not have an ending or cannot think of one, then he might narrate one for them:

> **T**: And so the complaint manager and the irate customer never got a chance to find out who would win the argument for the bell sounded for the closing of the department store. The complaint manager closed his window and the customer stormed out saying, "You haven't heard the last of this!! (Pause for the child's probable repeat.) I'm getting my lawyer!" (Pause) And to the strains of the Muzak playing "We Wish You a Merry Christmas," they all went home.

The leader may also play the part of the store manager, who works out an agreement with them.

EVALUATION

Audience Behavior

As before, the leader may have to guide for sensitive audience behavior. Some classes are not unduly critical of each other. They may, in fact, identify with the children who falter and be very sympathetic. Their attitude, of course, will be influenced by the teacher's attitude.

Sometimes children will become impatient with their friends when they are having difficulty. *They* know what to say in the same situation, and so they may call out a line. "Mae! Tell him you don't want to go on the picnic!" "Psst, George, you're suppose to say. . . ." Sometimes just a quiet reminder to anxious audience members will suffice. They sometimes need to have it explained that prompting from the audience isn't very helpful. It interrupts the player's thinking and does more harm than good.

After the children have played their scenes, it is useful to have them evaluate their efforts. Self-evaluation continues to be important.

> What did you like about your scene?
> In your scene, what moments were the most enjoyable for you? Why?
> If you could do it over again, what would you want to change? Why?
> In your opinion, how successful was the ending to your scene? Why?

When children have a great deal of confidence in their ability to create dialogue scenes, the leader may want the audience to give its evaluation of each scene. Positive evaluation is paramount; the leader's wording of the discussion questions is crucial.

> What did you *like* about that scene?
> What were the things that were said by certain characters that were *especially believable?*
> What lines of dialogue were *especially typical* of the characters?
> When did you notice moments when people helped each other?

The leader's own feedback to the children will also be important. This may be particularly true if the children in the audience insist on being overly critical. Or if the scene could benefit from additional challenges, the leader may need to suggest these. As in previous work, however, it may be that continued playing of the material, more than anything else, results in more involving and believable dramatization.

ACTIVITIES

1. *Filling in the Time* Children create short scenes in which people try to occupy the time. The following are examples:

   Two TV announcers trying to fill in the time before a delayed space launch, but they've said everything they've had to say!

   Your sister's new date has arrived, but she's late tonight and you're the only one around to make conversation.

Puppets can help in verbalizing. Left to right: a hand puppet, paper bag puppets, and a sock puppet.

A paper plate face, wig, skirt and blouse, and coat hanger make a broom puppet.

Your parents are unable to visit elderly Aunt Martha and you go in their place to talk with her.

Two radio announcers try to keep up a conversation during a very slow baseball game.

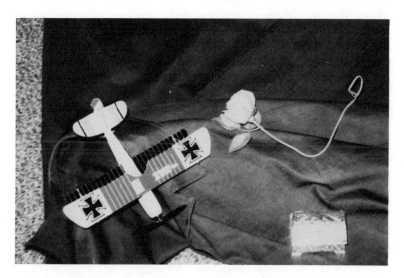

A cape, a plane, a silver chest, and a single rose might suggest a spy story.

2. *Solve the Problem* Children create dialogue around problem situations:

Nurse trying to get patient to take medicine.

Photographer tries to get a chattering group organized for picture-taking.

A waiter spills soup on your best clothing.

Cheering up a friend in the hospital.

Persistent salesman tries to sell his product in order to meet his quota for the day.

Real estate agent trying to sell an obviously poor house.

A customer orders a meal; gets the wrong one; waitress says she never makes a mistake.

3. *Nonsense Language* Children create a nonsense language. It might be just sounds, the alphabet, numbers, or one word repeated such as "applesauce." Create a situation in which several people are having an argument.

4. *Silent Movies* Children can create dialogue for old silent movies or films in which the sound has been turned off.

5. *Puppets* Puppets are useful for creating dialogue scenes since some children can talk for a puppet more easily than for themselves. Do not spend so much time making puppets that they become art objects that are never

functional. Simple stick puppets, or puppets from paper bags, are sufficient. One activity that is fun even for older children is to dress up two brooms for a dialogue scene as if they are two large puppets. Brooms can be turned upside down, decorated with paper bags, and draped with clothing. While two people move the brooms about, two others can speak for them.

6. *Talking Pictures* Children can create dialogue scenes based on pictures of people, animals, or inanimate objects that appear to be carrying on interesting conversations. It is also fun to create appropriate voices for the animals or inanimate objects.

7. *Talking Music* Some instrumental music suggests the idea of conversation between interesting personalities. After listening to the music, children can divide into groups and create a situation.

8. *Three-people Scenes*

Two people are trying to talk but they speak different languages (could be nonsense). A third is a translator.

Two people are arguing. A third tries to enter as a peacemaker, even though he does not know what the argument is about.

Three people sit together in a row. The person in the middle has to keep a conversation going with the other two, although they are talking about two different things.

9. *Making Excuses*

Someone trying to talk a policeman out of giving him a traffic ticket.

Someone trying to explain his tardiness to someone who is reluctant to believe him.

Someone trying to talk a friend out of entering a room in which people are arranging a surprise party for him.

Someone trying to get an advance on his allowance.

10. *Moments in History* Children can create dialogue scenes from historical moments. Information related to these moments may be given to the children on cards, or they can do the research in preparation for their dialogue. The following are some examples:

William Penn tells his father he wants to be a Quaker.

Cyrus McCormick tries to convince a doubtful farmer that the reaper is safe and workable.

Patriots at the Second Continental Congress try to convince the loyalists that independence is more important than loyalty to England.

11. *Teaching* Children can create situations in which people are trying to teach one another. For example:

A group of exasperated witches try to teach a scared apprentice how to fly the magic broom.

A patient but nerve-worn driving instructor tries to teach a student how to drive a car.

A master chef tries to teach an apprentice how to make a soufflé.

A father (or mother) tries to teach the daughter (or son) how to dance the afternoon before the school prom.

12. *Talking Settings* Plan a setting, either indoor or outdoor. Each person is a different part of the setting, either furniture or building, etc. They talk to each other when humans are not around. What do they talk about?

The scene might be continued with humans entering the setting. Now the setting remains quiet. When the humans leave, the scene may continue again.

13. *"Ad" Talks* The leader prepares a set of cards with clipped statements from ads in magazines. Each child has a card. In groups of twos or threes the children converse and each must try to work his "ad" statement into the conversation.

14. *Group Scenes*

People on a bus. A man gets on with a briefcase that is ticking.

People in an elevator that gets stuck.

Parents in a busy department store lose their child.

A group of elderly people discover what appears to be the fountain of youth.

A group of archeologists discover an unusual skull, which appears to be the missing link in man's past.

Laborers in a depressed area are told the union wants to strike.

15. *Stories From Unrelated Words* Prepare a set of cards with *places,* another set for *things* (props), another for *characters.* Groups select one card from each set. Shuffle cards to produce an infinite variety of combinations. Scenes can have interesting or unusual locations, people, or objects in them.

Setting	Characters	Props
elevator	alligator	bowl of soup
Island of No Return	mule	nest with eggs
museum	Joe Namath	roller skates
railway station	good fairy	rowboat
abandoned mine shaft	prehistoric monster	treasure chest
lost/found department	president	fire
attic	Harriet the Spy	giant tree
junkyard	statue that comes to life	bomb
information desk	Snoopy	bouquet of flowers
gangplank	Jack Frost	bubble gum
locker room	near-sighted ladybug	a magic wand

16. *Role-Playing Situations* There are a number of situations children can dramatize in order to explore acceptable ways to handle problems. Many of their dramatizations may demonstrate unacceptable ways, but they can serve to illustrate the consequences of unacceptable behaviors; from them more acceptable ways can develop.

Children have the habit of crossing an elderly woman's lawn. She confronts them one day.

A group of friends in a variety store decides to shoplift for the fun of it. Two children in the group argue that nevertheless it is stealing.

A child interviews for a newspaper delivery route or a babysitting job.

A group of children are throwing hard-packed snowballs at passing cars and shatter a windshield. The car stops and the driver confronts the group.

EXERCISES FOR THE COLLEGE STUDENT

1. Practice adding dialogue in storytelling. Select a story, and as you rehearse it or tell it to your classmates, add direct dialogue.
2. Practice generating dialogue through discussion. Select a situation in which dialogue is possible. Briefly describe the situation. List the questions you would ask to stimulate discussion for dialogue.
3. Select or create a dialogue scene. Plan your role in aiding dialogue. Lead your classmates in the activity. Be prepared to step in when necessary.
4. Create additional variations of the verbal activities given in this chapter.
5. Look for possible dialogue scenes in literature (stories and poetry), history and biography sources, and other curricular topics. Keep a file of these materials.

STORIES FOR DIALOGUE SCENES

The following stories are essentially dialogue scenes. They are arranged in alphabetical order. The following symbols are used to indicate the age level the story might be best suited for:

Y   young children in kindergarten, first, and second grades
M   middle-grade children in third and fourth grades
O   older children in fifth and sixth grades

Y   "Ask Mr. Bear," Marjorie Flack.   (46)
     Danny wants a birthday gift for his mother and goes to the animals for help.

Y   *The Bojabi Tree,* Edith Rickert. Doubleday, 1958.
     The hungry animals find a fruit that looks like appleorangeplumpear-banana but smells like a bananapearplumorangeapple. King Leo Lion tells them they have found a Bojabi, but they cannot remember the name.

M   "The Hare and the Bear," Yasue Maiyagawa.   (26)
     A bear accidentally injures a hare and tries to nurse him back to health. But the hare takes advantage of the situation.

M   "How Wihio Made a Trade," Grace Jackson Penney.   (48)
Wihio tricks some rabbits into his bag. Then he bargains with Coyote for a bigger bag, which turns out to have buffalo bones in it.

M   *Just Say Hic!* Barbara K. Walker. Follet, 1965.
Hasan, a simple fellow, is told to repeat the word salt (hic) to remember what to buy. He is overheard to say the word and there begins a series of misunderstandings as each person he meets tells him to say a different word.

O   "Justice," Harold Courlander.   (20)
Two deaf people misunderstand events, and a brief humorous situation is presented.

M–O   *The King's Fountain,* Lloyd Alexander. Dutton, 1971.
A king wants to build a fountain that would cut off the water supply to the people. A poor man tries to find someone to persuade the king not to build the fountain. Each has his excuse, and the poor man is left to speak to the king himself.

M   "Mrs. Peterkin Puts Salt in Her Coffee," Lucretia Hale.   (46)
The chemist tries a variety of chemicals, the old woman tries herbs, but no one can get rid of the salty taste.

M   *Not This Bear!* Bernice Myers. Four Winds, 1967.
A little boy in a furry coat and hat has to convince a bear family that he is not one of them.

M–O   "The Princess Who Always Believed What She Heard," Mary C. Hatch.(54)
A contest is held to see who can tell a story big enough so that the Princess will say, "It's a Lie!"

Y–M   "The Rabbit, the Bear and the Zinniga-Zanniga," Dr. Seuss. Houghton Mifflin Reader, *Bright Peaks*
A rabbit outsmarts a bear by convincing him he's sick.

M–O   "The Short Horse," Ellis Credle.   (49)
Uncle Bridger teaches Jess how to talk his way out of renting a horse.

M   "The Three Wishes," Olive Beaupré Miller.   (46)
The old tale of the husband and wife who wish foolishly for pudding, then for the pudding to be on the wife's nose, leaving the final wish to remove it.

M   *The Tiger in the Teapot,* Betty Yurdin. Holt Owlet, 1968.
A family tries to entice the tiger out of the teapot before teatime. The little sister succeeds.

Y–M   "The Tiger, The Brahman, and the Jackal," Flora Annie Steel.   (3)
A Brahman enlists the aid of a clever jackal to help him outwit a tiger who wants to eat him.

O   "A Travelled Narrative," Charles M. Skinner.   (61)
Ichabod, a "shiftless fellow," tries to sneak out of the general store with butter hidden under his hat. The other customers try to detain him with conversation so the butter will melt and give him away.

M-O *The Truthful Harp,* Lloyd Alexander. Holt, Rinehart & Winston, 1967.
     Fflam adds color to his stories and discovers that his harp breaks a string
     with each exaggeration.

  O "Waiting for Martin," Richard Dorson.   (61)
     A preacher in a haunted house tries to keep reading out of his Bible to
     scare the ghosts away.

M-O "Wicked John and the Devil," Richard Chase.   (22)
     An ornery blacksmith outwits the Devil who comes to claim him.

  M "The Zax," Dr. Seuss.   (40)
     Two Zax meet and neither will give way for the other — ever.

POETRY FOR DIALOGUE SCENES

The following poems pose interesting possibilities for creating dialogue scenes.
The actual dialogue used in the poetry is less specific than in the previous stories.
Therefore, it may take some discussion and imaginative thinking for them.

M-O "Barter," Sara Teasdale.   (1)
     "Life has loveliness to sell. . . ." What would Life as a salesman have to
     sell? What would Life say trying to convince someone to buy? What
     would you trade for Life's loveliness? This poem should be done with
     sensitivity to the mood and philosophy.

M-O "The Builders," Sara Henderson Hay.   (39)
     A person speaks critically of someone else's lack of building capabilities.
     There is a strongly implied reference to the story of the "Three Pigs."

  M "Cheers," Eve Merriam.   (39)
     The frogs and serpents have a football team with interesting cheerleading
     yells.

  M "Creep," Linda Kershaw.   (31)
     You are spying on a neighboring village and return to your own village to
     report what you saw.

M-O "Diddling," James Reeves.   (5)
     The people of this town are constant complainers.

Y-M "Doorbells," Rachel Field.   (4) (46)
     You never know who might be ringing your doorbell.

Y-M "Food and Drink," David McCord.   (47)
     Conversations take place between various foods and utensils on the table.

Y-M "The Grasses," James Reeves.   (59)
     What do the grasses talk about when they whisper to each other?

Y-M "The Grasshopper and the Bird," James Reeves.   (5)
     A grasshopper and a bird don't quite agree with each other.

M "Jonathan Bing," Beatrice Curtis Brown.   (4)
Poor Jonathan is forgetful, and each day dresses inappropriately for his visit to the King and must return home again.

Y-M "Little Talk," Aileen Fisher.   (51)
Bugs and other insects probably talk together if we could only hear them.

M "Mean Song," Eve Merriam.   (52)
Mean things are said in nonsense words. Who is the speaker, and what is he so angry about?

Y-M "The Mouse," Elizabeth Coatsworth.   (12)
A mouse complains how hard he has to work to find food.

Y-M "Overheard on a Saltmarsh," Harold Monro.   (39)
A goblin and a nymph argue over some green glass beads.

M-O "Phizzog," Carl Sandburg.   (4) (13)
Create a dialogue scene in which you receive your newly made face and, although it doesn't please you, you must make do with it.

M-O "Sir Smashum Uppe," E. V. Rieu.   (34)
Sir is very clumsy, and the poet keeps giving him assurance that his accidents are forgiven.

M-O "Southbound on the Freeway," May Swenson.   (39)
A visitor from "Orbitville" mistakes cars for Earth creatures and gives an interesting description of them. To whom is he reporting?

M-O "The Statue,," James Reeves.   (5)
What does the "stone gentleman" say and to whom does he speak?

M "Stones by the Sea," James Reeves.   (59)
What do stones say to each other?

M-O "Summons," Robert Francis.   (39)
What would be something important to summon a person to?

Y-M "Ticking Clocks," Rachel Field.   (58)
Different clocks have different voices and different things to say.

M-O "Two Friends," David Ignatow.   (41)
It seems that two friends who pass each other and talk hurriedly really don't listen to each other's comments.

12

Story Dramatization and Project Work

Many children and teachers have an interest in making a dramatization of a story. Sometimes there is also an interest in making a dramatization a part of a unit's work, correlating it with several areas of the curriculum. In this chapter, we will examine some ways of approaching story dramatization and project work.

STORY DRAMATIZATION

We have already referred to a number of stories and to various ways of dramatizing them. Some of the stories were essentially pantomime; others were essentially dialogue encounters. Other suggested possibilities for handling scenes and characters in stories include employing adaptation, editing, and creative elaboration.

Some stories that the children and the teacher want to dramatize may be quite complex. They may have a variety of characters or an involved plot or may require extensive dialogue to forward the action. For such stories a programmed approach is often needed. Programming means the leader analyzes and divides the story into all of the separate and unique experiences it offers. These experiences or scenes are played one at a time. To dramatize the entire story, the "rehearsed" scenes are played in their appropriate sequence.

Sometimes children have numerous ideas of their own for dramatizing a story, and sometimes they are mature enough to carry out their ideas with a fair degree of success. In this case, the leader's role is mainly one of guiding and organizing the playing. More frequently, however, the leader must help the children in selecting their material, in seeing the possibilities for dramatization, and in planning the dramatization.

Leader's Preparation

Usually the leader plans ahead of time some ideas of how the scenes might be played. In this way he can be more flexible in selecting the scenes for playing when he sees the group's reaction to the story.

The selection of the scenes for playing may be according to the children's interest in them. If the children seem to like the entire story, the leader may begin at any point. Or, he might ask the question, "Which scene (or part of the story) did you like the best?" If he gets a majority response for one particular scene, he may decide to begin with that one.

The scenes might also be played according to their difficulty. For example, the movement or action scenes might be played before the dialogue scenes are attempted. Or, scenes that can be narrated might precede those that require more creative thinking.

In an initial playing the leader may focus on one character or on one scene that everyone can play. The leader may narrate some action from the story or develop some pantomime activities related to the story that the characters perform. In this way the children can begin to identify with the characters immediately and can participate in at least part of the story right away. Often it is advisable to have the children play these activities individually at their desks or in limited space.

As the children continue to work with the story the leader may cast only a part of the class at a time while the rest of the class observes. Then the scene can be recast and replayed in order to give all the children a chance to play as many characters as possible.

Another way might be to discuss a scene and the characters in it and then divide into groups. Each group can work out its ideas for the scene, rehearse briefly, and then share the ideas with the rest of the class.

Often additional characters are created in the story so that more children can participate. Sometimes the number of people in crowd scenes are increased. Or, some parts may be double cast. The leader and the children may also think of ways to include sound effects, lighting, music, or other additions that the children can handle.

When the entire story is played, the children sometimes need assistance in remembering the sequence of events. There are several ways to help. The leader may participate in the playing, particularly when help with dialogue may be necessary. Or, the leader may serve as a narrator whenever the story needs to be forwarded. Another possibility may be to write a simple outline of the story on the board. Or, if there are a number of characters who appear one at a time, they may be lined up in the order of their appearance.

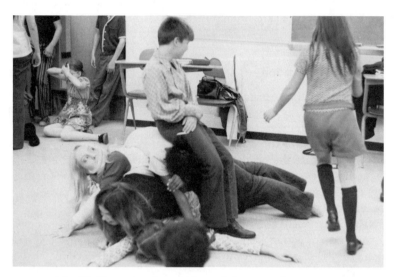

The Wolf ate six of the kids, and the seventh got away.

Mother Goat opens the Wolf's tummy and rescues the kids.

All of the possibilities suggested above should be kept in mind when the leader prepares a story for dramatization. The leader should plan for several alternatives in order to be as flexible as possible when guiding the children in the playing.

Discussion

Although children are usually satisfied with playing the action in the story, there may be deeper meanings to be probed. Depth of characterization and feeling usually cannot be reached without some discussion and analysis. Often the story and the characters are more meaningful to the children if the situations can be related to their own lives. Of course the age and maturity of the children will determine the extent to which they can participate in discussion.

While there may be many interpretations of meaning in stories, the leader may need to devote some thought to the theme he wishes to focus on. Superficial analysis of characters can cause problems, as one leader discovered when he used the book, *Horton Hatches the Egg* (p. 245) by Dr. Seuss. In this story, an elephant does a favor for a runaway bird, agreeing to sit on her egg for a day. The bird does not return, and Horton feels obligated to sit on the egg for a year until it hatches. In spite of the many difficulties he encounters he remains "faithful 100 percent."

In introducing this story the leader focused on the following question:

T: Have you ever made a promise and then wished you hadn't?

This question caused the children to think of many unpleasant experiences they had had and didn't wish to repeat. The leader ignored Horton's faithfulness to the egg, and the more the children discussed the story the stronger their conviction became that anyone who would go through such an experience would have to be stupid and dumb. Eventually they lost all interest in the story.

An introduction that focuses on the theme of the story more clearly might be the question, "Did you ever do a very nice favor for someone, even though it took a great deal of work on your part?"

Evaluation

Evaluation of the dramatization is usually made after each scene is played. Or, if things seem to be going well and evaluation would be an interruption in the proceedings, the leader may choose to wait until the entire story is dramatized.

One helpful way to evaluate pantomime scenes as objectively as possible is to utilize simultaneous playing. For example, several individual children or pairs may enact a brief moment or a scene at the same time. Then the children in the audience can be asked to look for all the specific details they note that indicate believability. One leader chose this method for a serious scene in "The Legend of the Moor's Legacy" (p. 246). Several children were paired to play in pantomime the scene in which the water carrier meets the dying Moor and takes him home with him. Some children played the scene with deep feeling and involvement, while others had difficulty. The audience readily saw which actions were convincing, and no comment was necessary for the unconvincing ones.

The points to consider in the evaluation center on whether or not the story is understandable. The action should be clear. The characters should be believable, both in their actions and in their dialogue.

When the evaluation is made, it is usually helpful to use the character's names rather than the children's names. This practice can be encouraged both in self evaluation and in audience evaluation.

> **T**: The King really seemed to care about his subjects.
>
> **C**: I spoke the Captain's orders in a gruff voice, but I tried to show that he was a kind person by smiling just a little.

A STORY FOR YOUNGER CHILDREN

The following extended illustration demonstrates one way of analyzing and playing the story, "Why the Bear Is Stumpy Tailed" (p. 248). In this story, which is usually enjoyed by young children, a bear is told by a sly fox that he can catch fish if he will just put his tail down in the water and wait for the fish to bite. Since it is winter time, the bear cuts a hole in the ice and begins to fish. He waits patiently, but in the meantime the water freezes over. When he gets up he discovers his tail is caught fast. As he pulls to free himself, he pulls off his tail, and that is why today bears have short tails instead of long ones.

When the leader analyzes this story, he will see that essentially it has two parts. There is an opening dialogue scene between the bear and the fox and an action scene with the bear fishing and finally pulling off his tail. Both scenes are written with very little detail and will need elaboration in order to create a dramatization.

Narrating

The leader may choose to narrate the story the first time through. Everyone can play the part of the bear, and the action can begin with his decision to go and fish.

> **T**: ... So the bear decides he will try catching fish the way the fox said *he* did. The bear goes off toward the pond. He feels very hungry and can hardly wait to catch a long string of fish.

Although the action scene in which the bear loses his tail is an exciting one, there is a minimum of movement during the bear's long wait. The leader's narration here will be most important in making the story interesting and exciting. Notice the sensory detail added to the following narration:

> **T:** The bear settled himself down and waited for the fish to begin to bite. His coat was thick and heavy and he felt snug and warm, even though his tail was in the ice water. He looked around at all the sights. Some animals were scampering nearby and he waved to them. He thought he could see some fish under the ice darting to and fro.
>
> Soon he began to get a little bit chilled, so he breathed on his paws to warm them. . . .

The story could be narrated with other characters as well. One group of second-graders suggested that skaters could be skating on the pond just before the bear got there. They also wanted trees, a sun, and snowflakes falling as night approached.

In order to give the trees and sun action to perform, the leader narrated, "The wind blew as it got colder and the trees bowed and waved and danced in the wind." It was decided that the sun would be in the background but should make a slow, arcing path to indicate rising and setting while the bear fished.

Creative Pantomime

The same scene of the bear fishing could be played as a creative pantomime activity. The children could be questioned about the equipment they would use; they might describe the pond as they think it would look; and what they could think of to do in order to pass the time waiting.

> **T:** What does the bear take with him in order to fish? How does he cut the hole in the ice? What sorts of ideas do you have about that?
>
> **C:** The pond is covered with snow, and the bear has to shovel it away before he can cut the hole.
>
> **C:** The bear cuts a hole with his sharp claws.
>
> **C:** He has an ice cutter and a tiny ice house and a small heater.
>
> **T:** When the bear had to sit there for such a long time, he must have gotten tired. I wonder what he did to pass the time. What do you suppose he might have looked at and heard while he sat there?
>
> **C:** I think he heard his stomach growling, and he counts to ten and he quits fishing.
>
> **C:** He gets cold and wraps his muffler around his ears and he twiddles his thumbs and then he hums a song about the summertime to himself.
>
> **C:** He reads a book.
>
> **C:** He keeps looking for someone to come and talk to him, but no one's there but the trees; so he counts all the trees he can see.

T: As the bear sits there, what do you think his feelings might be?

C: First he's happy because he thinks he's going to get some fish.

C: It hurts him when the fish bite. But the fox told him it would and it would be a good sign because he would be catching so many.

C: He gets real mad and decides to go and beat up the fox.

T: When I play the music, you start pretending to be the bear when he goes down to the pond. You can do any of the ideas we talked about. When you think you've got enough fish, you pull your tail. When I blink the lights you'll become boys and girls again. If you finish before other people do, just stay where you are and wait.

Dialogue

In order to play the dialogue scene in the beginning of the story, the leader might need to stimulate ideas in a discussion. He might ask:

T: When the bear sees all of the fish the fox has, what might he say to him?

C: "Those are good looking fish. Where'd you get them?"

C: "I want some fish like that. I'm hungry."

C: "Hello, fox. Where'd you get those fish? I'll buy some from you."

T: What do you think the fox tells the bear about getting some fish?

C: "See, you cut a hole in the ice and put your tail in it. They'll bite and you'll get some."

C: "It's real easy. You just cut a hole in the ice."

C: "You put your tail in the water, but you have to wait a long time. But it's really fun to do. And these fish are delicious."

The dialogue scene might be played in a preview. Four verbal volunteers might be double cast as the bear and the fox. Or, the leader may play one of the foxes or one of the bears. Or, the scene could be played by everyone in pairs. The scene is over when the bear decides to fish.

T: Now that you're in partners, decide who will be the bear and who will be the fox. You've just met, and you will be talking about the fish and the fox will suggest that you try ice fishing. When the bear is convinced that he will fish, stop your scene and sit down and wait for the other players to finish. . . .

Sometimes the leader and the children enjoy elaborating the story. Frequently these elaborations become as intriguing as the story itself, and when the story is put together, the children ask to include their elaborated ideas. The above story offers many possibilities. The following are some suggestions.

An additional dialogue scene might be created:

T: Let's suppose that the bear has suddenly discovered that he has been tricked by the fox and that he is stuck in the ice. But he doesn't want to admit what has happened because he is embarrassed about it.

Now, there might be a number of people who come by and see him there. Each has a reason for wanting the bear to leave, and they try to coax him away. Because he doesn't want them to see him stuck there, he has to make up a story.

Who do you suppose might pass by? What might be their reason for asking the bear to leave? What reason would the bear give for having to stay where he is?

C: His mother wants him to come home to dinner, but he says he isn't hungry.

C: A friend comes by and wants him to play but he says he would rather ice-fish.

C: Some little animals come by and wonder why he doesn't chase them like he usually does, and he tells them he is getting too old for that.

They may also invent additional creative pantomimes:

T: The story doesn't tell us, but what do you think the fox would be doing before he meets the bear?

C: He's planning on how he's going to trick the bear. He's writing all his ideas in a notebook.

C: He's down at the market buying fish. That's where he really got them.

C: He's really ice-fishing, but he's doing it with a real fishing pole.

A similar pantomime might be made up about the bear:

T: What do you think the bear is doing before he meets the fox?

C: He's combing his beautiful tail.

C: Searching for a good breakfast.

C: Sleeping. He loves to sleep.

A STORY FOR OLDER CHILDREN

A very popular story for dramatization with older children is Hans Christian Andersen's "The Emperor's New Clothes" (p. 245). Following is a listing of some of the possible activities a leader might use. Some of the activities may be played in pairs and groups as well as individually.

The first set of activities would probably be essential in dramatizing the entire story. They are listed in chronological order. The second set of activities elaborate on the basic story line. Some of the activities in the second set may be incorporated into the story dramatization if the leader or the children wish.

A

a. In a dialogue scene, pretend to be the rogues convincing the Emperor (and perhaps members of court) that they can weave magical material that becomes invisible to anyone who is unworthy of the office he holds.

b. Pantomime the rogues pretending to work at the looms with imaginary threads and materials.

c. Create the dialogue scene between the rogues and the various officials who come to view the wonderful new clothes and find they cannot see them. The officials must protect their positions, however, by pretending that they do see the fabric.

d. Create a dialogue scene between the Emperor and the rogues when the Emperor comes to view the new clothes. He, too, must pretend that he can see the imaginary fabric.

e. Create a dialogue scene when the rogues and the chamberlains carefully and with much showmanship dress the Emperor for the procession.

f. Be the Emperor, proudly walking through the streets of the city. He hears all the appreciative comments of the admiring crowd. Then there is the single voice of the child saying that he has no clothes on. Slowly everyone in the crowd agrees, but the Emperor decides to go through with the procession. (The voices of the crowd and the child who reveals the truth may be played first by the leader.)

B

a. Pretend to be the rogues when they are certain that no one is watching them work. What do they do to pass the time and to entertain themselves? (Pantomime or dialogue.)

b. Pretend to be the rogues rehearsing their description of the fabric they have woven. The description might include the lovely patterns, the magnificent weaving skills, the unusual color combinations, etc. (Monologue or dialogue.)

c. Pretend to be someone from the court or the kingdom. Pantomime something they would do, their recreation or work suitable to the period. The audience will try to guess the pantomimes.

d. Act out one idea of what happens when the Emperor arrives back at the palace after the procession is ended. (Pantomime or dialogue.)

A STORY CREATED
BY CHILDREN AND TEACHER

Occasionally it is possible for the teacher to guide a group of children to create a story collectively. The group has to be a cooperative one, which will accept each other's ideas. Although it is not always true, smaller groups may have an easier time with collective story creating.

Generally the leader selects some stimulus material and leads the discussion to develop the story. As the children give their ideas, the leader must think ahead and visualize a story forming. Sometimes he needs to suggest ideas or to clarify those the children offer. He must ask questions that will help formulate the plot, using many of the principles discussed in Chapter 8. The discussion will need to proceed carefully but quickly so that the plot does not become too entangled with subplots that cannot be resolved.

Again, the stimulus materials will vary in the amount of detail they provide. Sometimes it is easier to begin with fantastical material in order to allow more leeway for the plot. A fairy godmother or a magician can always come in at the end and save the whole thing, if necessary!

One teacher, using the nursery rhyme "Old King Cole" developed a story with a group of twenty fourth-graders:

> The leader's first question was, "Why was the king so merry?" The children began by commenting with description of how he was merry and the things he did to demonstrate his happiness. He whistled, he played games, and was always in a good mood.
>
> The leader then asked if his merriness was acceptable to everyone. (If it is not, then there is the possibility of a conflict for the story.) The children decided that it was not all right and that, indeed, the kingdom was actually populated with people who were glum most of the time, that only the King was happy.
>
> Then the leader asked the children, "How does the King feel about having a glum Kingdom to rule, and how do the people feel about him?" (Here the leader focused on the possible difference of opinion the King and his people would have, which could form the basis of the conflict.) The children suggested that the people grumbled because the King kept them awake nights with his partying. The King, on the other hand, wanted them to share his happiness.
>
> Then the leader asked, "What did the King do about this situation?" The children seemed to have difficulty thinking of an idea so the leader returned to the lines of the rhyme. "Why did the King call for his pipe, a bowl, and fiddlers three?" The children very quickly suggested that smoking the pipe helped the King think, and that he liked to have the musicians play to help him feel merry.
>
> Then one youngster suddenly threw in the idea that the bowl was a gift from a man in another country. The teacher asked, "Somebody important?" "Yes," was the reply. The teacher suggested, "Perhaps an ambassador?" The child agreed. When the teacher asked, "Why was the gift given?" the children said that it was to help solve the King's problem with his gloomy subjects.

At this point the leader asked a very general question, "What happened then?" Here the children might have easily bogged down. If they had run out of ideas, this open question might not have been very helpful. But for this group it did not pose a problem. Somehow all the pieces of the story began to fall into place.

One child said, "A page brought the bowl in and tripped and it broke. And then everyone started to laugh." The teacher then simply described the situation as he envisioned it. "I see. The people who had been glum for so long slowly broke out into smiles." His tone of voice and manner indicated that the moment was a dramatic one; it was the turning point and the solution to the problem.

Several children then offered their ideas to fill in the rest of the details. One said, "The King was mad at first because the gift was broken, but when the people smiled, he was happy again." Another said, "When they picked up the pieces of the bowl they suddenly saw the words 'Chained Laughter' in the bottom." The leader suggested, "The Ambassador had a bowl magically filled with laughter and when it broke the laughter was released. Is that it?" The children agreed. Then someone added, "And the Ambassador was from 'Gladland!'"

Because the children had been the authors of the story, it was easily dramatized. Half the children were cast in the first playing, while the rest were the audience. For the second playing, the two groups switched.

PROJECT WORK

Dramatizations may involve extended work over a long period of time and may integrate additional areas of the curriculum as well. Sometimes they are planned in skeletal fashion in advance; sometimes they are an outgrowth of the children's expressed interests.

The leader and the children may wish to take an idea and explore it in depth with a number of activities. For example, the theme of blindness might be selected. In order to help the children understand what it is to be blind, some initial activities might be considered. For example:

a. Have the children perform various simple tasks with their eyes closed. Some activities might include writing a brief letter, tying shoelaces, making an inventory of the items in their desk, and so forth.

b. Half the children are blindfolded and paired with a partner whom they must identify by listening to their voice or by touching facial features lightly. This activity is to be done as quietly as possible.

c. Have the children work in pairs for the activity "Leading the Blind." The blindfolded child is guided by his partner through the classroom, experiencing objects, textures, and so forth. The activity is to be done nonverbally so that the sensory experiences can be fully absorbed. Quiet music can help set the mood for this.

d. Select a number of everyday items and have the children try to guess them by shape, texture, and other clues. This activity might be done in small groups.

e. Special materials and aids for the blind might be examined: books for children written in braille with tactile illustrations, tape measures or watches with raised markings, and so forth.

Leading the blind.

Two selections dealing with the subject of blindness can be played as narrative pantomime. One experience is the book by Florence Parry Heide *Sound of Sunshine, Sound of Rain* (p. 129). This is the story of a young black child who is blind. He learns about the world of color from a friend, but experiences color discrimination from insensitive people. It is possible to play almost the entire book as a narrated experience.

Another experience might be taken from Glen Rounds' book *The Blind Colt* (p. 127). There are a number of episodes in this book, based on a true story, which can be played as narrative pantomime. The story is not only informative but sensitively written as well.

A poem on blindness might be "Mimi's Fingers" (19). In addition to the sensory experiences described in the poem, the final line offers possibilities for verbal exploration in pairs. Mimi asks if someone could describe "blue" to her, a challenging question indeed.

The class might also wish to dramatize episodes and events from the life of Helen Keller as presented in Catherine Owens Peare's book *The Helen Keller Story* (98). Helen, who was both blind and deaf, had only the senses of touch, taste, and smell available to her. There are many events in her life that lend themselves to dramatization: the family's concern about Helen's education, the search for a teacher, the arrival of Anne Sullivan to the home and Helen's first encounter with her, the adjustment of the family and Helen to Anne Sullivan's educational program, and the scenes of Helen's discoveries and newfound knowledge of the world. Some scenes can be enacted as narative pantomime, some as group pantomime, and some involve verbal interaction.

Children, playing the story of Helen Keller, hold out their hands for Anne Sullivan to finger-spell into their palms.

Sometimes teachers like to integrate additional learning activities around a dramatization experience. For example, *The Adventures of Tom Sawyer* (139) by Mark Twain offers many possibilities for dramatization and for other curricular work as well. The chapter on whitewashing the fence is perfectly designed for a dialogue scene. In this episode, Tom learns to use psychological strategy. Not only does he get his friends to whitewash his fence for him, he also gets them to barter for the privilege of such an honor!

The episode in the graveyard involves a dramatic fight and a murder; the oath-taking scene that follows is an example of a paired verbal interaction. The episode of the interrupted funeral offers possibilities of eulogy speeches, group dialogue scenes, and narrative pantomime.

Because of its historical setting, the book can stimulate social studies activities as well. The mid-1800's Hannibal, Missouri, setting may lead to an investigation of the customs of life, styles of clothing, early school curriculum, and occupations of the period. The children might become interested in studying the Mississippi River and what life on it was like in Mark Twain's day. The study might also include a consideration of the river's effect on the evolution of cities, agriculture, and transportation. The book may also stimulate interest in caves, spelunking, map reading, and mapmaking.

In working with story dramatization or with projects, the teacher and the children may find themselves developing an improvised play. If their interest remains high throughout their work, and they are satisfied with their efforts, they may want to share their work with other classes or with parents.

The presentation of any creative dramatics experiences should remain improvised rather than becoming a formal production with a written script. If the class has spent time with the project and it has been a meaningful experience for them, they will probably be thoroughly familiar with their ideas and how they want to present them. They will have no need to recite memorized lines because the experience will have become a part of them. The characters and events will be understood because they will be the children's creation and elaboration.

Presentations can easily be given in an informal style. There is no need for a staged production. Some presentations take place right in the classroom with the various scenes placed around three sides, and the audience sitting on the fourth side. Other semiformal arrangements are possible in other areas of the school.

Elaborate costuming, scenery, and props are not necessary. The story and the people in it are more important than any embellishments. If any additions are used they should be kept to a minimum so that they do not dominate the presentation.

In presenting creative dramatics experiences, the children are selecting the ideas and the materials that have appealed to them to share with an audience. Such experiences can be more enjoyable and more educationally beneficial than the presentation of a scripted play because the children have created a project uniquely theirs.

EXERCISES FOR COLLEGE STUDENTS

1. Select a story suitable for dramatization. Analyze the story in terms of pantomime and dialogue possibilities. Consider also the creative elaboration you see possible in it. Outline the dramatization plan as was done with "The Emperor's New Clothes" in this chapter.

2. Select a theme or a topic that can be studied in several ways through dramatization. List the various activities possible for this theme.

3. Select a book that could be dramatized and could correlate with other curricular areas as well. Outline the book's drama possibilities and list the related activities it could stimulate.

4. Select a story suitable for dramatization and lead your classmates in a playing of it. Discuss afterwards the other possibilities for dramatization.

5. Select other stories and books suitable for dramatization and keep a file of them.

6. Keep a file of the many books available that are of curricular interest and are also suitable for dramatization. Biographies, historical fiction, and books with social themes are some of the possibilities.

STORIES TO DRAMATIZE

The materials are arranged in alphabetical order. The following symbols are used to indicate the age level they might be best suited for:

Y   young children in kindergarten, first, and second grades
M   middle-grade children in third and fourth grades
O   older children in fifth and sixth grades

Y   "The Adventure of Three Little Rabbits," author untraced.   (46)
Three little rabbits get stuck in some spilled syrup and almost become rabbit stew.

O   "All Summer in a Day," Ray Bradbury. Follett, 1970, *The World of Language, Book 6.*
Children on Venus anxiously wait for the sun, which shines one hour every seven years. Minutes before the sun appears, they lock Margot into the closet and forget about her during their hour in the outdoors.

M   "Anansi and the Fish Country." Philip Sherlock.   (2)
Anansi tries to trick fish by playing doctor.

M   "Anansi Plays Dead," Harold Courlander and Albert Kofi Prempeh. (25)
Anansi pretends to die so that he will not have to be prosecuted for a crime, but the villagers trick him.

M   "Anansi's Hat-Shaking Dance," Harold Courlander and Albert Kofi Prempeh.   (25)
Anansi fasts and becomes so hungry he has to sneak food.

M   *Bartholomew and the Oobleck,* Dr. Seuss. Random House, 1949.
King Derwin of Didd gets tired of all the things that fall from the sky and orders oobleck to be substituted.

M   *The Bigger Giant,* Nancy Green. Follett, 1963.
Fin McCool, a giant, is afraid of a bigger giant. Fin's little wife outwits the bigger giant.

M "The Cat and the Parrot," Sara Cone Bryant. (3)
A cat with an insatiable appetite eats everyone he meets.

M–O "Clever Manka," Parker Fillmore. (4)
Czech folk tale about a girl who proves her intelligence on more than one occasion.

M "The Conjure Wives," Frances G. Wickes. (46)
Selfish witches are turned into owls.

Y *Corduroy,* Don Freeman. Viking, 1968.
A teddy bear in a department store looks for his lost button.

M *The Dragon Takes a Wife,* Walter Dean Myers. Bobbs-Merrill, 1972.
Delightful story of a dragon who needs to win a battle with a knight so that he can get a wife. A fairy tries to help him, but nothing works until she turns herself into a lady dragon! Told in the black idiom.

O "Dr. Heidegger's Experiment," Nathaniel Hawthorne. (43)
Elderly people who experiment with water from the Fountain of Youth change their mind about wishing to be young again. The version suggested is a simplified one.

M *The Duchess Bakes a Cake,* Virginia Kahl. Scribner's, 1955.
A duchess decides to bake a cake, which grows into an enormous size with the duchess on top! The problem is how to get her down. After several plans fail, the solution is to eat the cake.

M "The Elephant's Child," Rudyard Kipling. (28)
The elephant's child, who has an "insatiable curiosity" finds out some answers to his questions but also gets a long nose doing it. After he discovers all of the advantages a long nose has, his relatives decide they want one also.

M "The Emperor's New Clothes," Hans Christian Andersen. (46)
A vain Emperor is swindled by rogues posing as weavers of fabric invisible to those unworthy of the office they hold.

M *The Fence,* Jan Balet. Delacorte, 1969.
A poor family in Mexico is taken to court by a rich family because they sniffed the delicious aromas from the kitchen of the rich family's house.

Y–M *Gillespie and the Guards,* Benjamin Elkin. Viking, 1956.
Three brothers with powerful eyes become guards of the kingdom. The King offers reward to anyone who can get past them. Gillespie, a young boy, tricks the guards.

M "The Golden Touch," Nathaniel Hawthorne. (46)
The tale of a greedy king who wishes that everything he touches could be turned to gold.

Y–M *Horton Hatches the Egg,* Dr. Seuss. Random House, 1940.
Horton, the elephant, hatches an egg for lazy Maizie.

M *How Davy Crockett Got a Bear Skin Coat,* Wyatt Blassingame. Garrard, 1972.
Davy finds a bear and gets the skin, and the bare bear hibernates until his hair grows out.

M   "How Jahdu Took Care of Trouble," Virginia Hamilton.   (57)
Jahdu tricks Trouble and frees everyone from the huge barrel they have
been caught in. One of the lovely tales a grandmother tells to instill black
pride in her grandson.

M–O   "How Pa Learned to Grow Hot Peppers," Ellis Credle.   (49)
Pa is too easygoing to be able to raise peppers with zip in them, so the
family has to find a way to get him fired up.

M   "How the Animals Got Their Fur Coats," Hilda Mary Hooke.   (55)
All the animals get lovely new coats except Moose, who gets the
leftovers. Charming characters in an American Indian legend.

M   "How the Birds Got Their Colors," Hilda Mary Hooke.   (55)
Delightfully funny tale of how all the birds get colorful feathers except
the Sapsucker. American Indian legend.

Y   *Journey Cake Ho!* Ruth Sawyer. Viking, 1953.
The Journey Cake escapes Johnny as well as a variety of animals.

O   "Knights of the Silver Shield."   (60)
A young man carries out his commander's orders in spite of his dis-
appointment.

O   "The Legend of the Moor's Legacy," Washington Irving.   (46)
A water carrier inherits a secret passport to a cave of riches.

Y   *The Little Engine That Could,* retold by Watty Piper. Platt and Munk,
1954.
A little engine is able to take the stalled train over the mountain to
deliver Christmas toys.

Y   "The Little House," Valery Carrick.   (44)
A group of little animals make their home in a jar until a Bear comes
along.

M   *The Magician Who Lost His Magic,* David McKee. Abelard-Schuman,
1970.
Melric loses his magic because he misused it by helping people to do
things they should do for themselves. He gets the magic back in time to
save the day for the King.

M–O   *Many Moons,* James Thurber. Viking, 1943.
A princess wishes for the moon and finally gets it.

O   *The Nightingale,* Eva Le Gallienne, trans. Harper & Row, 1965.
The Emperor of China hears the nightingale's beautiful song and orders
him to stay in court and sing. When he receives a gift from Japan with a
mechanical bird that sings very well, the nightingale is banished, but
returns when the Emperor becomes ill.

Y–M   "The Peddler and His Caps," Geraldine Brain Siks.   (46)
This version of an old tale has been elaborated to include more characters
and dialogue.

M–O   *Pitidoe the Color Maker,* Glen Dines. Macmillan, 1959.
Pitidoe is the lazy apprentice of a color maker who ignores the recipes

for color and turns everything purple. All the color fades and is returned only when Pitidoe discovers color in his tears.

M-O "A Portrait Which Suited Everyone and Pleased No One," M. A. Jagendorf.   (46)
Tyll is commissioned to paint the court portrait, but each member wants a flattering picture of himself. One of the many tales about this legendary German prankster.

Y-M "The Princess Who Could Not Cry," Rose Fyleman.   (46)
A peasant girl solves the princess' problem with an onion.

Y-M *The Reluctant Dragon,* Kenneth Grahame. Holiday, 1953.
A peaceable dragon doesn't want to fight with a knight.

O "Rip Van Winkle," Washington Irving.   (46)
The American tale of a man who falls asleep for twenty years to return to a world that has forgotten him.

O "Robin Hood's Merry Adventure with the Miller," Howard Pyle.   (46)
Robin Hood and the Miller fight for the right-of-way on a log.

M-O "Salting the Pudding," B. A. Botkin.   (61)
Ma doesn't have time to salt the pudding so everyone else in the family does.

M-O *Six Companions Find Fortune,* Katya Sheppard, trans. Doubleday, 1969.
Retired soldier finds a strong man, a hunter, a blower, a runner, and a frost maker. They win a race. The King does not want to reward them so he tries to get rid of them in various ways, each of which is foiled by the specific skills of each man.

M *Sparrow Socks,* George Selden. Harper & Row, 1965.
A family's sock business falls off until the son makes socks for sparrows. All who see the socks decide they want a pair just like them. Scotland setting.

Y-M *The Star Thief,* Andrea di Noto. Macmillan, 1971.
A thief raids the night's sky and hides all of the stars in his cellar.

M-O "Stone In the Road," traditional.   (46)
A Duke, as a lesson to his lazy people, places a stone in the road with gold underneath. Whoever removes the stone will be rewarded.

M-O *Stone Soup,* Marcia Brown. Scribner's, 1947.
Three soldiers return from the war and stop in a village. The villagers are tired of feeding soldiers, and they hide all their food. The soldiers teach them how to make stone soup, with vegetables and meat added for flavor.

M *A Story-A Story,* Gail E. Haley. Atheneum, 1970.
The African tale of how all stories came to be Anansi's, the spider man. Anansi must capture and give to the Sky God a leopard, hornets, and a dancing fairy whom men never see.

M "Taper Tom," Thorne-Thomsen.   (46)

Tom, a magic goose, and a string of people stuck to it make a sad Princess laugh.

O   *Three Strong Women,* Claus Stamm, trans. Viking, 1962.
A wrestler meets his match with strong family of women. They train him and he becomes the champion. A Japanese tall tale.

M   "The Ugly Duckling," Hans Christian Andersen.   (3) (4)
The sensitive story of a "duckling" who is rejected by all other animals. He happily discovers that he is actually a swan.

O   "Urashima Taro and the Princess of the Sea," Yoshiko Uchida, ed. (4) (16)
Urashima is enticed to live in the sea and spends much more time there than he imagines. When he returns home, he finds how much has lapsed. A Japanese folktale.

M-O   *The Wave,* Margaret Hodges. Houghton Mifflin, 1964.
There is a small earthquake, and Grandfather knows a tidal wave will follow. The villagers are unaware of the danger, and Grandfather must burn his rice fields to warn them. Japanese setting.

Y-M   *Where the Wild Things Are,* Maurice Sendak. Harper & Row, 1963.
Max is sent to his room for punishment and imagines that he goes off to a land where wild things live.

Y-M   "Why the Bear is Stumpy Tailed," George Webbe Dasent.   (4)
The Bear is tricked into fishing in the ice with his tail and loses it.

The following is a list of traditional and well-known fairy tales that children enjoy dramatizing.

M   "Beauty and the Beast"
M   "Cinderella"
Y   "The Elves and the Shoemaker"
Y   "The Gingerbread Boy"
Y   "Goldilocks and the Three Bears"
Y-M   "Hansel and Gretel"
Y-M   "Jack and the Beanstalk"
Y   "Little Red Riding Hood"
Y-M   "The Musicians of Bremen"
M   "Rapunzel"
M   "Rumpelstiltskin"
M   "Sleeping Beauty"
M   "Snow White and the Seven Dwarfs"
Y   "The Three Billy Goats Gruff"
Y   "The Three Little Pigs"
Y-M   "The History of Tom Thumb"

13

The Leader
and the Group

The previous chapters have been devoted to guiding children in the varied experiences of creative drama. An important part of this process must include guiding children to be self-seeking, self-directed, authenticated individuals capable of integrating themselves into a democratic, cohesive group.

Every classroom is composed of a group, including the teacher, organized for the express purpose of education. The most effective accomplishment of this purpose requires a high degree of cohesive interaction. Effective group interaction also depends on each member's (including the teacher's) unique and honest contributions.

The methods of achieving group interaction cannot be specifically described because of the variables involved in the nature of groups themselves. No two children, leaders, or groups are alike. Neither do they remain consistent in their differences from day to day or even minute to minute. As every teacher knows, variations in demeanor and attitude can be caused by such things as: weather, time of day and year, physical aspects of the environment, material presented, presence or absence of individual members, and age, sex ratio and size of the group. Furthermore, every individual in the group, including the teacher, is a constantly growing and evolving human being — never static.

The leader must recognize these variables in order to guide the group most effectively. His own unique contribution to the group is to be responsible for

College students studying creative dramatics get acquainted with a demonstration class of youngsters. The students sometimes play with, sometimes observe, the children.

leadership. But his leadership also includes an awareness of when and how he can help the group to guide itself.

Each person in the group is unique in his total personality. He is exclusive because of his different experiences and background. What he does, what he thinks, and how he feels reveal his personality. However he presents himself, each human being as a group member is equally important because his individuality makes its own unique contribution.

The leader must also recognize his own uniqueness as a group member. The leader, guiding children in their self-realization, should be honest and objective about himself. He should acknowledge that his background with its unique experiences has contributed to the self he presently is. He will try to examine the source of his ideas, values, feelings, and behaviors. He will acknowledge that he favors certain curricular subjects; that he enjoys working on particular pet projects; that he likes or dislikes certain personalities; that he himself has a personality that can be labeled "jovial," "sensitive," "demanding," etc.; or that he values certain ideas above others.

In all classroom learning, the leader's total personality will probably influence the children more than any subject matter he teaches. Especially in experiences dealing with human emotions and interpersonal relationships, the leader's own behaviors will serve as a strong example. He will need to examine and understand his own sensitivities as a human being in order to teach human interaction to children with honesty and relevance.

The individual makes his best contributions when he feels confident and possesses a positive self-image. This attitude develops in a climate of acceptance, of psychological freedom, and of open communication.

Acceptance is the belief that all people are worthy individuals. They are accepted as they are, although certain behaviors and actions may be disapproved. Acceptance forms the very foundation for successful group interaction, which creative dramatics attempts to foster.

Psychological freedom means that a person is secure enough in his social, physical, and emotional environment to operate with ease. Everyone has known the feelings of fear and anxiety in uncomfortable and tense situations. At such times, all the eyes of the world appear to be staring at us and making impossible demands. Our insecurity with the situation may cause us to become shy and withdrawn, or hostile and aggressive. We are unable to operate with maximum effectiveness.

Creative dramatics is a natural medium for the free expression of ideas, feelings, and attitudes. Fostering open communication becomes fundamental and paramount in the leader's successful guidance of creative dramatics.

The teacher initiates acceptance and becomes the model for it. He accepts each child as a human being with important feelings and ideas. His guidance reflects an understanding of children's various stages of growth and development as well as their interests, needs, and concerns. He respects the right of every child to be treated with equality, and he teaches this attitude to the group by example and practice.

The leader must be responsible for establishing an atmosphere of psychological freedom. He must create the secure climate in which a child can express himself freely. He must value and respect the sincere, open and honest communication that creative dramatics can engender. Furthermore, he should be sensitive to his obligation to communicate his own thoughts and feelings with equal sincerity.

ACCEPTANCE

Ideas

Acceptance of children's ideas means giving them positive feedback as frequently as possible. We have already referred to the nonverbal and verbal comments the leader can make during discussions and playings. In addition, the leader can demonstrate acceptance in showing a genuine interest in the children's ideas and in trying to understand them.

Acceptance can also be given for the children's involvement in the process as well as for the product. That is, it is as important to encourage them for working on an idea or a problem as it is to praise them for the answer or solution they discover.

> I can see that you are really thinking about this idea. I can almost see the wheels turning around in your heads.
>
> We exercised our body muscles a moment ago; now we're exercising our brain muscles.

As we have discussed earlier, the teacher should not indicate that one child's idea is prized above that of another. General noncommittal statements are more helpful in the long run.

> That's one idea.
> That's an interesting way to interpret that idea.
> Umm, I hadn't thought about that.

When praising, it is best to include everyone and everyone's ideas.

> Those are all good ideas.
> You all have so many ideas.
> Good! (said to an entire group).

Because the leader becomes an accepting person, the children will often pick up on this model and begin to express acceptance and appreciation also.

> Teacher, what music were you playing when we were pretending? It's neat.

I liked watching Jim when he pretended he was that stubborn donkey and he rolled on his back.

You were good, Annette.

While it is important to accept the ideas of children, there is no need to claim creative genius for a rather ordinary idea. Children have an awareness of what is pretty good and what is outstanding, and exaggerated praise is usually recognized as phoney.

One leader discovered this fact from the children themselves. She had the habit of being overly enthusiastic with everyone and everything. When a group of children spontaneously praised one child for his ideas in playing a scene, the child expressed delight and was very pleased. The children reminded him that the teacher often praised his work, but his response was, "Oh, she says everything's good."

Creativity and Imitation

In creative dramatics, the children are usually creatively interpreting an idea as well as thinking of their own ideas to interpret. Sometimes children and teachers worry when children express their ideas in new or unconventional ways.

Teacher, John isn't doing it right. He's not the sun; he doesn't have his arms out.

The teacher may respond:

There are lots of ways to be the sun. John has a way; you have a way.

He may even want to use this teachable moment to help the children explore the various possibilities there are for expressing an idea. "How else can we pretend to be the sun?" he may ask. All the various ideas demonstrate versatility and the uniqueness of everyone.

Often in creative dramatics activities children will imitate each other. This is normal and natural; imitation is a basic way of learning. Yet some children (and teachers) feel that imitating is similar to cheating, and children often demonstrate considerable concern about it.

Mary's doing *my* idea!

Tom's copying!

In response to these protestations, the leader must communicate his acceptance of imitation in such a way that protects the child who is imitating yet reassures the child who has originated the idea.

When people see an idea that they like they enjoy using that idea. Tom must have liked your idea. . . .

Your idea must be so interesting that people like it and want to use it.

Throughout all dramatic experiences, the leader is encouraging the sincere and honest expression of ideas and feelings. If, for any reason, he rejects a sincere and honest response, he risks closing the channels of communication. The following examples demonstrate this point.

A group of fourth graders were pretending to be robots. In the first playing they were robots working hard all day long, performing a variety of tasks. For the second playing, the leader suggested that they be robots entertaining themselves on a night off. In the discussion that followed the playing, one boy said, "I had a fight with my wife and went to the gasoline station and got oil and got drunk."

The child's answer was logical, and delivered in a sincere way. The answer was accepted with a nod of the head. If the leader had given a shocked look or rejected the answer as inappropriate, he would have given reproof to a child's honest expression. From a pragmatic point of view, he could also have triggered other children into creating "drunken robots," too, if they thought it would get attention.

One six-year-old, pretending to be a witch casting an evil spell, said that he was "turning all the parents in the world into furniture." The teacher, playing the "oldest and wisest" witch, merely cackled and said, "I see."

If the teacher had remarked something to the effect, "Are you sure that's what you'd like to do to parents?" or "You shouldn't say things like that," he would have rejected the child's emotions.

Leader Participation

Acceptance can also be demonstrated when the leader participates and plays with the children. Of course, not all teachers will feel equally disposed toward participation. Each teacher must decide for himself what he can comfortably do. There are other techniques he can use to compensate, and he may feel more comfortable with participation as time goes on.

He need not be skilled in his playing; in fact he could intimidate some children by being too accomplished. His participation should, instead, emphasize

Accepting Self

Sometimes children have a difficult time accepting themselves. Often these are the feelings the teacher is most tempted to reject.

"That's a pretty sweater you have on, Mark," said the teacher at the beginning of the session.

"I don't like it, I hate myself in it," said chubby Mark who had not yet played with his classmates in creative dramatics although he had been attending the sessions regularly.

The teacher was tempted to say, "Well, I don't know why you don't like it. It is really a pretty sweater." Or, "You shouldn't hate anyone, not even yourself." But she knew that these statements would have been rejecting ones. She recognized that Mark's weight problem may have caused his concern, so she made no further comment at all. As it turned out, Mark played that day for the first time; and he continued to participate in succeeding days.

Accepting statements may be hard to give when the teacher appears to be under direct attack.

One seven-year-old boy in an early session in creative dramatics said to the teacher, "You're stupid."

The teacher, although stunned, asked, "Why do you think so, Rocky?"

"Because you pretend and make up things. That's stupid," was his reply.

The teacher reflected his feelings, "It's true that I do like to pretend and make up things. You feel that pretending is stupid."

Possibly Rocky had heard something similar before. He wasn't going to pretending if someone might call *him* "stupid" for doing it. He didn't want label, so in defense he applied it to someone else before it was applied to.

The teacher did not reject Rocky's statement but let him know that she erstood his feelings. In being allowed to express his concerns, and in knowing someone understood them, his anxiety had been relieved. Interestingly he inued to attend the volunteer sessions and in time participated very freely.

Accepting Mistakes

The process of learning also involves experimenting, often accompanied by ainty and mistakes. Many children have never been helped to realize that

the spirit of play rather than the skill. If he is enthusiastic and appears to enjoy himself, he encourages them to participate and to relax and enjoy themselves also. His positive attitudes influence their attitudes.

For example, as a child pretends to walk a tightrope, the leader may join him, walking the child's imaginary rope. These actions say to the child, "Your idea sounds like fun. I'd like to pretend it with you."

If the teacher allows himself to play with the children, he can directly interact and communicate with them. This communication is stronger than if the teacher simply observed from the sidelines. He becomes a stronger member of the group and establishes a meaningful, working relationship with it. As a result, he learns about himself and the other members more clearly. This insight can be valuable in assisting effective classroom interrelationships in all learning activities.

Feelings

In addition to the feelings played in drama experiences, the subject of feelings and emotions in the classroom is an important area in itself. Every experienced teacher knows the importance of a positive emotional climate in the classroom and of a learner's healthy emotional outlook. When we deal with the whole child, learning is only one aspect. Without a feeling of well-being, learning is not possible. If for no other reason, emotions must be dealt with because of their effect on learning.

Many children have a great many problems related to emotional feelings. Realistically the teacher will not be able to solve many of the child's problems. Neither can he assume the responsibilities of a therapist or a counselor who diagnoses and treats specific emotional problems. But simply in the number of waking hours spent together, perhaps the teacher, of all the people in the child's world, is in an ideal position to help him understand and cope with human emotions.

Creative dramatics, as an enjoyable, active experience, creates by itself a positive emotional atmosphere. The strong movement of marching around the room to a bouncy rhythm can help a child toward a fresh and renewed outlook on the rest of the day; or pretending to be on a raft with Tom Sawyer floating down the Mississippi may help a child forget, if only temporarily, his own struggles with life.

A teacher can deal even more directly with the subject of emotion. He can help the children understand what emotions are, how they are expressed, why people behave as they do, and how emotional responses differ. Such questions are also a part of other curricular areas such as social studies, literature, or health.

The subject of emotions is dealt with every time the leader guides the children in a discussion of the characters in stories and the motivations behind their behaviors. Children readily identify with certain characters. Often these are the ones they choose to play, and through those characters the children have the opportunity to release strong feelings.

As the children discuss particular characters, they can talk about their perceptions and understanding through their own experiences. Sometimes these insights are offered spontaneously. At times the leader can guide the children to see that they, too, have had experiences similar to those of the people in the story.

> . . . Did you ever do a favor for someone that took a lot of time and patience on your part, as Horton's favor for Maizie did? . . . (p. 245).
>
> . . . The person in Eve Merriam's "Mean Song" (52) is very angry about something. But he's making up nonsense words in talking about it. Have you ever felt that angry? . . .

We will want children to understand that all people have feelings. They are always present and usually normal. People all over the world share emotions of fear, love, hate, and joy. When the student hears someone expressing understanding of his emotion, he knows that his feelings are normal.

For some children it can be particularly helpful for the teacher to identify with them and their feelings. He can demonstrate his oneness with them in the experiencing of common human emotions.

> I know how you feel.
> I can understand how you must have felt.
> I felt the same way when I was in that situation.

We will want children to understand that even though feelings are neither good nor bad in themselves, some can be troublesome or painful.

> No one likes to be called names.
> Yes, one can feel hurt if everyone else is invited to a party and he isn't.

Learning to cope with emotions may mean learning to understand that feelings are normal and have a reason for existing. We do not reject feelings, but we do try to understand why they occur and what causes them.

The expressions of emotions are sometimes universal and sometimes quite different. Differences are influenced by the concepts and values held by various cultures. What people do reflects what has been learned culturally from families, communities, and nations.

No doubt it will be surprising for some children to learn that in some parts of the world, the men greet each other by kissing; or that fistfighting in some

cultures would be a shameful way to express anger. Even within the classroom community there may be some dissimilar values.

Because each person is unique, his individuality may show itself in what h likes or doesn't like; what he fears or doesn't fear. Children may be surprised find that there may be a classmate who doesn't like ice cream — something th think is universally liked. Or, they may find it curious that a child says he li the sound of thunder and is not afraid of it.

Understanding and appreciating these differences is a valuable lea experience. The common respect people must have for one another's fe begins with the teacher and children:

> One of the authors was guiding a class of third graders in creati drama. One of the boys did not like physical contact. The leac noticed his negative response on one occasion when she took hand to form a circle and at another time when she unthinki gave him a friendly pat on the head. She made a mental note Tom did not like contact and that she would not touch him.
>
> But the very next time she met the children, she forgo intentions. This time she was playing with the children, pret to be smoke slowly rising from the floor. The mood was mysterious, but it was quickly broken for Tom when the t smoke movements accidentally touched him.
>
> The teacher stopped playing and said quietly to Tom, "To you don't like for me to touch you. I'm sorry that I did I've told myself not to do it, but I seem to be having a making myself mind."
>
> There was a moment of absolute silence. By now e aware of what had happened. Tom's face changed fror disgust to one of surprise. Then the eight-year-old sai right, I understand." Tom appreciated her concern f and at that moment a bond of understanding was fc them.

Often the child is denied normal emotional feeling as, "Big boys don't cry"; or "It's silly to be afra statements say to the child that he must deny his feeli people's feelings can only cause them to question th more helpful to acknowledge that the child's feelings "Sometimes crying makes us feel better"; or "We a dark because we can't see what's there" are stateme of the child.

mistakes are natural and normal for everyone. Often they become distressed by mistakes; they have learned a societal attitude that says mistakes indicate failure and failure cannot be tolerated.

One of the most effective ways a teacher can communicate acceptance of mistakes is to acknowledge his own.

Boy I seemed to goof that time. Wonder how I can make it right? . . .

And, just as he can stop and acknowledge his own difficulties, he can also guide the children to do the same.

Some people didn't follow the rules. Perhaps they forgot them. Let's try it again and remember this time that you can use only the space at the side of your desk for this activity.

I sensed that some of you were not sure or had second thoughts about the way your scene was going. Would you like to try it again?

REJECTION

Even though the teacher accepts ideas and feelings, he is still able to set limits on behaviors. It would be ridiculous for any teacher to allow children to fight with each other, hurt others' feelings, shout obscenities, or refuse to follow rules.

The children need to learn that the specific things that people do with their emotions and feelings influence their ability to be a part of society. A person may feel angry, but if he kicks someone, he is likely to be avoided or even kicked in return.

Rejecting statements must be made with care. Rejections must not cause children to feel disgraced or to lose self-respect. "You're a bad boy," "Naughty girls like you. . ." "That's a mean thing to do. . . ." are not helpful, but destructive.

Children's self-concepts are formed on the basis of the opinions expressed about them. They are susceptible to fulfilling or living up to both the negative as well as the positive statements made about them. In addition, negative statements close off communication. Often the statements are simply ignored. Or, worse yet, a feeling of rebellion sets in and in the long run, little is gained.

It is possible to disapprove of behaviors and actions without rejecting the individual. It is important that the children feel *they* are not being rejected; it is what they are *doing* that needs to be controlled.

I know that you're angry; but fighting is not allowed in the classroom.

All your talking lets me know you're excited. But, you know the rules. We can't begin playing until everyone settles down. I'll know that you're ready when everything is quiet. . . .

> I know you're disappointed that you all can't play this first time. But in just a few moments we'll be repeating it, and everyone will have a chance.

There may be times when children's behaviors become disruptive to the rest of the class. When this happens, rules for participating should be reinforced as objectively as possible.

It is helpful to speak to the child as privately as possible so that he is able to "save face."

> Please sit down. When you feel that you can follow the rules to remain by yourself and not disturb others, you may rejoin the group.

Sometimes the child's behavior is such that the teacher cannot allow him to participate with the group at all.

> I'm sorry. I know you are disappointed: But I cannot allow you to poke and pinch other people who are trying to do their work. Perhaps it will be easier for you to follow the rules in class tomorrow.

Although the child can no longer physically participate, he should be allowed to watch if he wishes. Some children will quietly watch the others play; some prefer to read or rest privately. Although the participating children enjoy playing activities in a quieter setting, the aggressive child needs the activity as much as anyone else, and should be returned to it as soon as possible.

Sometimes children will demand attention. In their attempts, they will sometimes seek recognition by trying to do the opposite of what the teacher requests. Ignoring the child's demand may be most helpful in convincing him that this is not the best way to get attention.

In the following example, the child was an unusually loud and aggressive child. He needed much attention and found that contradicting the teacher or doing the opposite of the directions would draw attention to himself. The leader, who often gave in to his demands, decided to change tactics:

> **T:** I'll be the North Wind that blows all of the Snowmen inside the house. Ok. Here we go!
>
> **C:** I'm not going inside.
>
> **T:** OK. The rest of us will go inside and David, you can stay outside.
>
> **C:** I'm coming! I'm coming!

GROUP INVOLVEMENT

While creative dramatics emphasizes the value of individual expression, it also emphasizes the value of group involvement. Learning to function in a democratic society is a high educational priority. While the teacher encourages each child to develop his individual potential, he also emphasizes the importance of sensitive interrelationships with others. Ultimately the leader guides the group to learn that it functions best when everyone contributes his individuality. Organization, cooperation, group problem solving and decision making thus become an integral part of the group experience.

The group experience is an interesting one. Although a group may be composed of a wide range of individuals, it has a personality all its own — as if it were one huge individual embodying the separate individuals. The group is capable of growing and changing, just as individuals are.

Creative dramatics encourages group interaction, and sometimes the power of the group creates difficulty for both the children and the teacher. If the children have not had much experience with group work, and the leader does not understand his role in guiding it, a great many problems may occur. When the group is given the opportunity to work on its own, it begins to have a life of its own. A beginning teacher may panic at this power, especially if he sees his own contact and control diminishing.

When the teacher plans the activities carefully, instructs clearly, and when the group knows what is expected of them, group work should pose few problems. Strong direction as well as support may be required from the leader for beginning groups until the children can begin to have success and feel confident working in more independent ways.

Some children have an easy time of cooperating and integrating themselves within almost any group. For them democratic involvement is natural. The children demonstrate their maturity and readiness to accept each other. They enjoy working together.

A.

Maria and I have an idea. Can we do it together?

B.

John and I are going to be the ticket men and those guys are going to come and buy a ticket from us. What are you girls going to do?

C.

Oh, I know how we can do this story, teacher. You be the old lady and we'll be the rabbits.

They also have ideas for facilitating organization and interaction.

A.

I think everybody ought to put his hand up if he wants to say something.

B.

I think each group should have a corner of the room to plan and pretend their ideas so we're not bothered.

They listen to each other and empathize with feelings.

A.

Leslie: I know how the boy in that story felt. The saddest time for me was when my dog died. He was run over by a car.
Michael: That's sad.

B.

Sue: Robby was really funny when he pretended to come in the palace door and was singing that funny song.

They are interested in each other and spontaneously comment on and question further the ideas of their peers.

A.

Owen: I wanted a horse.
Teacher: Did you get one?
Owen: I'm too little. If I rode it, I'd fall off.
Eric: Oh, you're crazy. You can't have a horse because you gotta have a ranch to have a horse and you gotta have a saddle and you gotta have a bridle and you gotta have horseshoes and you gotta have a lot of food to feed 'em.
Owen: Oh no! You don't have to have all that stuff for the horse.
Eric: Well, maybe you're right.

B.

Dick: If I could have my wish I'd journey to another planet and help start a new civilization there.
Paul: Like the boy in *Farmer in the Sky* (88).
Clinton: You'd have to get used to living in pressurized buildings all of your life.
Paul: Maybe you'd save the rocket ship like Bill did.

There are some children who have difficulties in group interaction. Some choose to avoid any group. They are hesitant to participate, to contribute an idea or an opinion. Still others demand attention from the group; they refuse to listen to others and have difficulties compromising and cooperating. Their personal ego needs interfere with their ability to interact successfully with the group.

Democratic living is not easy! Cooperative interaction takes time, and as we have noted previously, social maturation is not necessarily contingent on chronological age. Furthermore, while group cohesiveness steadily grows, the group is dynamic and changing. There will invariably be days when the leader and the children wonder how they can ever get together or why in the world

Watching the action from the sidelines.

they would ever want to! These seemingly backward steps are a natural part of the group process. The children are constantly growing in awareness of themselves as individuals and as a part of the group.

Yet, the group is powerful. The need to belong to a group is strong, and the leader can count on this need to be the motivation for the child to continue to make attempts to integrate himself. For children who do have difficulties, the teacher will need to give special understanding, help, and support.

The leader may need to guide children to formulate the specifics of how to get along with each other.

> Because we like to have people listen to us, we will listen to others.
>
> Because I wouldn't want anyone to call my ideas "stupid" or "dumb" I don't say that about anyone's idea.
>
> Because I don't want anyone to make fun of the way I feel, I won't make fun of anyone else's feelings.
>
> I can have my own ideas as long as what I do does not interfere with the wishes of the majority.
>
> If I don't like the idea that the majority has, I don't have to play, but I should not disturb the others.
>
> Because I don't like being disturbed, I will not purposely disturb others.
>
> Because there are times when I want people to watch me, I'll give others my attention.

General discussions about group cooperation and compromise can help.

When people cooperate, what do they have to do?

What procedures can a group use to decide what ideas they will use?

How can a group make certain that everyone has a chance to speak and contribute?

Sometimes in a group only a few members do all the talking. When this happens, how do the other members feel? What can they do?

The subject of group cooperation and compromise can be the basis for dramatic experiences.

T: What specific situations can you think of when groups must compromise and cooperate?

C: Every summer my family decides where we'll spend our vacation. My dad tells how much money we can spend and how far that would take us and then we vote. Before we voted we used to argue a lot. My sister always screamed about going to the lake because she had a boyfriend there. I always vote for camping.

C: Well, this isn't about compromise, just the opposite. My brother's in Mr. Bender's class and when the art teacher wanted groups to make a mural they couldn't do it. They couldn't agree on anything. One of the kids even ripped up the paper. My brother said Mr. Bender just flipped and really got mad at them.

C: Our committee had a hard time planning the class Halloween party. Not to mention names, but *someone* wanted to bring in *real* eyeballs and guts for kids to touch when they had their blindfolds on. He was going to get them from the butcher. The girls said we'd be sick so we made him take a vote.

T: I can see you have a lot of ideas. Let's divide into groups of five. Each group decide on a specific situation when cooperation and compromise seems necessary. Plan that everyone has a part. And plan specific ways that you establish compromise. Try giving your situation an ending so that everyone will know when to stop the scene.

Before groups organize themselves, it is helpful if the leader reminds them of their challenge to cooperate and compromise:

T: Before your group can plan the building of your version of a "Wonder of the World" you'll have to decide what "Wonder" you will build. You may not like the idea that your group decides on as well as everyone else. But remember that you are a part of a group, and people in groups help each other when they compromise.

It is important to a democratic society and to the growth and development of individuals that children learn to handle their own problems and make their own decisions. The decisions the children make may not always be the ones the leader would have made, but the process of thinking through an idea and experimenting with trial and error is an excellent learning experience.

The teacher can grant the children the opportunities to be self-directed in many ways:

> Let's see, how can we do this? Does anyone have a suggestion?
>
> We've been playing this story for quite a while. Are you still interested in it or should we go on to something else?
>
> Do we need a preview playing this time?
>
> Do you think everyone can play all at the same time, or should we start out with just a few people first?
>
> How much space do you think we can handle today?

Of course, whenever the children make their own decisions they must also accept the consequences. If things don't work out, then stopping the playing to reanalyze the situation is inevitable. Just as the teacher can make mistakes and miscalculations about what a group is ready to do, so can the children in managing themselves. The important point is that they have had a hand in the decision making.

In addition, the leader can help the group deal with its own problems of human interaction. Often these situations occur in regular day-to-day classroom living. In the example below, the teacher uses a teachable moment to help a group of second-graders see alternatives in handling a particular behavior problem. The teacher and the children had just begun a discussion when a rather constant and minor problem reoccurred.

> **George:** Troy's hitting me again.
>
> **Teacher:** Troy seems to be a problem for you, George. What are you going to do about it?
>
> **George:** What am *I* going to do about it?
>
> **Teacher:** Yes, how are you going to solve your problem?
>
> **George:** Well . . . I'll . . . (shouts to Troy) STOP DOING THAT!!!!
>
> **Teacher:** That's one way that might work. Is there anything else you could do?
>
> **George:** I'd hit him too.
>
> **Teacher:** That's another thing to do. Do you think it will work in this case?
>
> **Angela:** Troy would hit you back, would't you, Troy? (Troy doesn't respond.)
>
> **Cindy:** Ask him nice to leave you alone.
>
> **Teacher:** If you did ask nicely and it still didn't work, what else might you do?

Jimmy: Just don't play with him any more.

Rusty: Go sit by somebody else.

Teacher: Sometimes when people don't leave us alone we can move away from them. That's one thing we can do. There might be other things we can do to help us solve our problem. Let's take a few minutes to imagine that someone keeps hitting you but you have a plan for solving this problem. I'll count to ten and all of you act out what you would do or say if someone had just hit you again. One . . two . . three. . . . I saw different solutions. Let's talk about them. (The children discuss what they did.)

In a previous chapter we suggested that a group usually works best when the members are free to choose their co-workers. Because planning and sharing with others can be difficult, many children find it more comfortable talking and working with their selected friends.

Yet for the sake of class unity and cohesiveness as well as the children's social growth, the leader will want to widen their experiences in interacting with various groupings. He will want them to have the opportunity to learn that everyone can contribute to a group relationship.

When he plans to break up the usual groupings or cliques, it is best to explain his reasoning:

T: For this activity we're going to form new groups. I know that it is enjoyable to work with people you particularly like. But I'm concerned that we are all able to be flexible and to recognize the contributions that every single person in our class can make. You may discover that the unfamiliar ideas that new people have can stimulate new ideas in you. So just for today, and for all those reasons, we're going to experiment.

Throughout all experiences in creative dramatics, the goal is to help children understand and empathize with others; to learn to put themselves into other people's shoes. We want them to discover their common bond of feelings with people they know; people they read about; historical figures; famous personalities; people of other countries. We want them to know each other better and appreciate themselves as viable human beings. This understanding is important to drama. And it is this understanding and awareness that frees us from alienation in a world whose future ultimately depends on sensitive human interrelationships.

EXERCISES FOR THE COLLEGE STUDENT

1. Consider your own individual uniqueness. What are your values, feelings, likes, dislikes, etc.?

2. Discuss with your classmates those specific incidents during your elementary years when a teacher demonstrated acceptance of you. Recall specific incidents when you felt rejected.

3. Practice verbally accepting ideas. Brainstorm with your classmates the verbal feedback a teacher can give to accept ideas.

4. Practice verbally accepting feelings. Use the procedure suggested above.

5. Practice rejecting behaviors without rejecting the child. Brainstorm with a partner behaviors that can be rejected; take turns verbally rejecting them. Check each other to see that the language does not inadvertently reject the individual. Books suggested in the bibliography can help you.

6. Make a list of situations that can be dramatized focusing on democratic living in the classroom.

7. Read Chapter 9 of Elizabeth George Speare's *The Witch of Blackbird Pond* (148), in which Kit leads children in a dramatization of "The Good Samaritan." Also read the episode beginning in Chapter 7 of Louise Fitzhugh's *Harriet the Spy* (97), in which the gym teacher attempts an enactment of a Christmas dinner. Analyze the problems each teacher faced. What solutions can you offer?

8. There are many books for children that deal with emotions. The following are only a few. Read some of them and discuss their themes.

   Brooks, Gwendolyn, *Bronzeville Boys and Girls*. New York: Harper & Row, Publishers, 1956.

   Cohen, Miriam, *The New Teacher*. New York: The Macmillan Company, 1972.

   Cohen, Miriam, *Will I Have a Friend?* New York: The Macmillan Company, 1967.

   Hoban, Russell, *The Sorely Trying Day*. New York: Harper & Row, Publishers, 1964.

   Preston, Mitchell Edna, *The Temper Tantrum Book*. New York: The Viking Press, 1969.

   Steptoe, John, *Stevie*. Harper & Row, Publishers, 1969.

   Viorst, Judith, *I'll Fix Anthony*. New York: Harper & Row, Publishers, 1969.

   Viorst, Judith, *Alexander and the Terrible, Horrible, No Good, Very Bad Day*. New York: Atheneum Publishers, Inc., 1972.

   Wondriska, William, *All the Animals Were Angry*. New York: Holt, Rinehart and Winston, Inc., 1970.

   Yashima, Taro, *Crow Boy*. New York: The Viking Press, Inc., 1955.

   Zolotow, Charlotte, *The Quarreling Book*. New York: Harper & Row, Publishers, 1963.

9. Collect stories, poems, books, and articles that can help children understand emotions.

Amidon, Edmund, and Elizabeth Hunter, *Improving Teaching*. New York: Holt, Rinehart and Winston, Inc., 1966.

A valuable text for making the teacher aware of his specific verbal behaviors and their consequences.

Axline, Virginia M., *Play Therapy*. New York: Ballantine Books, 1969.

Discussion of play therapy techniques including special attention to uses for the classroom teacher.

Berger, Terry, *I Have Feelings*. New York: Behavioral Publications, Inc., 1971.

Situations and pictures covering seventeen different feelings and an explanation of them.

Borton, Terry, *Reach, Touch, and Teach*. New York: McGraw-Hill, Inc., 1970.

A book devoted to the importance of understanding feeling and expanding self-awareness as a significant part of the educational process.

Evans, Eva Knox, *People Are Important*. New York: Western Publishing Company, 1951.

A helpful text for children (as well as teachers) about people, cultures, and values the world over.

Ginott, Haim G., *Between Parent and Child*. New York: Avon Books, 1965.

A best-seller book by a noted educator and therapist with practical suggestions for developing meaningful relationships.

Ginott, Haim G., *Between Teacher and Child*. New York: The Macmillan Company, 1972.

Helpful suggestions for strengthening interpersonal relationships in the classroom and at home.

Grambs, Jean Dresden, *Intergroup Education Methods and Materials*. Englewood Cliffs, New Jersey: Prentice-Hall, Inc., 1968.

A useful source for the teacher who wishes to focus on human relations activities in the classroom. Extensive bibliography included.

Greenberg, Herbert M., *Teaching With Feeling*. New York: The Macmillan Company, 1969.

An exploration of teacher's feelings toward themselves as well as children, supervisors, parents, and colleagues.

Jones, Richard M., *Fantasy and Feeling In Education*. New York: New York University Press, 1968.

Deals with the importance of including a consideration of the emotions, cultural values, and feelings in certain curricular topics.

LaMancusa, Katherine C., *We Do Not Throw Rocks at the Teacher!* Scranton, Pennsylvania: International Textbook Company, 1966.

An amusingly written but thoroughly practical guide to classroom management.

LeShan, Eda, *What Makes Me Feel This Way?* New York: The Macmillan Company, 1972.

A noted educator, writer, and family counselor explores the emotional feelings common to us all. Written for children but helpful for adults as well.

Lederman, Janet, *Anger and the Rocking Chair.* New York: McGraw-Hill, Inc., 1969.

One teacher's approach in dealing with children's emotions in the classroom.

Limbacher, Walter J., *Here I Am.* Dayton, Ohio: George A. Pflaum, Publisher, 1969.

————, *I'm Not Alone.* Dayton, Ohio: George A. Pflaum, Publisher, 1970.

————, *Becoming Myself.* Dayton, Ohio: George A. Pflaum, Publisher, 1970.

Text books for a mental health program in grades four, five, and six written by a psychologist. The books deal with feelings and growing up.

Moustakas, Clark, *The Authentic Teacher: Sensitivity and Awareness in the Classroom.* Cambridge, Mass.: Doyle Publishing Company, 1966.

A helpful text in inviting awareness of the importance of a meaningful relationship between teacher and child.

Neisser, Edith G., and the Staff of the Association for Family Living, *How to Live With Children.* Chicago: Science Research Associates, Inc., 1950.

A booklet for parents and teachers containing practical chapters such as "They Need to Know What to Expect" and "The Importance of Not Being Too Earnest."

Now That You Are 5, Charlotte Steiner.

Now That You Are 6, Dorothy Marino.

Now That You Are 7, Eleanor Clymer.

Now That You Are 8, Sydney Taylor.

Now That You Are 9, Iris Vinton.

Now That You Are 10, Frieda Friedman.

All published in New York by The Association Press, 1963.

Texts that concentrate on various developmental levels and the feelings that accompany them.

Rogers, Carl R., *Freedom to Learn.* Columbus, Ohio: Charles E. Merrill Publishing Company, 1969.

A psychotherapist and teacher discusses his approach to education based on his theory of personality.

Shaftel, Fannie, and George Shaftel, *Role Playing for Social Values.* Englewood Cliffs, N. J.: Prentice-Hall, Inc., 1967.

Explanation of techniques in role playing. Includes story situations to dramatize.

Tester, Sylvia, *Moods and Emotions.* Elgin, Illinois: David C. Cook Publishing Co., 1970.

A booklet discussing various ways to teach the subject of emotions in the classroom. Includes sixteen large photos illustrating emotions.

Bibliography
of Story and Poetry
Anthologies
and Books for
Dramatization

(1) *All the Silver Pennies,* Blanche Jennings Thompson. New York: The Macmillan Company, 1967.

(2) *Anansi, the Spider Man,* Philip M. Sherlock. New York: Thomas Y. Crowell Company, Inc., 1954.

(3) *Anthology of Children's Literature,* Edna Johnson, Evelyn R. Sickels, Frances Clarke Sayers. Boston: Houghton Mifflin Company, 1959.

(4) *The Arbuthnot Anthology,* May Hill Arbuthnot. Glenview, Illinois: Scott, Foresman and Company, 1961.

(5) *The Blackbird in the Lilac,* James Reeves. New York: E. P. Dutton & Co., Inc., 1959.

(6) *Catch a Little Rhyme,* Eve Merriam. New York: Atheneum Publishers, 1966.

(7) *Catch Me a Wind,* Patricia Hubbell. New York: Atheneum Publishers, 1968.

(8) *Childcraft – the How and Why Library.* Chicago: Field Enterprises Educational Corporation, 1972.

(9) *Children's Literature for Dramatization: An Anthology,* Geraldine Brain Siks. New York: Harper & Brothers, Publishers, 1964.

(10) *A Child's Book of Dreams,* Beatrice Schenk de Regniers. New York: Harcourt Brace Jovanovich, Inc., 1957.

(11) *Cinnamon Seed,* John T. Moore. Boston: Houghton Mifflin Company, 1967.

(12) *Compass Rose,* Elizabeth Coatsworth. New York: Coward-McCann, Inc., 1929.

(13) *The Complete Poems of Carl Sandburg.* New York: Harcourt Brace Jovanovich, Inc., 1970.

(14) *The Cow-Tail Switch and Other West African Stories,* Harold Courlander and George Herzog. New York: Henry Holt & Company, 1947.

(15) *The Crack in the Wall and Other Terribly Weird Tales,* George Mendoza. New York: The Dial Press, Inc., 1968.

(16) *The Dancing Kettle and Other Japanese Folk Tales,* Yoshiko Uchida (ed.). New York: Harcourt, Brace & World, Inc., 1949.

(17) *Eleanor Farjeon's Poems for Children.* Philadelphia: J. B. Lippincott Company, 1951.

(18) *Favorite Stories Old and New,* selected by Sidonie Matsner Gruenberg. Garden City, New York: Doubleday & Company, Inc., 1955.

(19) *Fingers Are Always Bringing Me News,* Mary O'Neill. Garden City, New York: Doubleday & Company, Inc., 1969.

(20) *Fire On the Mountain and Other Ethiopian Stories,* Harold Courlander. New York: Holt, Rinehart & Winston, Inc., 1950.

(21) *God's Trombones,* James Weldon Johnson. New York: The Viking Press, Inc., 1955.

(22) *Grandfather Tales,* Richard Chase. Boston: Houghton Mifflin Company, 1948.

(23) *Green Pipes,* J. Paget-Fredericks. New York: The Macmillan Company, 1929.

(24) *Gwot! Horribly Funny Hairticklers,* George Mendoza. New York: Harper & Row, Publishers, 1967.

(25) *The Hat-Shaking Dance and Other Tales from the Gold Coast,* Harold Courlander and Albert Kofi Prempeh. New York: Harcourt, Brace & World, Inc., 1957.

(26) *The Hare and the Bear and Other Stories,* Yasue Maiyagawa. New York: Parent's Magazine Press, 1971.

(27) *I Feel the Same Way,* Lilian Moore. New York: Atheneum Publishers, 1967.

(28) *Just So Stories,* Rudyard Kipling. Garden City, New York: Doubleday & Company, Inc., 1952.

(29) *Little Bear's Visit,* Else Holmelund Minarik. New York: Harper & Row, Publishers, Inc., 1961.

(30) *The Martian Chronicles,* Ray Bradbury. Garden City, New York: Doubleday & Company, Inc., 1958.

(31) *Miracles,* Collected by Richard Lewis. New York: Simon and Schuster, Inc., 1966.

(32) *The Moon and a Star,* Myra Cohn Livingston. New York: Harcourt, Brace & World, Inc., 1965.

(33) *Now We Are Six,* A. A. Milne. New York: E. P. Dutton & Co., Inc., 1927.

(34) *Oh, What Nonsense!* selected by William Cole. New York: The Viking Press, Inc., 1966.

(35) *Once the Hodja,* Alice Geer Kelsey. New York: Longmans, Green & Co., Ltd., 1943.

(36) *On City Streets,* Nancy Larrick (ed.). New York: M. Evans and Company, Inc., 1968.

(37) *Poems of Edgar Allen Poe,* Dwight Macdonald (ed.). New York: Thomas Y. Crowell Co., 1965.

(38) *Prefabulous Animiles,* James Reeves. New York: E. P. Dutton & Co., Inc., 1960.

(39) *Reflections on a Gift of Watermelon Pickle,* Stephen Dunning, Edward Lueders, Hugh Smith (eds.). Glenview, Illinois: Scott, Foresman & Co., 1966.

(40) *The Sneetches and Other Stories,* Dr. Seuss. New York: Random House, Inc., 1961.

(41) *Some Haystacks Don't Even Have Any Needle,* compiled by Stephen Dunning, Edward Lueders, Hugh Smith. Glenview, Illinois: Scott, Foresman and Company, 1969.

(42) *Someone Else,* Hollis Summers. Philadelphia, Pennsylvania: J. B. Lippincott Company, 1962.

(43) *Stage: A Handbook for Teachers of Creative Dramatics,* Natalie Bovee Hutson. Stevensville, Michigan: Educational Services, Inc., 1968.

(44) *Storytelling,* Ruth Tooze. Englewood Cliffs, New Jersey: Prentice-Hall, Inc., 1959.

(45) *The Storytelling Stone,* Susan Feldman (ed.). New York: Dell Books, 1965.

(46) *Stories to Dramatize,* Winifred Ward. Anchorage, Kentucky: Children's Theatre Press, 1952.

(47) *Take Sky,* David McCord. Boston: Atlantic-Little, Brown and Company, Inc., 1962.

(48) *Tales of the Cheyennes,* Grace Jackson Penney. Boston: Houghton Mifflin Company, 1953.

(49) *Tall Tales from the High Hills,* Ellis Credle. Camden, New Jersey: Thomas Nelson & Sons, 1957.

(50) *That Was Summer,* Marci Ridlon. Chicago: Follett Publishing Company, 1969.

(51) *That's Why,* Aileen Fisher. Camden, New Jersey: Thomas Nelson & Sons, 1946.

(52) *There Is No Rhyme for Silver,* Eve Merriam. New York: Atheneum Publishers, 1962.

(53) *The Thing At the Foot of the Bed and Other Scary Tales,* Maria Leach. New York: The World Publishing Company, 1959.

(54) *Thirteen Danish Tales,* Mary C. Hatch. New York: Harcourt, Brace & World, Inc., 1947.

(55) *Thunder in the Mountains: Legends of Canada,* Hilda Mary Hooke. Toronto: Oxford University Press, 1947.

(56) *The Tiger and the Rabbit and Other Tales,* Pura Belpré. Philadelphia, Pennsylvania: J. B. Lippincott Company, 1965.

(57) *The Time-Ago Tales of Jahdu,* Virginia Hamilton. New York: The Macmillan Company, 1969.

(58) *Time for Poetry* (rev. ed.) May Hill Arbuthnot. Glenview, Illinois: Scott, Foresman and Company, 1959.

(59) *The Wandering Moon,* James Reeves. New York: E. P. Dutton & Co., Inc., 1960.

(60) *Why the Chimes Rang,* Raymond Macdonald Alden. Indianapolis, Indiana: The Bobbs-Merrill Company, Inc., 1954.

(61) *World Tales for Creative Dramatics and Storytelling,* Burdette S. Fitzgerald. Englewood Cliffs, New Jersey: Prentice-Hall, Inc., 1962.

(62) *Yertle the Turtle and Other Stories,* Dr. Seuss. New York: Random House, Inc., 1958.

BOOKS FOR DRAMATIZATION

The following books have been referred to throughout the text. They are listed here alphabetically according to title. The books are only a representative sampling. Some are literary classics. Others have been selected for their historical and geographical settings, social themes, and variety of heroes. They contain many situations and episodes for dramatization with both pantomime and dialogue scenes.

The following symbols are used to indicate the age level it might be best suited for:

  Y young children in kindergarten, first, and second grades
  M middle-grade children in third and fourth grades
  O older children in fifth and sixth grades

(63) *O* *Adam of the Road,* Elizabeth Janet Gray. Viking, 1942.
    A minstrel and his son are separated when the boy goes off in search of his stolen dog. His search leads him to many exciting adventures. Thirteenth-century English setting.

(64) *M-O* *Alice in Wonderland and Through the Looking Glass,* Lewis Carroll. Many editions.
    The classic stories of Alice's unusual adventures.

(65)   M   *All Alone,* Claire Huchet Bishop. Viking, 1953.
Two boys who are in charge of the herds in the French Alps violate the rule of constant vigil.

(66)   O   *Amos Fortune, Free Man,* Elizabeth Yates. E. P. Dutton, 1950.
The biography of a slave who struggles for and gains his freedom.

(67) M–O   *... And Now Miguel,* Joseph Krumgold. Crowell, 1953.
The story of a sheepherding family in New Mexico.

(68) M–O   *The Apple and the Arrow,* Mary and Conrad Buff. Houghton Mifflin, 1951.
The legendary William Tell leads the people of Switzerland in their revolt against Austria. Middle Ages.

(69) Y–M   *A Bear Called Paddington,* Michael Bond. Houghton Mifflin, 1958.
A charming human-like bear arrives in London and is adopted by a family. Life becomes full of adventures that border on the disastrous.

(70) M–O   *The Black Cauldron,* Lloyd Alexander. Holt, Rinehart and Winston, 1965.
Taran and his friends must find and destroy the evil Black Cauldron.

(71)   M   *The Borrowers,* Mary Norton. Harcourt, Brace & World, 1953.
The adventures of the little people who live under the floorboards of the house and borrow small objects to furnish their home.

(72)   O   *The Bronze Bow,* Elizabeth George Speare. Houghton Mifflin, 1961.
The setting is Israel during the time of Jesus. Daniel desires to play a part in driving the Romans from his land. His hate and revenge dissolve in understanding.

(73)   M   *Caddie Woodlawn,* Carol Ryrie Brink. Macmillan, 1935.
The adventures of Wisconsin pioneers.

(74)   M   *Carolina's Courage,* Elizabeth Yates. E. P. Dutton, 1964.
Carolina, a pioneer girl on a wagon train, is able to assist in the advance through Indian territory.

(75) M–O   *Centerburg Tales,* Robert McCloskey. Viking, 1951.
The further adventures of Homer Price and the people in his small town.

(76)   M   *Charlie and the Chocolate Factory,* Roald Dahl. Alfred Knopf, 1964.
A young boy wins the opportunity to tour a famous and unusual chocolate factory. English setting. The teacher should avoid the racial overtones suggested by the characters of the Oompa Loompas.

(77)   M   *Charlotte's Web,* E. B. White. Harper & Row, 1952.
Actually two stories in one. One story is about Wilbur the pig, who, with the help of his barnyard friends and most particularly Charlotte the spider, develops into a most unique pig. The second

story is about the girl who owns the pig and her experiences growing up.

(78) *O* *A Christmas Carol,* Charles Dickens. Macmillan, 1950.
The classic story of Scrooge and the Cratchit family.

(79) *Y-M* *Christmas on the Mayflower,* Wilma P. Hays. Coward-McCann, 1956.
A dramatic conflict is presented when the crew of the *Mayflower* wants to return to England before the safety of the Pilgrims is assured.

(80) *O* *The Count of Monte Cristo,* Alexandre Dumas. many editions.
Dantes' adventures during the revolutionary period in France.

(81) *Y-M* *The Courage of Sarah Noble,* Alice Dalgliesh. Scribner's, 1954.
The true story of a little girl who bravely accompanies her father into the Connecticut territory in the early 1700's.

(82) *M* *The Cricket in Times Square,* George Selden. Farrar, Strauss, Giroux, 1960.
A cricket brings music, happiness, and some prosperity to a family in New York City. There are two stories in one. One story centers on the animals and insects; the other on the family's struggle with their newsstand business.

(83) *O* *The Crimson Moccasins,* Wayne Dyre Doughty. Harper & Row, 1966.
The story of a half white Indian who painfully learns that he must be a bridge between his peoples.

(84) *M-O* *The Door in the Wall,* Marguerite de Angeli. Doubleday, 1949.
The story of Robin, son of a great lord, who is left crippled after an illness. He proves his courage and is rewarded. Fourteenth-century England.

(85) *Y-M* *The Drinking Gourd,* F. N. Monjo. Harper & Row, 1969.
A New England boy learns of the Underground Railroad in the 1850's.

(86) *M* *The Enormous Egg,* Oliver Butterworth. Little, Brown, 1956.
A dinosaur is hatched, and the scientific world is astounded.

(87) *M-O* *The Family Under the Bridge,* Natalie Savage Carlson. Harper & Brothers, 1958.
Armand, a hobo who lives under one of the bridges of Paris, "adopts" a family during the housing shortage after WW II.

(88) *O* *Farmer in the Sky,* Robert A. Heinlein. Scribner's, 1950.
The realities and adventures of living on another planet.

(89) *O* *Friedrich,* Hans Peter Richter. Holt, Rinehart & Winston, 1970.
A Jewish family find their world slowly falling apart as they struggle to survive in Germany during the rise of Hitler and the Third Reich. A powerfully moving story.

(90) *M-O* *From the Mixed Up Files of Mrs. Basil E. Frankweiler,* Elaine L. Konigsberg. Atheneum, 1967.

Claudia and her brother run away to live for a week in New York City's Metropolitan Museum of Art. A modern adventure.

(91)   M–O   *The Good Master,* Kate Seredy. Viking, 1935.
Kate, a mischievous child, is understood and helped by her uncle. Hungarian setting.

(92)   M   *The Great Cheese Conspiracy,* Jean Van Leeuwen. Random House, 1969.
A gang of mice, who have learned about burglaries from old gangster movies, decide to rob a cheese store.

(93)   M   *The Great Quillow,* James Thurber. Harcourt, Brace, 1944.
Quillow outwits a giant and saves his town.

(94)   M   *Hah-Nee of the Cliff Dwellers,* Mary and Conrad Buff. Houghton Mifflin, 1956.
A terrible drought has made the Cliff Dwellers afraid. They blame Hah-Nee, an adopted boy.

(95)   M   *The Half-Pint Jinni,* Maurice Dolbier. Random House, 1948.
The adventures of a small jinni who can only grant half a wish.

(96)   M   *The Happy Orpheline,* Natalie Savage Carlson. Harper & Brothers, 1957.
A happy orphan is afraid she will be adopted by a woman who claims to be the Queen of France.

(97)   M   *Harriet the Spy.* Louise Fitzhugh. Harper & Brothers, 1964.
To counteract the loneliness caused by affluent and indifferent parents, Harriet keeps a notebook on her observations of people.

(98)   M–O   *The Helen Keller Story,* Catherine Owens Peare. Crowell, 1959.
The biography of a great American woman.

(99)   M–O   *Homer Price,* Robert McCloskey. Viking, 1943.
Humorous adventures of a boy in a small town.

(100)   O   *The House of Dies Drear,* Virginia Hamilton. Macmillan, 1970.
A family moves into a house that was once a station on the Underground Railroad. The house is full of mysteries, which make for a fascinating, suspenseful story.

(101)   M–O   *How Many Miles to Babylon?* Paula Fox. David White, 1967.
James is kidnapped and involved in a dog-stealing racket.

(102)   M   *The Hundred Dresses,* Eleanor Estes. Harcourt, Brace, 1944.
Wanda, a daughter of an immigrant family, is rejected by her classmates.

(103)   M   *James and the Giant Peach,* Roald Dahl. Knopf, 1961.
Inside the magic peach James finds many insect friends, and together they have a fantastic journey across the ocean.

(104)   M   *John John Twilliger,* William Wondriska. Holt, Rinehart & Winston, 1966.
A young boy and his dog discover the secret of the mean, mysterious stranger who has taken over a town.

(105)   *O*   *Johnny Tremain,* Esther Forbes. Houghton Mifflin, 1943.
Johnny, a young silver apprentice in Boston, struggles to maturity during the 1770's.

(106)   *O*   *Journey Outside,* Mary Q. Steele. Viking, 1969.
Dilar leaves the dark world of the Raft People to search for the Better Place. He learns a great deal about ignorance and wisdom. It is both an adventure and an allegory.

(107)   *M*   *J. T.,* Jane Wagner. Dell, 1969.
Taken from the television play, *J. T.* is the story of a boy growing up in the crowded city. He finds an old battered cat and through his love for the animal begins to find himself.

(108)   *M*   *The Little House in the Big Woods,* Laura Ingalls Wilder. Harper & Brothers, 1959.
The true story of an American pioneer family in Wisconsin.

(109)   *Y*   *Little Pear,* Eleanor Frances Lattimore. Harcourt, Brace, 1931.
The amusing adventures of a little Chinese boy.

(110)   *M–O*   *The Lotus Caves,* John Christopher. Macmillan, 1969.
A science fiction story of two boys who live on the Moon. They leave their community to explore one day and become entrapped underground in a plant which possesses superintelligence.

(111)   *M–O*   *Magic at Wychwood,* Sally Watson. Knopf, 1970.
Elaine does not conform to the stereotype of a princess. Her undaunted nature is the cause of conflict in this satire on chivalry.

(112)   *M*   *Mary Jemison: Seneca Captive,* Jeanne Le Monnier Gardner. Harcourt, Brace & World, 1966.
The exciting biography of a courageous white girl who was captured and adopted by Indians in the late 1700's.

(113)   *M*   *Mary Poppins,* P. L. Travers. Harcourt, Brace & World, 1962.
Mary, a nanny for Michael and Jane, entertains them with many magical adventures.

(114)   *M*   *Mystery of the Musical Umbrella,* Friedrich Feld. Random House, 1962.
A brother and sister help a gentleman find his stolen invention – a musical umbrella. Very easy to dramatize. English setting.

(115)   *O*   *Penn,* Elizabeth Janet Gray. Viking, 1938.
The story of William Penn, who became a convert to the Quaker way of life. He suffers religious persecution as well as his father's wrath.

(116)   *Y–M*   *Peter Pan,* Sir James Barrie. Scribner's, 1950.
The classic story of a boy who doesn't want to grow up.

(117)   *M–O*   *The Phantom Tollbooth,* Norman Juster. Random House, 1961.
Milo has many adventures in a fantastical land. He tries to be the

mediator between two kings who are having a dispute over the importance of mathematics and language.

(118)   *Y-M*   *Pinnochio,* C. Collodi (pseud.). Macmillan, 1951.
The adventures of a puppet who wants to become a real boy.

(119)   *M*   *Pippi Longstocking,* Astrid Lindgren. Viking, 1950.
Pippi, a superhuman girl, lives by herself and is independent. Her adventures are unorthodox.

(120)   *O*   *The Pushcart War,* Jean Merrill. William R. Scott, 1964.
A humorous spoof on the traffic problems in New York City in the Year 1976. Push cart vendors and truck drivers start a war with pea shooters.

(121)   *M-O*   *Queenie Peavy,* Robert Burch. Viking, 1966.
Queenie's father is in jail and her mother works hard at a factory. She is always in trouble but gradually learns to control her actions, attitudes, and destiny. Depression years in Georgia.

(122)   *Y-M*   *Quiet on Account of Dinosaur,* Jane Thayer. William Morrow, 1964.
Mary Ann finds a dinosaur and takes him to school. A problem arises when the dinosaur is frightened by noise.

(123)   *Y-M*   *Rabbit Hill,* Robert Lawson. Viking, 1944.
The small animals are concerned about the "new folks" who are moving into the empty house.

(124)   *O*   *(The Merry Adventures of) Robin Hood,* Howard Pyle. Scribner's, 1946.
The legendary adventures of the outlaw-hero of England.

(125)   *M*   *Roosevelt Grady,* Louisa R. Shotwell. Grosett & Dunlap, 1963.
A nine-year-old boy wants to live in one place and stop migrating from fruit crop to fruit crop.

(126)   *Y-M*   *Sam, Bangs and Moonshine,* Evaline Ness. Holt, Rinehart & Winston, 1966.
Sam, a fisherman's daughter, makes up fanciful stories. Trouble begins when she tells her friend Thomas about her mermaid mother.

(127)   *Y-M*   *Sarah Whitcher's Story,* Elizabeth Yates. E. P. Dutton, 1971.
Based on a true account, this story is of a little pioneer girl in New Hampshire who becomes lost in the woods for four days.

(128)   *O*   *Secret of the Andes,* Ann Nolan Clark. Viking, 1952.
Cusi, an Indian boy, lives with the Inca llama herder and helps him tend the sacred flock. The young boy leaves to search for his heart's desire, but returns to learn the secret of the Andes and to take the vow to be the Inca llama herder.

(129)   *O*   *Shadow of a Bull,* Maia Wojciechowska. Atheneum, 1964.
Everyone expected Manolo to be a great Spanish bullfighter like his father, but he has many fears.

(130)   *M-O*   *Shan's Lucky Knife,* Jean Merrill. William R. Scott, 1960.

Shan, a country boy from the hills of Burma, is taken advantage of by the sly boatmaster he works for. In the end Shan outwits him and gains great wealth.

(131)   *O*   *Sing Down the Moon,* Scott O'Dell. Houghton Mifflin, 1900.
A fourteen-year-old Navaho girl tells her story of slavery and forced migration. Mid 1860's setting.

(132) *M-O* *Sounder,* William H. Armstrong. Harper & Row, 1969.
A young sharecropper's son sets off to find his father who has been imprisoned.

(133) *Y-M* *Squaps, the Moonling,* Artemis Verlag. Atheneum, 1969.
A shy moonling hangs on the suit of an astronaut and is taken back to earth. He can only say "squaps," he likes the rain, and he can float when there's a full moon.

(134) *Y-M* *The Story of Ferdinand,* Munro Leaf. Viking, 1936.
Ferdinand the Bull prefers to smell flowers rather than fight. A study of Spanish customs surrounding the bullfight may be correlated with this story.

(135)   *M*   *Strawberry Girl,* Lois Lenski. Lippincott, 1945.
A story, set in Florida in the early 1900's, of two quarreling families. Eventually the women serve as peacemakers.

(136) *Y-M* *Sumi's Prize,* Yoshiko Uchida. Scribner's, 1964.
Sumi, a little Japanese girl, is the only girl to enter a kite flying contest.

(137) *Y-M* *Thy Friend, Obadiah,* Brinton Turkle. Viking, 1972.
A young early American Quaker boy tries to reject a friendly seagull.

(138)   *O*   *Tituba of Salem Village,* Ann Petry. Crowell, 1964.
Tituba, a slave from Barbados, is slowly drawn into the Salem witch hunts, and is, herself, accused of witchcraft.

(139) *M-O* *(The Adventures of) Tom Sawyer,* Mark Twain. many editions.
The American classic of a Missouri boy's adventures on the Mississippi River in the 1800's.

(140)   *O*   *Tomás Takes Charge,* Charlene Joy Talbot. Lothrop, Lee & Shepard, 1966.
When his father disappears, Tomás must find shelter and food for his sister in the tenements of New York City.

(141)   *O*   *Treasure Island,* Robert Louis Stevenson. many editions.
Young Jim Hawkins and the villainous rogue, Long John Silver, sail to a tropic isle and become involved in a climactic battle for treasure.

(142)   *M*   *Venture for Freedom,* Ruby Zagoren. Dell, 1969.
The son of an African king, Venture, was sold into slavery in America in the 1700's. This account is based on his auto-biography.

(143)   *O*   *Walk the World's Rim,* Betty Baker. Harper & Row, 1965.

Three Spaniards and a Negro slave, the survivors of an expedition of 1527, befriend a young Indian boy and take him to Mexico with them. The boy's friendship with the slave teaches him greater meaning in life.

(144) *M-O* *"What Then, Raman?"* Shirley L. Arora. Follett, 1960.
Raman, a boy of India, is the first in his village to learn to read. From his teacher he learns of the responsibility that education carries with it.

(145) *M-O* *The Wheel on the School,* Meindert De Jong. Harper & Row, 1954.
The children of Shora, a little Dutch fishing village, involve the whole town in their project to get the storks to return.

(146)   *M* *Wind in the Willows,* Kenneth Grahame. Scribner's 1935.
The charming adventures of Mole, Rat, Badger, and Toad.

(147) *Y-M* *Winnie-the-Pooh,* A. A. Milne. Dutton, 1954.
Winnie, a stuffed Bear, and his animal friends have many delightful days.

(148)   *O* *The Witch of Blackbird Pond,* Elizabeth George Speare. Houghton Mifflin, 1958.
After leaving her home in Barbados, Kit Tyler feels out of place in a Puritan community in Connecticut. Her spirited personality arouses suspicion, and she finds herself accused of witchcraft.

(149) *M-O* *A Wrinkle in Time,* Madeline d'Engle. Farrar, Straus, Giroux, 1962.
Children's search for their missing father in outer space.

(150) *M-O* *Zeely,* Virginia Hamilton. Macmillan, 1967.
A sensitive story about Geeder, a girl who fantasizes that an older girl, Zeely, is a Watusi queen.

Index